BENJAMIN GRAHAM AND THE POWER OF GROWTH STOCKS

LOST GROWTH STOCK STRATEGIES FROM THE FATHER OF VALUE INVESTING

Frederick K. Martin

with Nick Hansen, Scott Link, and Rob Nicoski

New York   Chicago   San Francisco   Lisbon   London
Madrid   Mexico City   Milan   New Delhi   San Juan
Seoul   Singapore   Sydney   Toronto

1 2 3 4 5 6 7 8 9 10   QFR/QFR   1 9 8 7 6 5 4 3 2 1

ISBN   978-0-07-175389-0
MHID   0-07-175389-3

e-ISBN   978-0-07-175456-9
e-MHID   0-07-175456-3

This publication is designed to provide accurate and authoritative information in regard to the subject matter covered. It is sold with the understanding that neither the author nor the publisher is engaged in rendering legal, accounting, securities trading, or other professional services. If legal advice or other expert assistance is required, the services of a competent professional person should be sought.
> —*From a Declaration of Principles Jointly Adopted by a Committee of the American Bar Association and a Committee of Publishers and Associations*

McGraw-Hill books are available at special quantity discounts to use as premiums and sales promotions or for use in corporate training programs. To contact a representative, please e-mail us at bulksales@mcgraw-hill.com.

This book is printed on acid-free paper.

To my three sons, Peter, Ted, and Will:
May you each follow your dreams.

CONTENTS

FOREWORD

first met Fred Martin more than three decades ago, in 1979. I was the assistant administrator for a neurological clinic in Minneapolis, and he was a young investment manager at a local firm. My clinic was shopping around for a new investment manager for our pension fund, and I was given the task of selecting candidates and making the final recommendation. Fred was one of several managers that we invited in to pitch their services.

Most of the managers came well prepared, with slick multimedia presenta tions with fancy graphics, charts, and tables that documented their investment expertise. Fred had none of that. He came into the boardroom, sat down, and just started talking in earnest about his investment philosophy. He was anything but slick, but he had something that none of the other investment managers had: substance. He explained to us in intricate detail exactly how he would manage our pension fund and make our money grow.

At the end of the vetting process, when I announced that Fred was my choice, the physicians expressed great surprise that I had chosen Fred over the more polished candidates. But there was an honesty and integrity and a quiet sense of confidence about Fred that set him apart from the field. I defended my decision and refused to budge, so we hired Fred to manage our pension fund beginning in 1980.

When he first started, we required him to come in and give us a report once a month. After a couple of years, as our confidence in his ability began to grow, we reduced those meetings to quarterly, and then yearly. In recent years, he hasn't been asked to come in at all. The return we've earned on our money speaks for itself.

When he took over management of the account in 1980, we had a total of $841,338 in the pension fund. Since then, some money has been added and some has been withdrawn, adding up to a total net addition to the original amount of $967,943. That means that, in all, we have contributed a net total of about $1.8 million. Under Fred's management, that sum had grown to $96.9 million as of April 30, 2011—an increase of more than 5,000 percent. Fred managed the pension fund as a balanced account—some stocks and some bonds. The total return for the account during that period was 13.8 percent per year. The stock portion of the portfolio grew by 16.1 percent per year. Those returns are almost unheard of for a 30-year period. During the same time span, the Standard & Poor's 500 grew by just 11.4 percent per year.

Once I made the decision to hire Fred, the rest was easy. Early on, it was obvious to all of us what an honest and ethical individual Fred was. He always spoke his mind, he told us exactly what he was going to do, and then he did exactly what he said he would. What you see is what you get. We took him at his word and maintained complete confidence in his approach—not that we would have had any other choice. Fred made it very clear that he worked only with clients who had the patience and the confidence to allow him to do his job. If you wanted to constantly second-guess him, chances are you would soon be looking for another investment manager.

Over the years, our business relationship has slowly evolved into a personal friendship. When I was contemplating retiring several years ago at the age of 55, Fred persuaded me to change my mind. He said I had a special gift that gave me a unique opportunity to contribute to the greater good. I took his advice and continued in my career, and I have never had a moment's regret since.

After watching Fred consistently rack up impressive performance numbers with our portfolio year after year, decade after decade, I am particularly eager to read this book and find out exactly how he works his magic.

I already have a good sense for who this man is and for the patience and discipline he has exhibited in building our portfolio. But I want to learn more. I want to learn about the stock valuation formula he adopted from Benjamin Graham, and I want to learn about the stock selection process, the margin of safety, and the elements he considers in determining whether a company has a sustainable competitive advantage. I want to learn about the patience, persistence, and discipline that are necessary to invest successfully in the market and the challenges that can affect your decision-making process. I think I already know how this man thinks, but I still want to read the details and find out exactly how he managed to take the net $1.8 million we put into our pension fund and turn it into $96.9 million. Fred Martin has a great story to tell, and I'm glad he has finally had a chance to put it into words for all the world to see.

CRAIG R. WEFLEN
Administrator
Noran Neurological Clinic

ACKNOWLEDGMENTS

There are many people I would like to thank:

Benjamin Graham and Warren Buffett—Ben Graham for his seminal work on investing and his love for our profession, and Warren Buffett for his willingness to share his investment approach so candidly in his many writings.

My colleagues Nick Hansen, Scott Link, and Rob Nicoski. Nick for writing Chapter 1. Nick is a young man with an incandescent future. Scott for writing Chapter 7. Scott is a brilliant analyst and competitive to the very core of his being. Rob for writing Chapter 6. Rob combines impeccable logic and great personal courage in his investment work. Each of these chapters was largely untouched by me.

Gene Walden. Gene helped me write this book. Not only did he write many parts of the book, but he also served as editor. Perhaps most important, he encouraged me to press on during those times when I just did not see the finish line.

Dennis Senneseth, Paul Becker, and Brad Anderson. Denny showed me very early on that it was possible to analyze companies systematically. He also taught me that it is OK to think about the world differently from others. Paul Becker taught me to look everywhere for good ideas and to apply the same discipline across all ideas. Brad taught me to think deeply about the overall environment for stocks.

John Parker, posthumously. John was a client and the closest to a mentor that I had. He was the best natural risk manager I ever met.

Craig Weflen. Craig wrote the Foreword to this book. He also exemplifies the very best in clients.

My brother Frank. Frank showed me that there is more than one way to invest.

Robert Buss. Robert was the instigator for this book. The thought of writing a book was not on my bucket list.

Evan Almeroth. Evan used his creativity and technical skills to make the charts in the book easy to understand. Since a picture is worth a thousand words, Evan might be the most prolific writer in the book!

All of the employees of DGI. Their competence and dedication made me feel comfortable taking on an endeavor like this book.

The many clients of DGI, too many to mention. They allowed us to translate our beliefs into action and to gain knowledge from those actions.

James Dobesh. Jim had the unenviable task of teaching me to fly turboprops and jets and then was graceful enough to become my fellow pilot. In addition to his superb flying skills, he showed me how to apply the margin of safety to flying.

My wife Sue. She is the wind beneath my wings.

1

■ ■ ■

Benjamin Graham and the Evolution
of Value Investing

uring an investment career that spanned more than half a century,
Benjamin Graham had a greater influence over the way stocks are
analyzed, bought, and sold than any other investor in the history of the
stock market. Graham practiced his trade during an era in which the stock
market evolved from an investment that was utilized almost exclusively by the
very wealthy to a pervasive investment that was used by almost everyone with
a job and a retirement savings account. As a professor, author, and stock market
trader, Graham turned stock market investing from a frenzied, speculative
practice based on intuition, emotion, and momentum to a precise science that
relied on strict formulas, meticulous analysis, and methodical timing.

Graham, who died in 1976 at the age of 82, has been referred to as the
"Dean of Wall Street," the "Father of Security Analysis," and the "Father of
Value Investing." As an author, he expounded on his methodology in two of
the most successful investment books ever published: *Security Analysis*, which
he wrote in 1934 with David Dodd, and *The Intelligent Investor*, which he
wrote in 1949. Both books have been periodically updated and still sell
briskly today.

To understand Graham's impact on the financial world, all you really
need to know is that he was Warren Buffett's mentor for more than two
decades before Buffett struck out on his own.

Graham is probably most widely recognized for his contribution to value investing, a methodology that relies on strict analysis and timing to acquire undervalued stocks when they're trading at a discount to their intrinsic value and sell them once they've earned a suitable return.

But until now, one of Graham's most brilliant revelations has been all but lost to the investing public. Although his name is nearly synonymous with value investing, Graham also began to see the value of growth stock investing late in his career. He even developed a formula and a methodology for growth stock investing that he introduced in the 1962 edition of *Security Analysis* in a chapter entitled "Newer Methods for Valuing Growth Stocks." Unfortunately, although *Security Analysis* was reissued in 1988, 1996, and 2009, this chapter was omitted from all the subsequent editions.

There's no real explanation for why this chapter was removed—a decision, oddly enough, that was made long after Graham's death in 1976. (The chapter is reprinted in Chapter 3 of this book.) Regardless of the reasons for the omission, investors who have read the newer editions of Graham's book over the past two decades have been denied one of the most significant investment insights ever offered by Graham.

The primary objective of this book is to unlock Graham's lost formula and methodology so that investors—both individual and professional— can take advantage of his insights on analyzing and buying growth stocks. I consider myself one of the fortunate few investment managers to have come across Graham's formula early in my career, and I have used it with great success ever since.

THE MAN AND HIS METHODOLOGY

Graham's investment philosophy was rooted in two important premises: that a security should be analyzed independently of its price, and that the future performance of any security is uncertain. He suggested that intelligent investors should aim to purchase a security at a discount to its assessed value in order to provide a margin of safety that can protect their investment against loss. Both the risk and the return of the investment are dependent on the quality of the analysis and this "margin of safety."

Graham did not stop there. With these principles firmly in hand, he laid out a comprehensive series of treatises on successful investing for the professional and lay investor alike. In *Security Analysis*, he focused primarily on the proper emphases and techniques to apply in the selection of investment securities. In *The Intelligent Investor*, which is widely considered his most influential work, Graham turned his attention to the investors themselves and laid out his philosophy of investment.

If the power of Graham's work was due to the simple truth at its foundation, its timelessness has been due to the quality of the craft Graham built upon it. He didn't construct a philosophy of investment in an academic vacuum; he derived it from long years of hard experience.

Graham was born in England in 1894 and moved with his parents to America the next year, where his father opened an import business. But the business failed, and his father died while Ben was still a child. In 1907, an economic crisis wiped out what little was still left of his mother's savings. But Graham excelled as a student and was able to get into Columbia University, where he graduated as class salutatorian at the age of 20. Columbia offered him a job teaching mathematics, English, or Greek and Latin philosophy, but he declined the offer to seek his fortune on Wall Street. He began working there for Newburger, Henderson & Loeb in 1914, and rose quickly in the firm. Within five years, he was making more than half a million dollars a year—a vast sum for a 25-year-old in 1919.

But that fortune didn't last. Graham and Jerome Henderson, who became Graham's business partner in the 1920s, nearly lost their business in the crash of 1929. But with the help of friends and the sale of most of their personal assets, Graham and Henderson were able to retain their business and rebuild it from the ground up. The lessons Graham learned from his early mistakes shaped his investment philosophy for the rest of his life.

Graham worked until the 1950s and continued writing into the 1970s, and during this period, he endured some of the greatest price dislocations and economic upheavals in modern history. Throughout, he refined his understanding and insight in subsequent editions of his published work. He was a successful practitioner and brilliant thinker living through extraordinary times, and he left us one of the most important bodies of work on investing ever written.

Not only was Graham a groundbreaking investment manager and prolific author, but he also taught evening classes in finance at Columbia from 1928 to 1955. One of his students was Warren Buffett, who managed to persuade Graham to hire him at his investment firm after he graduated from Columbia. It was there that Buffett learned the principles of investing that ultimately led him to become perhaps the most famous and successful stock market investor in America. Buffett subsequently built upon Graham's work over the course of his career. In fact, Buffett claims that Graham was the inspiration behind his widely read annual letters to shareholders that he writes for the Berkshire Hathaway annual report. In these letters, not only does Buffett provide readily accessible insight, but he does so in a fashion that is consistently both intellectually honest and humorous.

GRAHAM AS A GROWTH INVESTOR

To say the least, describing Graham as a growth investor is highly controversial and almost heretical among his many value investing disciples. The two strategies are considered almost polar opposites. Value investing focuses on paying a lower price for current assets or earnings in order to risk less capital against an uncertain future, while growth investing is traditionally characterized by the willingness of investors to pay a higher price for a company's current assets or earnings in the expectation that the future growth of the company will stimulate a rising stock price.

To support this assertion concerning Graham, then, we must refashion the traditional understanding of growth and value investing. In its simplest sense, "value" represents a purchasing style, not an investing style. The relationship between the two terms *growth* and *value* is confused. We believe that, thanks to Graham and Buffett, a "value" mindset has actually become a critical component of the growth investing process.

To make our case, it will be helpful to review the works of Graham and Buffett and speculate on their inspiration and development.

In his first job out of college at Newburger, Henderson & Loeb, Graham began as a junior bond salesman and was quickly elevated to a statistician. It was in that role that he refined his understanding of and appreciation for the raw numbers underlying each investment. But it was only after his fortune and his business were nearly wiped out that Graham truly began to put together the investment philosophy that was to form the foundation for his complex approach to security analysis. Graham's misfortunes were brought on by liquidity issues on margin calls, overly optimistic investments in "hot" stocks, and the Great Depression itself. Simultaneously, he continued to make money by purchasing securities with substantial non-operating assets, significant yields, and generally undervalued, unrecognized, or unpopular assets. These experiences were to guide his views on price, value, and conservatism, which would permeate the body of his written work.

It was the market's crash from 1929 to 1932 that spurred Graham to write in order to supplement his income. In addition to *Security Analysis* and *The Intelligent Investor*, Graham wrote several other books, articles, and papers.

The key to understanding the evolution of Graham's thinking lies in recognizing the source of his knowledge. While he had trained in the classics in school, Graham already had 20 years of practical experience in the field by the time he published the first edition of *Security Analysis*. Further editions benefited even more from his ongoing professional experience and his commitment to empiricism. Graham did not seek to create a mathematically pure or cohesive theory of investment; he brought a dynamic, bottom-up perspective to the development of his ideas. His philosophy reflects this origin.

Any investment, and the subsequent return on that investment, depends first and foremost on the price paid for that investment. That price—the vote taken by the market on value—can be an almost irresistible argument for a company's worth. Graham resisted this argument: between his own family's travails and the extreme vacillation of the market during the boom of the 1920s, the crash of 1929, and the subsequent recovery and bull run of the late 1940s and 1950s, Graham came to recognize the frequently irrational nature of market prices and the psychological effects of the consequent vacillations in wealth. This experience probably formed the genesis of his "Mr. Market" metaphor, in which he describes the stock market as a bipolar business partner that arrives daily without fail to quote you a price at which he will buy or sell portions of the partnership from or to you, and is sure to return again, unfazed, if you decline his offers. It also probably underlies his frequent admonitions to investors themselves: "The investor's chief problem—and even his worst enemy—is likely to be himself." Graham knew that separating value from price was easier said than done, and he provided practical advice to supplement the principle.

Graham disregarded price as an indicator of value and sought to develop a logically rigorous and more stringent methodology for evaluating an investment. His chief insight, encapsulated in his own words as the most important principle of investment, was a "margin of safety." He stressed that regardless of the quality and breadth of your information and analysis, the future of any stock is fundamentally uncertain. As a result, you must always account for your inevitable errors in forecasting and valuation by purchasing an investment at a significant discount to its assessed value. Graham pointed out that you are less likely to lose money if you have paid less money in the first place: you cannot control the future of the investment, but you can control the price paid.

The margin of safety implicitly reiterates that one *can* effectively assess the value of a security independently of the rest of the market. Graham's experience with wildly gyrating expectations for the future led him to initially appreciate more stable evidence of value, such as marketable nonoperating or off-balance sheet assets, over less tangible or less reliable sources of worth, such as future earnings growth. In his earlier writings, he repeatedly emphasized the valuation of the assets of the business. Only later in his career did he begin to focus on evaluating the long-term earnings potential of a company.

As with all aspects of his philosophy, Graham's appreciation of the power of growth was the consequence of experience. As his career progressed, he developed an appreciation for the long-term power of growth, which he first brought to light in his chapter "Newer Methods for Valuing Growth Stocks" in the 1962 edition of *Security Analysis*. In a later edition of *The Intelligent Investor*, Graham explained, "The risk of paying too high a price for good-quality stocks—while a real one—is not the chief hazard confronting the average buyer of securities . . . the chief losses to investors come from the purchase of *low-quality* securities at times of favorable business conditions."

The most powerful argument for growth in Graham's experience came later in his career, when he purchased a major stake in GEICO. That single transaction, which accounted for about a quarter of his assets at the time, ultimately yielded more profit than all his other investments combined. He paid $27 per share for GEICO stock and watched it rise over the ensuing years to the equivalent of $54,000 *per share*. Ironically, although Graham is universally associated with value investing, his greatest profit came from a growth company. In the concluding chapter of the final edition of *The Intelligent Investor*, he stated:

> The philosophy of investment in growth stocks parallels in part and in part contravenes the margin-of-safety principle. The growth-stock buyer relies on an expected earnings power that is greater than the average shown in the past. Thus he may be said to substitute these expected earnings for the past record in calculating his margin of safety. In investment theory there is no reason why carefully estimated future earnings should be a less reliable guide than the bare record of the past; in fact, security analysis is coming more and more to prefer a competently executed evaluation of the future. Thus the growth-stock approach may supply as dependable a margin of safety as is found in the ordinary investment—provided the calculation of the future is conservatively made, and provided it shows a satisfactory margin in relation to price paid.

While he never exclusively endorsed growth stock investing, Graham, over the course of his career, began to appreciate the power of that approach. And where Graham left off, Warren Buffett picked up.

BUFFETT AND GRAHAM

After working for Graham in New York, Buffett moved back to Omaha in 1956 and founded a limited partnership, Buffett Associates. Ultimately, Buffett melded that firm with several other partnerships and mostly liquidated it in 1969. He distributed the remaining shares of Berkshire and Diversified Retailing to the partners, observing that he was "unable to find any bargains in the current market." He then proceeded to take control of Berkshire and make several acquisitions, building the investment conglomerate that today is known as Berkshire Hathaway. In the first 10 years of his original partnership, Buffett's investments grew by 1,156 percent versus just a 123 percent rise in the Dow Jones Industrial Average. Berkshire Hathaway's success has been similarly incredible, registering a total gain of 434,057 percent from 1965 to 2009 versus a total return on the S&P 500 of 5,430 percent. That translates into a 20.3 percent compounded annual growth rate, versus 9.3 percent for the S&P 500.

However, Buffett did not totally buy into Graham's perspective on investing. He initially focused more on traditional value investing, but over time, he came to appreciate the value of growth companies. The fact is, the largest and most profitable positions in Buffett's portfolio have not been typical "value" stocks, but rather companies such as Coca-Cola, GEICO, Procter & Gamble, American Express, and Walmart—companies that have all profited immensely from long-term earnings growth. He definitely did not get rich by investing in the original business of Berkshire.

So while Buffett cleaved closely to Graham's emphasis on a margin of safety and an independent analysis of the true value of underlying assets, he began to focus more closely on the underlying earnings power, the value of competent management, and intangibles, such as brand and other competitive advantages. These focuses did not contradict Graham's principles, but were permutations of them. They represented a growing understanding of the nature of the value of a company and its ability to hold that value in the future.

Buffett's contribution to Graham's philosophy, similarly derived from decades of actual experience in the field, was a more refined sense of the ingredients of value in a business. Buffett, having benefited deeply from Graham's "intellectual generosity," was free to develop an understanding of valuation that went beyond the balance sheet. Buffett emphasized a conservative approach to this strategy. Whereas Graham was reluctant to attribute value to assets that he could not quantify, Buffett was suspicious of investing in companies whose business model or product he could not comprehend.

But both men were in agreement on the simple assertion that investing in something one does not understand can be a recipe for disaster. This concept of risk stands in contrast to the popular notion that fluctuations in price indicate a collective and more superior indication of uncertainty, and thus of risk. Moreover, this collective assessment of risk is then posited to be the prime determinant of return. Not only does Graham challenge that assertion (he believed that risk is simply the chance that the investors might permanently lose their capital), but he stated flatly that risk and return are erroneously interconnected. As he put it, "There has developed a general notion that the rate of return which the investor should aim for is more or less proportionate to the degree of risk he is ready to run. Our view is different. The rate of return sought should be dependent, rather, on the amount of intelligent effort the investor is willing and able to bring to bear on his task."

If Graham recognized that both risk and return were products of intelligent effort, it was Buffett who recognized that the amount of effort available to any one investor was finite and must be allocated judiciously. Graham never wrote much about the "buy-and-hold" strategy that Buffett utilized—this strategy was more a consequence of Buffett's increasing focus on capturing the value of long-term earnings growth. If investors were required to regenerate their portfolios anew each year, their understanding of the assets they held would necessarily be limited, and thus their portfolios would be riskier.

Similarly, it was unlikely that investors would be compensated for the value of long-term growth over such a short period.

EMPIRICAL EXPERIENCE

Graham and Buffett developed their philosophy from empirical experience; it was not a theory that sprang into the world wholly formed, but an ongoing attempt to understand and profit from reality. When viewed through this lens, the development of their philosophy reflects the growing sophistication of the lessons they learned as their experiences grew. Against sufficient evidence, any aspect of this philosophy was mutable.

Graham's philosophy began with primary principles: evaluate the fundamental worth of a security, and then purchase it with a margin of safety to protect against error. He began with an analysis of a company's most evident, concretely valuable assets: the components of the balance sheet. Over time, Graham recognized the potential for *reliably* evaluating the worth of more intangible assets, such as the potential for earnings growth. Buffett carried this insight further, delineating such intangible components as brand, competent and responsible management teams, competitive advantage, and culture. As each became comfortable with the proper relationship among price, value, and uncertainty, they were freed to refine their ability to better value the more subtle elements of a business.

Their philosophy is often misconstrued by investors, who interpret it as a static dogma, an unchangeable bible of investment. Buying a company inexpensively based on tangible assets is not a principle. It is simply Graham's earlier application of the principle of buying a company after proper analysis and with a margin of safety between the price paid and the value. Buying cheaply is the principle. It is not a dictate to buy cheaply based only on assets, or based on present earnings.

That philosophy is not now (nor will it ever be) complete. There are areas that merit further development. While Buffett identified many of the less tangible but more important determinants of a company's value, he did not delve deeply into the details of their nature. In this book, we will build upon his work on sustainable competitive advantage, culture, management, and other drivers of growth. We will also further expand upon the Mr. Market analogy; that is, we will cultivate a more nuanced manner in which to use the market's misevaluation of companies to supply both a margin of safety and further profit. But even more important, we will make the case that growth companies are the superior investment choice for the Graham–Buffett investor.

While this book will by no means be the final word on effective investing, we believe the strategies and methodologies presented here will represent the next step in a natural progression begun by Benjamin Graham.

2

■ ■ ■

Value versus Growth

All intelligent investing is value investing—acquiring more than
you are paying for. You must value the business in order
to value the stock.
—CHARLIE MUNGER

O
ver the past two decades, equity money managers have been divided
into two broad categories: growth managers and value managers. The
Frank Russell Company has even developed separate indexes for
growth stocks and value stocks.

Some investors—Warren Buffett among them—would argue that this is
a distinction without a difference. "In our opinion the two approaches are
joined at the hip," says Buffett in his book *The Essays of Warren Buffett: Lessons*
for Corporate America. "Growth is *always* a component in the calculation of
value, constituting a variable whose importance can range from negligible to
enormous and whose impact can be negative as well as positive."

He also scoffs at the notion of "value investing." "We think the very
term 'value investing' is redundant. What is 'investing' if not the act of seeking value at least sufficient to justify the amount paid? Consciously paying
more for a stock than its calculated value—in the hope that it can be sold
for a still higher price—should be labeled speculation (which is neither
illegal, immoral nor—in our view—financially fattening)."

This arbitrary splitting of the investment environment into value and growth categories can offer helpful insights for investors that will aid the process of understanding and valuing companies. Whether you favor value stocks or growth stocks, a consistent, understandable (by the investment manager and the client) discipline is a minimum condition for successful stock market investing.

Every investor faces two key questions with the purchase of any stock: (1) what kind of company am I buying, and (2) have I built in an adequate margin of safety for purchase of that stock? Knowing whether you own a growth company or a value company can help clarify your thinking about how to approach each type of investment.

In this chapter, we are going to focus on the distinctions between growth investing and value investing; we'll highlight the pitfalls and dangers of investing in each type of company and, ultimately, make the case that investing in growth companies gives investors a far better chance of long-term success than investing in value companies.

GROWTH COMPANIES AND GROWTH INVESTORS

A growth company is a company that grows faster than the average company over the long term and earns a satisfactory return on its investors' capital. If the average company grows earnings per share at perhaps 4 percent per year, then a growth company would grow faster than 4 percent per year and earn a satisfactory return on shareholders' capital.

Benjamin Graham offered his own definition of a growth company in the 1949 edition of *The Intelligent Investor*: "A growth stock may be defined as one which has done better than average over a number of years in the past and is expected to do so in the future." He expanded on the definition in the 1962 edition of *Security Analysis*: "The term 'growth stock' is applied to one which has increased its per share earnings in the past at well above the rate for common stocks generally and is expected to continue to do so in the future."

A growth investor is someone who seeks to invest in growth companies.

VALUE COMPANIES AND VALUE INVESTORS

Ironically, a value company has never been universally defined. For our purposes in this book, we are going to take the liberty of offering our own definition of a value company: a mature company that is growing more slowly than the average company. This category could include many companies with no long-term growth whatsoever.

A value investor is someone who seeks to invest in value companies.

GROWTH STOCKS AND VALUE STOCKS

Investors should constantly remind themselves of the difference between a company and a stock. A company is a real set of people engaged in the business of dispensing products or services. Every company has some reasonably definable value (intrinsic value), based on an analysis of its current earnings and cash flow and its future prospects. A stock is traded publicly and offers a daily price at which investors are willing to buy or sell shares in that company. The daily stock price and the intrinsic value for every company can and will differ widely.

Growth stocks are the publicly traded entities of companies that are growing faster than the average company. Value stocks, by our definition, are the publicly traded entities of companies that are growing more slowly than the average company.

Ironically, the disparity between the intrinsic value of a company and the price of its stock can at times make a growth company into a value stock and vice versa. In fact, the disparity between intrinsic value and stock price has made the classification of stocks difficult. Does the analyst classify the stock of a growth company as a growth stock if the stock price is low? When developing their growth and value stock indexes, the analysts at Frank Russell must have struggled with how to identify a growth stock and a value stock. It appears that they chose to populate their indexes on the basis of the stocks rather than the companies. The stocks in the Russell Growth Index tend to be higher-priced stocks, measured by price/earnings and price/book value. The stocks in its value index tend to offer lower valuations when measured by the same metrics.

In evaluating investment choices, it's better to focus on the company than on the stock. And the companies that we believe offer the best potential for long-term growth are growth companies—not value companies. Even Benjamin Graham conceded that given the choice between growth and value companies, "It seems only logical that the intelligent investor should concentrate upon the selection of growth stocks," although he added, "actually the matter is more complicated" (*The Intelligent Investor*, 1949 ed., p. 91). In his later edition, Graham allowed a further endorsement of growth stock investing: "Obviously," he said, "stocks of this kind are attractive to buy and own, provided the price paid is not excessive."

Graham ran his portfolio as a value investor through much of his career—executing countless transactions and buying and selling stocks on the price swings, with the practice of buying very well and selling opportunistically. And yet in his most notable foray into growth stock investing—buying shares of GEICO when it was a young company and holding them for many years—Graham earned far more money on that single transaction than on all of his value stock transactions combined. In other words, Graham spent his life pursuing a value investing strategy, but made his fortune as a growth stock investor.

HOW TO PROFIT FROM VALUE COMPANY INVESTING

Investing in value companies has many of the same attributes as investing in fixed-income securities. Neither endeavor offers much in the way of future growth potential, but that doesn't mean that investing in value companies is unprofitable. In fact, it is entirely rational to expect reasonable profitability from such an effort.

Investing in value companies offers two sources of potential profit: dividends and capitalizing on the disparity between stock price and intrinsic value.

The Value of Dividends

The value of dividends has been overlooked during the past several decades, even though most studies of long-term total returns from stocks show that dividends play an important role in generating those returns. Dividends have become more important recently, in part because of the meager yields available from fixed-income securities. A retired couple living on the income from their investments might see a great benefit in investing in a stable company with a good dividend.

Dividends are particularly important for value companies, although many of those companies could do more with their dividends. In the best possible scenario, a value company in a no-growth industry with a good business model, a secure customer base, and a return on equity of 12 percent per year could theoretically pay out 100 percent of its earnings in the form of dividends. If you could buy that stock at its book value, you would earn a very attractive 12 percent annual dividend yield.

Unfortunately, nearly all value companies choose to pay out something less than 100 percent of their earnings in dividends. In recent years, many value companies have paid a dividend yield in the range of 3 to 5 percent.

We would guess that most investors would not be satisfied with an average annual return of only 5 percent from a stock, but would like at least an 8 percent annual return to justify the risk of investing in the stock. How does an investor gain a long-term return of 8 percent from a value company whose stock is yielding 5 percent? Since stock prices and intrinsic values rarely coincide, there are times when an investor can buy a value stock for less than its intrinsic value. This variance gives the investor the potential to improve his return from 5 percent to 8 percent by intelligently exploiting the difference between stock price and intrinsic value.

For example, if Company A has an intrinsic value of $10 per share, earns $1 per share, and pays out 50 percent of its earnings (50 cents) in dividends, let's examine three possible scenarios an investor might face.

The three scenarios, laid out here, include the chance to buy the stock at $8, $10, or $12 per share:

Purchase price	$8	$10	$12
Dividend yield	6.3%	5.0%	4.2%
Average annual price appreciation*	2.3%	0.0%	–1.7%
Average annual total return	8.6%	5.0%	2.5%

*The 2.3 percent price appreciation for the $8 stock assumes that stock price and intrinsic value will coincide in ten years. If the stock price and the intrinsic value coincide in less than 10 years, the annual return may be higher.

From this example, it is clear that value investors must typically buy below intrinsic value in order to earn a reasonable return on their stock purchases.

PROFITING FROM GROWTH COMPANY INVESTING

An investor in a growth company has three sources of potential return: (1) dividends, (2) exploiting the disparity between stock price and intrinsic value, and (3) long-term growth in intrinsic value.

Far too often, growth companies choose not to pay a current dividend. This practice reflects management's opinion that retained earnings are better invested in growing the business. For those fortunate growth companies that can concurrently grow and generate free cash flow, a dividend payment can be an important source of return for investors. Eventually, all growth companies become mature. If the management has developed the business properly so that the company has a significant and sustainable free cash flow, a substantial dividend payout can, in some cases, exceed the original purchase price of the stock!

A careful investor in growth companies should always seek to exploit any disparities between stock price and intrinsic value, especially at the time of purchase. While a value company investor must pay below intrinsic value in order to achieve a reasonable return, a growth company investor must seek to purchase the stock at a price of fair value or less.

If you buy stock in a growth company with an intrinsic value of $10 a share and the intrinsic value grows by 15 percent per year, in 5 years the stock will be worth $20; in 10 years, it will be worth $40; and in 15 years, it will be worth $80 in intrinsic value. Even at a 10 percent annual growth rate, after 7 years, the company's intrinsic value would have grown from $10 per share to $20. After 14 years, it would have grown to $40; and after 21 years, it would have grown to $80.

SHORTCOMINGS OF BOTH GROWTH AND VALUE COMPANIES

There are at least four potential shortcomings that apply to both value and growth company investing:

1. *The company reinvests its retained earnings poorly.* Every corporate management can distribute after-tax earnings to shareholders in the form of dividends, reinvest the earnings in the company, or some combination of the two. (Share repurchases are clearly not a return of net earnings or cash to shareholders!) For both value and growth companies, if the management reinvests retained earnings poorly, this dissipation of shareholders' capital will drag down the company's return on capital. Over longer periods of time, the stock market has been ruthless in punishing the shareholders of these companies.

2. *Predicting the future requires both vision and conservatism.* Yogi Berra once said, "It's hard to make predictions—especially about the future." Whether you're investing in growth companies or value companies, you're still relying on expectations of future performance. In the case of value companies, you are hoping that the value company will continue to manage its business well. If the company pays dividends and you are reinvesting the dividend payments, you are hoping that future interest rates will not be unreasonably low. If you are investing in a growth company, you are hoping that the company will achieve a

satisfactory rate of growth and manage its business well. Investing in stocks requires the investor to use some level of imagination about what the future will bring. But that imagination has to be tempered by a sense of moderation about what is likely to occur. In general, investors are best served by the idea of cautious optimism. Before you invest, develop a vision for where you believe the company can go, and make sure its odds of achieving that vision are well within reason.

3. *The company is stingy with its dividends.* The managements of most companies (both value and growth) tend to overestimate their ability to reinvest retained earnings in order to earn a reasonable return. This means that they tend to follow stingy dividend payout policies that are adverse to shareholder interests. In the case of the no-growth value companies, management often allocates the return on equity to various investments designed to achieve corporatewide growth. Frequently, these efforts involve acquisitions of other companies, which far too often fail to provide a reasonable return on invested capital. What the management should do instead is admit that this is a no-growth company and pay out all of its earnings to its shareholders in the form of dividends. Many growth companies today have such superior business models that they have been able to both grow at rapid rates and generate extra cash. Companies such as Apple Computer and Cisco Systems now have tens of billions of dollars in cash on their balance sheets and pay no dividend. Their refusal to pay an annual dividend has been a disservice to their long-term shareholders.

4. *The disparity between intrinsic value and market value doesn't narrow.* Benjamin Graham said that the stock market is a voting machine in the short run and a weighing machine in the long run. Implicit in this statement is the idea that the price of the stock and the intrinsic value of the company will tend to coincide over the long term. However, it is possible that the stock price may remain well below

the intrinsic value for a long period. If a major component of the expected return from a stock is the narrowing of the disparity between the stock price and the intrinsic value, a lengthy delay in closing that disparity would diminish the return from that stock.

CHALLENGES SPECIFIC TO VALUE COMPANY INVESTING

When you invest in a value company, you must accept that you are buying an asset that is likely to experience little or no long-term growth in intrinsic value. Investing in value companies can be roughly compared to investing in bonds.

Here are six challenges associated with value company investing:

1. *You will probably have to trade to enhance your return.* It is prudent to assume that most value companies will experience little or no growth in intrinsic value. Let's say an investor wants to earn a compound return of 9 percent per year over the long term. If the dividend yield of Company A is 5 percent and the company is likely to grow at less than 4 percent, the investor must trade the stock in order to enhance her return. The investment life of a value investor is one of researching and buying stocks at a price below intrinsic value and selling them at a price equal to or higher than intrinsic value.

2. *Time is not in your favor.* In order to earn an acceptable return on invested capital, the market value and the intrinsic value of a value company must true up quickly enough to meet the target return on investment. For instance, you might buy a stock that is trading at a 20 percent discount to its intrinsic value in hopes that the market price will ultimately catch up with the intrinsic value. If that happens in the first year or two, you could earn an enhanced return. But if it takes 5 or 10 years for the market price to reach the intrinsic value, the annual rate of return could be dramatically less. For a value investor, time really is of the essence.

3. *Your losers control your returns.* Let's say you invest $100 each in three value companies. Two of the companies perform as expected and provide a total return (dividends plus interest) of 50 percent over the next five years. The third investment is a disaster and falls by 50 percent during that period. The portfolio would have earned a return of only $50 (an increase from $300 to $350). Although your success rate was high (66 percent), your winning positions were barely profitable enough to offset your single losing position.

4. *Value company managements need to control their urge to grow.* Company executives are often reluctant to accept a no-growth strategy, even in a no-growth industry. Worse, far too often, shareholders push no-growth companies into unsustainable growth strategies. These companies can be tempted to seek bad growth through inept acquisitions and product line extensions rather than simply allocating retained earnings to shareholders in the form of dividends. The result can be disastrous for shareholders, as Eastman Kodak demonstrated over the past three decades. As Roben Farzad succinctly explained in *Bloomberg Businessweek* (July 12, 2010), Eastman Kodak "blew upward of $15 billion on abortive acquisitions and product development in the 1980s and 1990s as its core film business shriveled. The whole company is now worth just $1 billion; wouldn't shareholders have preferred to get some of that $15 billion back?"

5. *The "concrete rowboat" or "value trap."* When value investors buy a stock, they generally make the assumption that the company's management will continue to operate its business as effectively in the future as it has in the past. They anticipate that even a no-growth company will continue to maintain a consistent return on equity, supporting the current intrinsic value of the company. With a "value trap," the investor buys into a strong, mature company. The investor buys stock at a price that reflects a healthy discount to intrinsic value. The strong, mature company then

slowly mismanages its business, and the intrinsic value of the company sinks like a concrete rowboat. For example, since the 1960s, General Motors shareholders have continued to believe that the once-dominant company would perform well enough to maintain its intrinsic value. In fact, I must confess, we were also tempted by this siren song for far too long. Unfortunately, General Motors continued to slowly dissipate shareholder capital until its bankruptcy in 2009.

On rare occasions, an entire industry can collapse, sinking a whole fleet of concrete rowboats—a fate that sank investment manager Bill Miller, who was perhaps the most prominent value investor of the modern era. Miller, who managed the Legg Mason Value Trust, outperformed the Standard & Poor's 500 Index for 15 consecutive years, from 1991 through 2005. That incredible feat earned Miller a flotilla of honors and accolades from throughout the financial industry. *Money* magazine named him "The Greatest Money Manager of the 1990s," Morningstar designated him the "Fund Manager of the Decade" in 1999, and *BusinessWeek* dubbed him one of the "Heroes of Value Investing." Unfortunately for Miller, he had allocated much of his fund's assets to a fleet of concrete rowboats in 2009, when his portfolio of value companies in the financial sector was capsized by the global financial crisis. Shares of the Miller-led Legg Mason Value Trust plunged 77 percent—from a high of $78.93 in June 2007 to a low of $18.48 in March 2009. (Within the next two years, the shares recovered to about $38 a share.)

6. *Reinvesting the dividends.* Value investors typically buy stocks that pay dividends, so they also need to find a way to reinvest those dividends to keep their money working. It's a lot like bond investing. You might find a bond that pays 10 percent, but what do you do with the 10 percent payout? Can you find other stocks or bonds that match that rate? If not, the annual rate of return from your portfolio will decline.

CHALLENGES SPECIFIC TO GROWTH COMPANY INVESTING

Here are six key challenges for growth company investors:

1. *Paying too much.* There is a temptation to pay too much when you buy the stock. For instance, if a company's intrinsic value is $10 per share, but you decide to pay $80 per share to buy the stock, the company will have to grow 15 percent per year for the next 15 years before its intrinsic value will reach the price you paid for the stock. This was the root problem of the tech-led bear market from 2000 to 2002. There are some investors who are still waiting for the intrinsic value of the Internet and tech stocks they bought in the 1990s to catch up with the market price—and their wait may continue for years to come.

2. *Expecting too much.* It is far too easy to overestimate the future growth rate of a growth company. We are continually amazed at the casualness with which Wall Street analysts forecast growth rates of 20 percent or higher. Consider that a company that is growing at 20 percent per year will double in size every 3½ years! This means that half of the employees will have been with the company less than four years, and the customer base is likely to be relatively new. Internal budgeting is very challenging: the company will have to approximately double its physical space every 3½ years. And, adding to the challenge, fast-growing industries often attract tough new competitors.

3. *Pursuing a bad growth strategy.* The growth company you invest in could pursue a bad growth strategy instead of a good growth strategy. For instance, it could make some bad acquisitions or line extensions just for the sake of growing the company when a better strategy might have been to simply build on its strengths in order to become a more dominant player in its field. That could enable the company to continue to grow organically—even if the pace of the growth was slower. When you purchase a stock, you're essentially betting on the management to continue to make sage decisions that

will keep the company growing with a reasonable return on invested capital. Many technology companies invested poorly after the 2000–2002 bear market. Harmonic, a broadband hardware provider, was trading at over $150 a share in 2000 with a P/E of more than 100. In recent years, the stock has been hovering at $6 a share and is still struggling to post positive earnings. BroadVision, an e-commerce software maker that once was a darling of Wall Street, was recently trading at less than a penny on the dollar after reverse splits of 1-for-9 and 1-for-25. The stock had been trading in recent years at about $12 a share, down from a split-adjusted high in 2000 of about $19,000 a share. Commerce One, one of the hottest e-commerce companies in the 1990s, was trading at well over $100 a share in 1999 and 2000—despite having no earnings—before it spiraled into bankruptcy and was sold off in parts in 2004. Other onetime high-flyers, such as Exodus Communications, have long since declared bankruptcy and closed their doors.

4. *The temptations of trading.* Growth stocks tend to be more volatile than value stocks, which sometimes leads investors to believe that trading these stocks is a surefire way to enhance their returns. Only the most highly skilled traders can trade these stocks profitably; most likely, the trading activity will create profits for the brokers, not the client. Incredibly, many growth company institutional investors who should know better exhibit annual levels of trading activity that indicate that they have fallen prey to the temptations of trading.

5. *Trees do not grow to the sky.* Even the best growth companies eventually mature and slow down in growth. The investor needs to be able to plan accordingly. Even Microsoft, one of the most successful technology stocks of all time, ultimately reached a plateau and saw its growth slow to a crawl. Medtronic, the world's leading heart pacemaker producer, also saw its growth hit the wall after many years of double–digit returns. Graham addressed that issue in *The Intelligent Investor*: "Unusually rapid growth cannot keep up forever. When a company has already registered

a great expansion, its very increase in size makes the repetition of its achievement very difficult. At some point the growth flattens out and, in many cases, turns downward."

6. *Winners control your returns.* In a growth company portfolio, the winning stocks can appreciate many times over and will eventually dominate the losers. The mathematics of this concept is simple. If you invest $100 each in three stocks and lose everything on two stocks over the next five years but make 10 times your investment on the third stock, your success rate is low, but the portfolio has appreciated from $300 to $1,000, a gain of 333 percent. For a growth company investor, the old saying, "let your winners run," is particularly appropriate.

Now that we've defined growth companies and value companies and identified some challenges that are common to both and some that are specific to each, let's examine some of the key issues facing long-term investors. As you'll see, growth company investing, if done properly, offers a better chance of long-term success than value company investing.

The average investor has an "investing life" of approximately 50 years. Most investors think, incorrectly, that the returns achieved over the last one, three, five, or ten years are the most important factor in determining how to proceed going forward. Instead, the number one issue facing every investor is the need to achieve a reasonable compound return over his entire lifetime.

THE POWER OF COMPOUND INTEREST

Compound interest has often been dubbed "the eighth wonder of the world." It is the interest paid on interest from previous periods as well as on the principal. Though small at first, the additional returns can become substantial over time. An investment of $100, if compounded over time at the rate of 10 percent, would grow to $260 over 10 years, $673 over 20 years, and $11,730 over 50 years. Figure 2.1 visualizes the "layers" of compound interest.

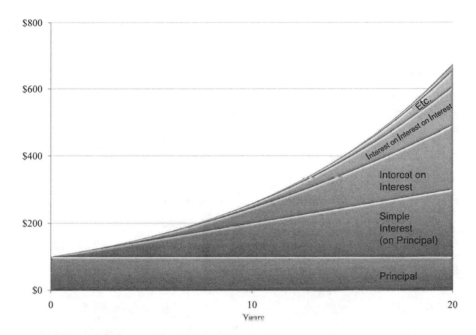

Figure 2.1 Compound Interest Tranches

The equivalent yearly rate is also referred to as the annual percentage rate, the annual percentage yield, and similar terms. These terms, which are often required by the government, assist consumers in comparing the actual cost of borrowing money more easily. By contrast, *simple interest* refers to interest that is not added to the principal. But compound interest is the type of interest that is generally referred to in finance and economics.

Let's look at the difference that compound interest can make over a lifetime of investing. Since the average investor has an investment lifetime of approximately 50 years, let's look at the difference that compound interest can make over long periods of time. Let's begin by examining shorter periods.

Investors A, B, and C begin their investment foray with $100,000 each. Investor A earns 5 percent per year compounded, Investor B earns 7 percent per year compounded, and Investor C earns 9 percent per year compounded. For most investors, these differences in performance do not seem that significant. Indeed, after five years, Investor A has $127,628, Investor B has

$140,255, and Investor C has $153,862. Investor C has less than 10 percent more than Investor B and about 20 percent more than Investor A.

The spread begins to grow over time. After 10 years, Investor C has $236,736, Investor B has $196,715, and Investor A has $162,889. Investor C now has 45 percent more assets than Investor A and 20 percent more than Investor B. After 20 years, Investor C now has $560,441, Investor B has $386,968, and Investor A has $265,330. Even though Investors A and B have made nice profits over the 20 years, Investor C has 45 percent more assets than Investor B and more than twice the assets of Investor A.

After 50 years, the differences are staggering. Investor C (9 percent per year) is now worth $7,435,752, Investor B (7 percent) is worth $2,945,703, and Investor A (5 percent) is worth $1,146,740. Investor C is worth more than 2.5 times as much as Investor B and nearly 7 times as much as Investor A.

In Figure 2.2, you can see the importance that a couple of percentage points can make over the long term. Seemingly small annual differences in investment returns can produce extreme differences in investment results over long periods of time.

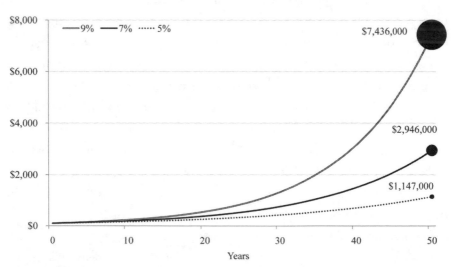

Differences in Rates ($000s)

Figure 2.2 Power of Compounding

INVESTORS SHOULD ESTABLISH A TARGET RETURN

Looking at tables of compound returns is straightforward, but actually using the concept of compound interest in the real world is much more complicated.

The first key to thinking about compound interest is to understand the difference between a goal and a target. Let's say Investor A's goal is to earn 9 percent per year compounded over 50 years. This would mean that Investor A's initial investment of $100,000 would grow to a nice sum of greater than $7 million. What target return should Investor A shoot for in order to ensure reasonable odds of achieving a 9 percent compounded annual return?

A quick scan of the compound interest tables yields a very interesting answer. (Compound interest tables should be a part of every investor's library, right next to your copy of Graham's *The Intelligent Investor* and *Security Analysis*, as well as *The Selected Essays of Warren Buffett: Lessons for Corporate America* and, we hope, this book.)

We looked at the effects of two events on the long-term compound rate of return. The first event is a one-year 50 percent decline in market value. To add clarity, let's assume that Investor A compounds her portfolio at 9 percent per year for 49 years and suffers a 50 percent decline in year 50. Investor A is still wealthy, with a portfolio value of nearly $3.4 million. However, her long-term compound return has declined from 9 percent to slightly greater than 7 percent. It does not matter whether Investor A suffers a loss in the first, tenth, or fiftieth year; the effect is still the same. Figure 2.3 shows how, when an investor sets an appropriate target, setbacks would not necessarily cause her to miss her goal. She may miss her target return of 9 percent but will still make her goal of 7 percent.

Investor B avoids the one-year 50 percent decline but suffers in a different way. It seems that about every 40 years or so, the markets experience a decade of no return. The years from 1929 to 1939, 1965 to 1975, and 2000 to 2010 come to mind. If Investor B compounds his portfolio at 9 percent per year for 40 years but suffers through a decade of no returns, the effect on his compound return is approximately the same as if he had had a one-year

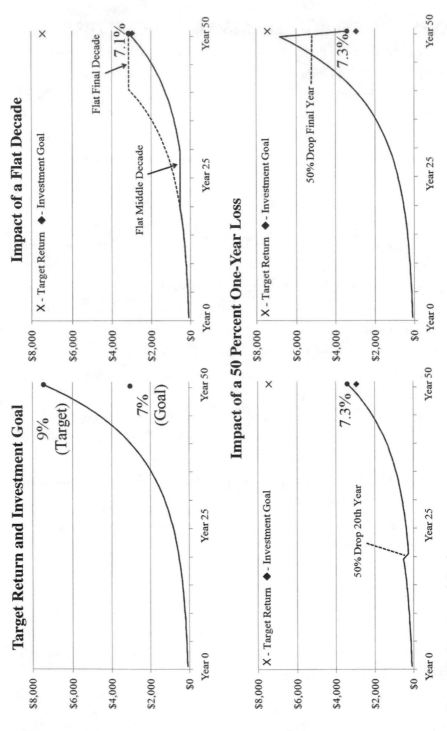

Figure 2.3 Targets and Goals

50 percent loss. His long-term return would decline from 9 percent to slightly greater than 7 percent.

We think it is prudent to assume that one of these two events is likely to occur within an investor's lifetime. This means that investors should make their target return about 2 percent higher than their long-term compound interest goal. In other words, if you want to achieve a compound return of 9 percent per year, you must have a target return of 11 percent per year. If you want 7 percent per year, you must target 9 percent.

(Please bear in mind that this discussion refers to returns before fees. Excessive fees often associated with frequent trading or mutual fund ownership can have a significant impact on your long-term returns.)

For the investor who is seeking a 9 percent long-term return (11 percent target return), the case for growth stocks becomes intuitively more appealing. How many value companies are going to provide a combination of dividend yield and growth rate equal to 11 percent? The challenge here is daunting. A value company with a generous 5 percent dividend yield must grow at a rate of 6 percent (faster than the average company) in order to achieve an 11 percent return.

The only path we know to achieving double-digit returns with value companies is to engage in high-turnover strategies.

The problem with trying to achieve double-digit returns with value companies is very similar to that of an average golfer who is trying to play at the level of the pros. You must constantly try to make difficult shots that you are simply not capable of making on a consistent basis. You might make those shots some of the time, but by stretching the limits and increasing the risk, you would also put yourself in some very difficult positions—sand traps, roughs, trees, and water traps.

As an investor, if you shoot for a hurdle rate that is too high (particularly with value companies), you must constantly take chances and constantly buy stocks at deep discounts that may have underlying problems that you haven't detected or don't understand. As a result, you will make some mistakes, pick some bad stocks, and find yourself on the losing end of too many investments.

Those losses will drag down your overall return on investment—even if you choose correctly for some of your picks. In fact, based on the published returns of the leading value stock funds, even professional money managers have been unable to sustain double-digit growth with a strategy that relies on high turnover and deeply discounted stocks.

Whether you are investing in growth companies or value companies, it's important that you choose a rate of return modest enough that you can avoid excessive risk and make good choices in your stock selection process.

CALCULATING INVESTMENT PERFORMANCE: HOW AM I DOING?

Along with compound interest tables, we encourage every investor to understand the basics of performance calculation. The first question is whether you have made or lost money on your investments. Please do not laugh at this question; far fewer investors actually earn a profit than is commonly perceived. The simple formula to calculate a return is

> Ending market value − (beginning market value + net contributions or − net withdrawals)

In the simplest example, let's say your portfolio doubled from $100,000 to $200,000 over 10 years with no additions or withdrawals. Your portfolio would have achieved a compound annual return of 7 percent per year. If an investor has a portfolio worth $200,000 and began with $100,000, did she double her portfolio? Not if she put in an additional $100,000 over the 10 years of investing. Here's how that calculation would read:

> $200,000 − [$100,000 (beginning market value) + $100,000 (net contributions)] = 0

For those who want to move to the next level of performance measurement, a study of time-weighted, linked performance is in order.

Time-weighted, linked performance attempts to adjust your performance for additions and withdrawals. You can then measure how your portfolio performed relative to other options, such as an index fund. (For those who are interested in learning how to calculate time-weighted, linked returns, we refer you to the Wikipedia link, http://en.wikipedia.org/wiki/True_time-weighted_rate_of_return.)

Investors should develop a simple understanding of the difference between dollar-weighted return and time-weighted return. The following article by David Spaulding, president of the Spaulding Group, published in *Pensions and Investment Magazine* (Feb. 21, 2011), succinctly summarizes the distinction between the two.

Flaw in Time-Weighting Return

Many pension funds are still trying to recover from the devastation they've suffered as a result of the market downturn. And many are seeing that using market indexes are the inappropriate metric to perform against, substituting absolute and/or liability-related benchmarks. But how many also see that the return they're using is inappropriate?

Most pension funds, I would guess, only use time-weighting to measure performance. And why? Probably for a few reasons: because that's the way they've always done it; because that's what the GIPS, or Global Investment Performance Standards, require; because that's the measure their consultants use and recommend.

They fail to recall that time-weighting was developed in the 1960s as a way to measure the performance of their managers, not their performance. The Bank Administration Institute, on the heels of Peter Dietz's landmark thesis, put forward the first standard on performance measurement in 1968. This was followed in 1971 by the Investment Council Association of America's standard. Both promulgated time-weighted measures, which eliminate, or reduce, the impact of cash flows. And why would they do this? Because managers don't control the flows, their clients do.

So great, if you want to know how your managers are doing, use time-weighting. But when it comes to wanting to know how the fund itself is doing, why on earth are you going to eliminate the very cash flows which you control? To utilize time-weighting makes absolutely no sense. Money-weighting is the measure to be using. Yes, this means you'll be calculating returns two ways, but that's because you're asking two different questions: How is our manager doing? And how are we doing?

We have had increasing success at convincing firms of their error and are hopeful that more will see the light, have an epiphany, or simply recognize what has been known for nearly 50 years. If a pension fund stops using the wrong benchmark, they're only half the way to properly assessing their performance; they also need to measure it properly.

The Sharpe Ratio

Over the last two decades, an even more mathematically sophisticated method of performance analysis has emerged—the Sharpe ratio.

The Sharpe ratio offers a risk-adjusted performance metric in the financial industry. Mathematically stated, it is

$$(R_p - R_f)/\sigma_p$$

Where

R_p = the return of the portfolio

R_f = the risk-free rate (typically the rate on a U.S. Treasury security)

σ_p = the standard deviation of the return of the portfolio

In conceptual terms, the Sharpe ratio is supposed to measure the ratio of the extra returns a portfolio earns above the return on a riskless investment to the variability of those returns. Since variability of returns is equated to risk in modern portfolio theory and its derivatives, the Sharpe ratio simply shows how much extra returns cost in terms of additional risk.

The Sharpe ratio has been criticized for many reasons, and similar ratios have been invented to correct some of these shortcomings. However, they all tend to overlook one glaring shortcoming: the impact of time and compounding. The Sharpe ratio considers investment returns as unrelated quanta associated with a singular period and compares these returns against the average variability during that period. For a long-term investor, this is a highly misleading comparison.

Returns compound over the long term, while variability does not; in fact, the magnitude of variability is generally very sensitive to the horizon it is measured over. If one were to measure the standard deviation of returns for stocks over 30-year periods, instead of daily variations, the compounding of the stock returns would come to dominate the noncompounding nature of the stocks' standard deviations, and the Sharpe ratio would consequently be much higher *even though* it is measuring the same portfolio.

A long-term investor derives almost no value from a metric that erroneously evaluates the risk of the portfolio in the context of short-term variability. It is confounding that most investors in equities have long-term designs on their portfolios, yet misguidedly measure risk using a blindly mechanical ratio that is disproportionately fixated on short-term pricing variability.

REINVESTMENT RATES ARE A BIG CHALLENGE TO LONG-TERM RETURNS

Let's imagine you have a choice of two stocks; one is a value company (V), and the other is a growth company (G).

Let's assume that Company V is an outstanding value company. It earns $1 per share, pays out $0.60 per share in dividends, and will grow at 5 percent per year over the next 50 years. If the stock is purchased at $10 per share, then the investor would forecast a nominal 11 percent compound return, with 6 percent per year from dividends and 5 percent from growth.

On the other hand, let's assume that Company G (the growth company) earns $0.50 per share and pays out $0.10 per share in dividends. Company G will grow at 10 percent per year over the next 50 years. If an investor could purchase Company G at $10 per share, the nominal expected return would also be 11 percent per year.

Most investors would select Company V as the superior investment. The combination of a nice yield and a nice growth rate would make Stock V less volatile over the short term. But the reality is, for the long-term investor, Company G is the obvious choice. The reason: the need to reinvest the dividends leaves investors in Stock V vulnerable to future levels of stock prices because it's impossible to predict what level stocks will be trading at in the future.

For our purposes, we have made four important assumptions: (1) investors hold both stocks for 50 years, (2) neither investor pays taxes, (3) neither investor pays transaction costs, and (4) all dividends are reinvested in the stocks.

Under these purchase conditions, both companies would purportedly yield an 11 percent total return (price increase plus dividend yield). Unfortunately, this total return calculation assumes that the stock market is continuously and rationally priced each year over the next 50 years. The reality is different; stocks do fluctuate around their intrinsic value. We need to account for these fluctuations in our analysis.

The issue here is simple. The greater the dividend yield, the more dependent our total return is on future stock prices. For example, over a 14-year period, the investor in Stock V must reinvest dividends totaling $18.06 per share in the company's stock, which is the sum of the dividend stream on the original investment, the growth of the dividend per share, and the dividends received on reinvested capital. In total, the dollar amount of reinvested dividends exceeds the original purchase price of the stock, which was $10. The investor in Company G must reinvest only $3.01 in dividends over the 14 years. Stock price fluctuations are far less important to the Company G investor than to the Company V investor.

Over a 50-year time span, investors in Company V must reinvest more than $1,000 in Stock V, while investors in Company G need invest only $167 in Stock G. This assumes that all dividends are reinvested in their respective stocks with no change in the future valuation of either stock.

Figure 2.4 shows the compound return distribution for each stock based on varying levels of stock prices.

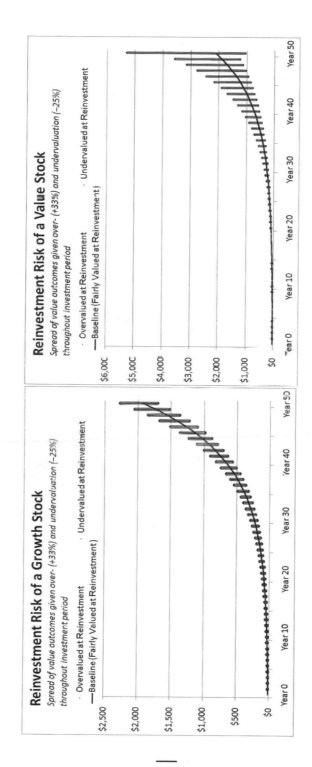

Figure 2.4 Reinvestment Risk

To glean further insight into the reinvestment issue, let's take a look at bond investing. During the 1970s and 1980s, when interest rates were high, the concept of bond duration was developed. This was an attempt to account for the high interest rates that were prevalent then.

Consider the example of a bond with an 8 percent coupon, a 30-year maturity, and selling at par. If an investor were to buy 100 bonds for $100,000, he would earn $8,000 per year in interest payments. He would earn $96,000 in the first 12 years and $240,000 over the life of the bond. If he wants to continue to compound his portfolio at 8 percent per year, he faces massive reinvestment-rate risk. He must reinvest the equivalent of nearly his entire original investment in the first 12 years and nearly 2½ times his original investment over the life of the bond.

His return distribution is likely to look like Figure 2.5.

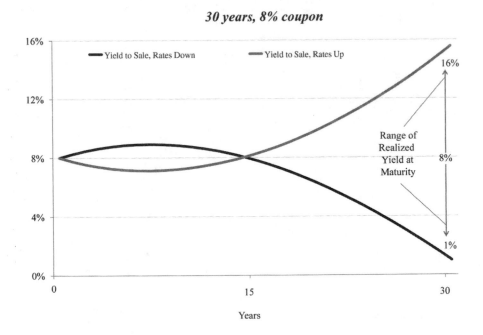

Figure 2.5 Coupon-Paying Bond Yield to Sale

Figures 2.5 to 2.7 show the variance in the cash-on-cash yield achieved (*y* axis) if an investor were to sell the bond at that future point in time (*x* axis) in an atmosphere of rising or falling interest rates.

In the case of the 30-year coupon bond, the "fish" chart (Figure 2.5) can be explained by the interaction of the value of the principal and the value of the reinvested coupons. For example, if rates are rising, the present value of the future principal repayment falls, but the value of the reinvested coupons compounds at a higher rate and over time dominates the capital markdown on the principal. The converse, however, is that in an environment of falling rates, the present value of the principal is marked up, since the discount rate drops, but the reinvested coupons are reinvested at lower rates, and eventually, as they accumulate, overwhelm the beneficial effects of the rise in the present value of the principal repayment.

In the case of the 30-year zero (Figure 2.6), the present value of the principal is marked up or down based on a decrease or increase in the prevailing discount rate, but the future value remains certain, since no variance caused by coupon reinvestment occurs. The value converges back to face value as the impact of a compounded discount rate diminishes with time. However, there is risk if an investor needs to reinvest the proceeds from the bond at maturity.

Let's examine another type of bond to understand this concept more fully. Suppose the same investor buys a zero coupon bond offering 8 percent for 30 years. This bond will pay no coupon payments but will pay a one-time principal payment in 30 years. The investor invests $100,000 in the bond. He will receive one payment of approximately $1,000,000 in 30 years. His distribution of returns is shown in Figure 2.6.

If we combine the investment experience of the two bonds in the same chart, we find the distribution shown in Figure 2.7.

Figure 2.7 demonstrates that the 8 percent coupon bond structure reduced the volatility of the return in the early years. In the later years, the range of possible returns began to expand because it's impossible to predict what future

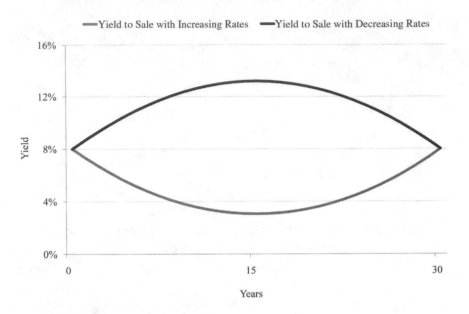

Figure 2.6 Zero Coupon Bond Yield to Sale (PV)

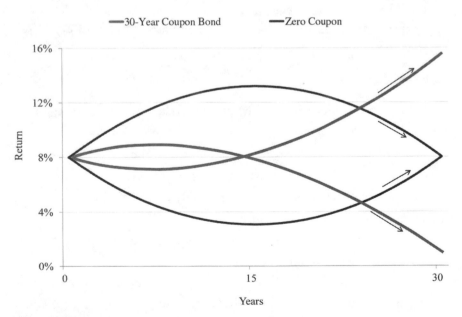

Figure 2.7 Returns Potential: Zero versus Coupon Bond

interest rates will be available for reinvestment of the coupon income. The zero coupon bond experiences significant price volatility in the early years, but the range of returns narrows as the bond approaches maturity. For the investor with a 30-year time horizon, the zero coupon bond has a much higher chance of achieving the desired 8 percent per year compound return goal.

In the example of the two stocks, V and G, we deliberately made Company V an attractive value stock. Now let's borrow from our bond example and consider two companies, Company ZG (zero growth) and Company HG (high growth).

Company ZG earns $1.10 per share and has no growth. The company pays out all of its earnings in the form of dividends. If you could buy the stock at $10 per share, you would have a hefty 11 percent dividend yield.

By contrast, the high-growth company, HG, earns $0.33 per share and reinvests all of its earnings back into the company, so there are no dividends. Company HG also sells for $10 per share and will grow at 11 percent per year over the next 50 years.

Investors in both companies face internal reinvestment risk (that is, either company could make poor future investments).

From the point of view of a shareholder, investors in Company ZG (zero growth) face massive reinvestment risk. During the next 50 years, investors who reinvest the dividend in Company ZG will have to reinvest about $1,836 into ZG common stock, assuming that ZG common stock retains the same P/E over the 50-year period. We have used an extreme example in the case of ZG; very few companies pay a dividend of 11 percent for 50 years. What if investors discovered ZG and elevated the stock price from an 11 percent yield (P/E of 9) to a 6.6 percent yield (P/E of 15) the year after the first purchase? As an example, if the P/E ratio on ZG were to increase from 9 to 15 the year after investors bought the stock, those investors would be able to reinvest only about $400 into ZG.

The future profitability from the purchase of a zero-growth company is heavily dependent on the future price of the stock.

By contrast, investors in the high-growth company (HG) have no reinvestment risk.

DIVIDEND GROWTH: HAVE YOUR CAKE AND EAT IT, TOO

Dividends are a prime source of return for long-term investors. If you buy a stock and never sell it, how else can you be compensated for owning the stock?

The power of long-term dividend growth can be significant. In the example of Company G (the growth company discussed earlier), if we buy the stock at $10 per share, current earnings per share are $0.50, and the earnings grow at 10 percent per year for 50 years, the earnings of the company will have increased by 117.4 times. In 50 years, Company G will be earning $58.70 per share. If, in year 50, Company G decides that it is a mature company and begins to pay out all of its earnings in dividends, then its annual dividend would be $58.70 per share—nearly six times the original investment of $10 per share. And this dividend is paid each year.

Let's put this stock in the portfolio of a 25-year-old investor. The investor invests $20,000 in Company G. When the investor is 75 years old, the potential dividend income from this stock alone would be $117,400, certainly enough to fund a reasonable, healthy retirement in today's dollars.

This is called having your cake and eating it, too.

THE POWER OF BIG IDEAS

Here is a pivotal question on the issue of whether to invest in growth companies or value companies: if you were limited to only one great stock in your lifetime, would you buy a growth company or a value company? We believe the answer is unequivocal: a growth company.

For those of you who would still prefer to buy (and trade) value companies, here are two great stories for you.

To demonstrate the power of buying and holding growth stocks, let us return to an event in the depths of the greatest bear market of the twentieth century: the reconstitution of the Dow Jones Industrial Average in May of 1932. At that point, the Dow had fallen nearly 90 percent from its 1929 peak, which in hindsight represented a tremendous short-term buying opportunity.

At the time, the combined market capitalization of these 30 companies was about $5 billion. It should be noted that these were not necessarily "value" companies; they were among the largest, most important companies in the world. Had an investor simply purchased an equal dollar amount of stock in each of these companies, how would her investments have fared?

She would have ended up holding four or five companies that had gone bankrupt, such as General Motors. She also would have held onto another seven or so companies that have remained public, but haven't performed very well, including Eastman Kodak, Goodyear, US Steel, and Fortune Brands. These "survivors" amount to nearly $50 billion in market value today.

There were also 12 companies from the 1932 Dow Jones Index that were either acquired by another public company or taken private in the subsequent 80 years, such as Honeywell, Chrysler, Westinghouse, and Texaco. The total value paid to shareholders for those 12 companies was $195 billion. Assuming that the investor could have achieved an 8 percent annual compound return for each acquisition from the date of the transaction, the investor's value would have grown to about $490 billion by 2011.

The true profit, though, came from a select six companies: Coca-Cola, General Electric, IBM, Procter & Gamble, Chevron, and Exxon. These six companies today represent a market capitalization of about $1.3 trillion; they pay approximately $35 billion in dividends annually. It should be noted that the gain in market capitalization is strictly that: there was no assumption made concerning the nearly 80 years of dividends received from these companies (nor was there any allowance made for their dilution).

Add it all up, and the original share of that $5 billion would have grown to an equivalent share of nearly $2 trillion of value, ignoring dividends—a gain of nearly 400-fold. And the annual dividends themselves would dwarf the original investment.

So should you buy and hold great companies that are capable of generating substantial gains and intrinsic value, or should you constantly trade static companies in hopes of earning a solid return on your dividends and trades? We believe the answer is obvious. Growth stocks give you a far better opportunity for superior long-term returns.

The second story comes from a postscript from the last edition of *The Intelligent Investor*, in which Graham refers to the two partners in his company, Jerome Newman and Graham himself. In this postscript, Graham is describing their investment in GEICO, which was originally known as the Government Employees Insurance Company. The lesson for investors from this story is stunning: the profits from their GEICO investment far exceeded the sum of all the other profits realized through 20 years of wide-ranging operations—and countless individual decisions. Here is Graham's account:

We know very well two partners who spent a good part of their lives handling their own and other people's funds on Wall Street. Some hard experience taught them it was better to be safe and careful rather than to try to make all the money in the world. They established a rather unique approach to security operations, which combined good profit possibilities with sound values. They avoided anything that appeared overpriced and were rather too quick to dispose of issues that had advanced to levels they deemed no longer attractive. Their portfolio was always well diversified, with more than a hundred different issues represented. In this way they did quite well through many years of ups and downs in the general market; they averaged about 20 percent per annum on the several millions of capital they had accepted for management, and their clients were well pleased with the results.

In the year in which the first edition of this book appeared an opportunity was offered to the partners' fund to purchase a half interest in a growing enterprise. For some reason the industry did not have Wall Street appeal at the time and the deal had been turned down by quite a few important houses. But the pair was impressed by the company's possibilities; what was decisive for them was that the price was moderate in relation to current earnings and asset value. The partners went ahead with the acquisition, amounting in dollars to about one-fifth of their fund. They became closely identified with the new business interest, which prospered.†

In fact it did so well that the price of its shares advanced to 200 times or more the price paid for the half-interest. The advance far outstripped the actual growth in profits, and almost from the start the quotation appeared much too high in terms of the partners' own investment standards. But since they regarded the company as a sort of "family business," they continued to maintain a substantial ownership of the shares despite the spectacular price rise. A large number of participants in their funds did the same, and they became millionaires through their holding in this one enterprise, plus later-organized affiliates.

Ironically enough, the aggregate of profits accruing from this single investment decision far exceeded the sum of all the others realized through 20 years of wide-ranging operations in the partners' specialized fields, involving much investigation, endless pondering, and countless individual decisions.

Are there morals to this story of value to the intelligent investor? An obvious one is that there are several different ways to make and keep money in Wall Street. Another, not so obvious, is that one lucky break, or one supremely shrewd decision—can we tell them apart?—may count for more than a lifetime of journeyman efforts. But behind the luck, or the crucial decision, there must usually exist a background of preparation and disciplined capacity. One needs to be sufficiently established and recognized so that these opportunities will knock at his particular door. One must have the means, the judgment, and the courage to take advantage of them.

Of course, we cannot promise a like spectacular experience to all intelligent investors who remain both prudent and alert through the years. We are not going to end with J. J. Raskob's slogan that we made fun of at the beginning: "Everybody can be rich." But interesting possibilities abound on the financial scene, and the intelligent and enterprising investor should be able to find both enjoyment and profit in this three-ring circus. Excitement is guaranteed.

† Veracity requires the admission that the deal almost fell through because the partners wanted assurance that the purchase price would be 100% covered by asset value. A future $300 million or more in market gain turned on, say, $50,000 of accounting items. By dumb luck they got what they insisted on.

Quantifying the "Big Idea" Strategy

To invest in one big idea among many is a matter of odds; to find and invest in several big ideas is a matter of methodology. Without a viable growth investment methodology, an investor conforming to the tenets of prudent diversification is unlikely to fully benefit from the best growth ideas. Consequently, an investor's rate of return is ultimately determined by the quality of the portfolio not by the quality of a single issue within it. And the quality of the portfolio will be determined by the quality of the investor's methodology.

When constructing a growth stock portfolio with a prudent level of diversification, the danger is not from a failing stock—which is (painfully) remedied by the addition of another stock with more potential—but from a successful stock, which can test the principle of prudent diversification. When one stock grows to a large position in the portfolio and could be considered to constitute an imprudently large-sized portion of an investor's total assets, investors face a dilemma: should he or she let the winner run and gain performance or prudently cut back the position for diversification purposes?

It is important to understand the cost of selling winning stocks far too early. For those who seek to understand the power of long-term compounding, analysis will show that the true benefit of holding a great stock is realized in the latter half of the compounding period. If a stock is trimmed before this occurs, this upside is diminished, as Figure 2.8 shows.

One of the ways to manage the risk of owning a single large position is to commit to finding and investing in more than one big winning stock. We think this is more a matter of methodology than luck. If an investor owns several major winning positions, his or her portfolio has a reasonable chance of remaining balanced, where no portfolio position is outsized.

Even if an investor applies a disciplined growth investing strategy, he or she may still end up with one large winning position. This is not necessarily a bad problem. Assuming the rest of the portfolio of stocks has achieved at least average results, the investor has a successful portfolio and is dealing from a position of strength. But the investor must acknowledge that his or her portfolio has become highly concentrated and that an extended collapse in the large position could harm the portfolio returns for years.

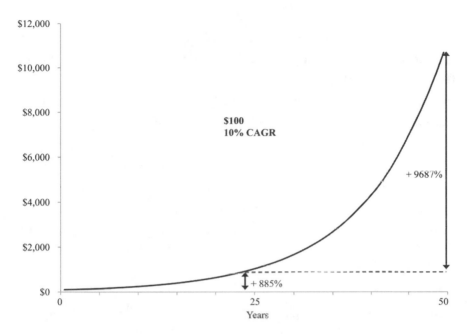

Figure 2.8 The Effects on Performance from Trimming Positions

Portfolios with one or two highly concentrated positions force the investor to emphasize the margin of safety for those particular holdings. In Chapter 5 we discuss how to honor the margin of safety when buying growth stocks. The concept of margin of safety can also be applied to a decision to maintain ownership of a stock, especially a highly concentrated position. We understand this is a highly subjective and difficult subject. As a general rule, if the margin of safety in a given investment has deteriorated so significantly so as to threaten the future return of that investment, consideration must be given to trimming or eliminating the position. For truly great companies these conditions occur rarely, perhaps once or twice in an investor's lifetime. The clearest and most recent example of this issue was the extreme overvaluation of stocks like Cisco and other high-tech and Internet stocks in 2000. After a major increase in the prices of technology stocks in the late 1990s, it was reasonable to conclude that the margin of safety for those shareholders was seriously compromised, based on the prices of the stocks. Prudent investors may have decided to trim or eliminate those positions.

To realize the true benefits of growth stock investing, then, it is not enough to simply purchase a stock that will appreciate 100-fold. As Ben Graham noted, "the big fortunes from single-company investments are almost always realized by persons who have a close relationship with the particular company . . . which justifies them in placing a large part of their resources in one medium and holding on to this commitment through all vicissitudes." Without such a "close relationship" to justify such a commitment, one needs a number of big ideas, such that their simultaneous long-term appreciation preserves prudent diversification and allows the power of compounding to benefit each in particular. Multiple good ideas jointly create the room for each to grow, without which they might be pruned before their time.

The Reality of Value Companies

In discussing reinvested dividends, we painted what we believe is the best possible scenario for value stocks as a viable alternative to growth stocks. But the chances of actually finding a value company with a dividend yield of 6 percent and a long-term growth rate of 5 percent or a no-growth company with a dividend yield of 11 percent are very slim. We made such optimistic assumptions to highlight the structural differences between growth stocks and value stocks, as opposed to the valuation differences.

In the real world, dividend yields above 5 percent are relatively rare, and these yields are typically associated with the stocks of companies that are growing more slowly than average, 4 percent per year or less.

Yet investors continue to pour their money into value companies in the belief that these companies provide the best possible avenue for consistent long-term returns. Their reasoning might be that a bird in the hand is worth two in the bush. In other words, they believe it is better to have a small real advantage than to strive for the possibility of a greater one.

That misguided philosophy, plus a lack of understanding of the power of compound interest, has cost most value company investors a considerable amount of money. Too many investors are willing to settle for a small real advantage—perhaps a better dividend—rather than take their chances on superior long-term returns with growth stocks. Not only are they passing up the potential for greater returns with growth stocks, but they are also often overpaying for the high-dividend stocks they do buy.

One way to look at this is that shoppers in a value stock market tend to let their emotions dictate their investment decisions and are willing to pay extra for the peace of mind that steady high-dividend stocks can offer. Shoppers in a growth stock market can often (although not always) find much better values for their money, but they must sacrifice that peace of mind.

Value company "shoppers" have chosen to look for their merchandise in the "safe" area. This does not mean that they cannot find undervalued securities within that sector. It does mean that they are shopping for merchandise along with many others. It also means that such investors are probably prudent to assume reasonable returns (mid- to high-single-digit returns), unless they are especially adept at trading.

The problem with value companies is their relative homogeneity—they all tend to trade in the same range relative to their value. That makes it harder to find the outliers—the good value companies that are trading at a significant discount to their intrinsic value—unless the investor is willing to settle for the so-called deep value companies, which typically represent extreme financial risk. By contrast, the volatility of the growth stock universe gives you a steady stream of opportunities to buy growth companies at a discount to their intrinsic value.

Diversity of the Growth Company Universe

The enduring characteristic of growth companies is their dynamism—they are constantly in flux. Ten years ago, Apple Computer was a washed-up personal computer maker. Today it is a powerhouse producer of clever electronic devices that hang off the end of the Web. The challenges of investing in growth companies mean that there has been (and is likely to continue to be) an endless roster of companies available for purchase at prices that should yield double-digit returns.

The question is not whether the universe of growth stocks is expensive, but whether you can find individual opportunities to build an investment position. Successful investment in growth companies is anything but easy. It's hard work. But with the proper effort and persistence, a studious investor should be able to build an outstanding portfolio of growth company stocks.

The Clear Favorite

If you were an investor, where would you rather shop—the growth company superstore or the value company superstore? Bargain shoppers might prefer the Walmart approach, the cheapest stuff at the lowest prices.

But for long-term investors, the choice is clear. The growth company universe simply offers far greater potential for significant long-term returns than the value company universe.

Here are the key benefits of growth stock investing:

1. *Fewer decisions and fewer trades.* With growth stock investing, you're required to make fewer decisions and fewer trades. The object of growth investing is to buy great stocks and hold them for the long run. The object of value investing is to find cheap stocks and sell them when they move up in price. Adept trading is an integral part of the value company investment strategy. Effective trading is rare; it is also costly.

2. *Time is your friend.* To earn a suitable compound return on your investment in a growth company, you simply need patience. You do not have to gamble on random, short-term market movements as you would with value companies. Instead, you're relying on the long-term ruthless efficiency of the market. With growth companies, time is your friend. If the company keeps growing, the stock market will ultimately make it well worth your wait.

3. *The power of the big idea.* With growth stocks, you can succeed through the power of the big idea. You can earn an above-average compound annual return with just one or two great stocks—even if the rest of your stocks achieve only average returns. But if you invest in value companies instead, you will significantly reduce your odds of landing that one big idea. If you invest in growth companies, you put yourself

in a position to invest in that one "lucky" huge long-term stock idea. Are there any guarantees that you will invest in such a company? No, but your chances are greatly enhanced with growth stocks.

4. *You have a better chance of earning double-digit annual compound returns.* As we illustrated earlier, long-term compound returns are not easy to achieve. Because growth investing is a buy-and-hold strategy, you can watch your stocks grow and multiply for many years without paying a dime of taxes. Value investing, with its active buying and selling strategy, requires you to donate generously to Uncle Sam on an ongoing basis—and it requires you to continuously beat the bushes to find more stocks that are worth your risk of investment.

Now that you understand the distinctions between value and growth investing and the opportunities that growth companies provide for investors, the next few chapters will help guide you through a well-conceived strategy for investing prudently in growth companies. We'll offer our insights on finding true growth companies, using Mr. Market to buy them well, and building a margin of safety when investing in growth companies. We will also tell a few "war" stories.

3

■ ■ ■

Graham's Valuation Formula

The intrinsic value of a company lies entirely in its future.
—Warren Buffett

During a typical flight in an aircraft, the landing phase is one of the most dangerous stages. A jet pilot must conduct the aircraft along a gradual descent path at about 140 miles per hour and then stop the descent just above the runway. No wonder most aircraft accidents occur within five miles of the airport.

The key to a safe landing is the pilot's ability to put the aircraft on a gradual descent path with a stable airspeed. But an aircraft operates in a three-dimensional space—pitch, roll, and yaw—and during the landing phase, those three dimensions must come together flawlessly. If a plane is above the desired gradual descent path, the pilot may choose to increase the downward pitch (i.e., push the nose down). While this action may bring the aircraft back to the desired descent path, it also causes the airspeed to increase, which, in turn, causes the lift produced by the wings to increase, which, in turn, may cause the aircraft to climb instead of descend. I hope you get the idea.

Many years ago—probably in response to an excessive number of landing accidents—someone discovered that freezing one variable might make it easier to track that nice desired descent path. The accepted practice became to freeze the pitch of the aircraft and adjust power to control the rate of descent. This simple technique gave pilots an important tool for achieving a safe flight.

Investing is also a multidimensional activity. To cope with this complexity, investors have resorted to increasingly powerful computers that purport to capture the interrelatedness of many variables. But this approach tends to lose the most valuable input of all: human intuition.

A far better solution for the investment process would be to "freeze" some variables so that analysts could focus on a reasonable number of factors. Benjamin Graham provided all stock market investors (both growth and value) with a critically important tool that freezes one of the key variables of the investment process to simplify the purchase decision. His valuation formula, which he introduced in the 1962 edition of *Security Analysis*, is so beautifully and simply constructed that it allows investors to easily compute the value of any company. Graham's formula is valid for both growth companies and value (or no-growth) companies. By using Graham's formula, investors are freed to consider other important factors when evaluating a public company.

We have reprinted Chapter 39 of the 1962 edition of *Security Analysis* in its entirety later in this chapter (beginning on page 66).

THE "SECRET" FORMULA

What was Graham's simple formula for calculating the intrinsic value of any public company? To calculate intrinsic value, multiply the earnings growth rate by 2 and add 8.5 to the total, then multiply that by the current earnings per share. Here's the formula:

$$8.5 + (2 \times growth) \times earnings\ per\ share = intrinsic\ company\ value\ per\ share$$

Let's look at some examples of how the formula works. The following examples show how the formula is used to value a no-growth company, an average-growth company, and a faster-growing company:

1. *A no-growth company*. For this example, Company A has annual earnings of $2 per share. Here's how the equation would look:

   > 8.5 + [2 × 0% (growth)] = 8.5 × $2 per share (earnings)
   > = $17 per share in intrinsic value

   An intrinsic value of $17 seems appropriate for this company. With earnings of $2 a share and a stock price of $17, the company would have a P/E ratio of 8.5 (and an earnings yield of 12 percent), which is a fairly typical P/E for a mature company.

2. *An average-growing company*. Company B has annual earnings of $2 per share and earnings growth of 5 percent per year. This is a typical growth rate for companies in the Standard & Poor's 500. Here's how the equation would look:

   > 8.5 + [2 × 5% (growth)] = 18.5 × $2 per share (earnings)
   > = $37 per share in intrinsic value

   Perhaps not coincidentally, most analysts use a P/E range of 15 to 20 times earnings for the S&P 500. The P/E ratio for this stock, as derived through the use of Graham's formula, would be 17.5 ($37/$2), which would be precisely in the middle of the typical range for an average-growth stock in the S&P 500.

3. *A faster-growing company*. Company C has annual earnings per share of $2 and earnings growth of 10 percent per year. Here is how the equation would look:

   > 8.5 + [2 × 10% (growth)] = 28.5 × $2 per share (earnings)
   > = $57 per share in intrinsic value

The P/E ratio for this stock would be 28.5, which is fairly typical for the faster-growing companies in the S&P 500.

OTHER VALUATION FORMULAS?

There are a number of other formulas that analysts use to value stocks. Let's examine some of the more common formulas and see how they compare with Graham's formula.

The PEG Ratio

One of the most common formulas used today is the "PEG ratio." Here is the formula:

Intrinsic value per share = growth rate × earnings per share

Using this formula, a company earning $1 per share and growing at 10 percent per year would sell at $10 per share:

$10 per share = 10% growth rate × $1 earnings per share

The PEG ratio is simple, but it has several major flaws. The most obvious involves the valuation of a mature company. According to the PEG ratio formula, a company with no growth would be worth nothing!

Intrinsic value per share = 0% growth rate × earnings per share
= 0 × $1 per share = 0

The PEG ratio tends to understate the value of all companies. A company that is growing at 5 percent per year would sell at 5 times earnings. Even a tremendous growth company with 12 percent growth would sell at 12 times earnings. As a result, most analysts overestimate the future growth rates of their universe of stocks—both value and growth companies—in order to justify purchase of the stocks.

Discounted Cash Flow (DCF) Approach

Another commonly used valuation model is the discounted cash flow (DCF) model. Because the theory behind the DCF approach is very robust, we have compared the valuations yielded by the Graham model to those yielded by a DCF model (see Appendix). We found that the Graham model closely approximates the results of the DCF model under a reasonable range of assumed growth rates.

For the mathematically inclined, consider that the capitalization multiple awarded by the DCF model is equal to the next year's earnings divided by the difference between a hurdle rate and a growth rate:

Intrinsic value per share = EPS year 1/($h - g$)

Where
    h — hurdle rate
    g = growth rate
EPS year 1 is next year's EPS

If we were to use a hurdle rate of 12 percent and a growth rate of 7 percent, the spread would be 5 percent. This would yield a P/E ratio of slightly greater than 21.4 times earnings. For the same stock, Graham's formula would yield a P/E ratio of 22.5 times, which is right in the ballpark with the DCF model.

The problem with the DCF model is that it has too many variables, and these variables can interact with each other. Since this formula deals with both a hurdle rate and a growth rate, it can be tempting to change one or the other in order to justify the valuation of the company. In general, complexity in valuation formulas can be mischievous. Simplicity is better. The valuation of companies is an inexact science. The simpler and more straightforward the valuation model, the easier it is for the investor to focus on other components, such as earnings, cash flow, and future growth.

TWO FLAWS IN THE VALUATION MODELS

All valuation models have flaws. Models such as Graham's value a company based solely on its earnings. This leaves out the possible positive effects of nonoperating assets or negative effects of nonoperating liabilities.

For example, suppose an investor is trying to value two companies to determine which would be the preferable investment. Company A and Company B both earn $1 per share and are forecast to grow at 10 percent per year over the next seven years. Both stocks sell at $10 per share. Which stock should the investor buy?

P/E-to-growth models would say that there is no difference between the two stocks. This can be misleading. Suppose Company A has $5 per share in cash on the balance sheet and no debt, whereas Company B has $5 per share in debt on the balance sheet and no cash. Although the valuation formulas don't show it, it seems obvious that the stock of Company A (the cash-rich company) is a better choice than that of Company B.

That's why investors need to look beyond earnings and examine company balance sheets prior to purchase to look for nonoperating assets and liabilities.

A second flaw has to do with the potential competition from high interest rates. Should the P/E ratio of stocks be immune to high interest rates? Of course not. Graham himself addressed this issue when he suggested that P/E ratios should be adjusted downward if long-term interest rates on corporate bonds exceeded 4.4 percent. Graham picked 4.4 percent because the AAA corporate rate averaged 4.4 percent in 1964. He introduced his revised formula at a seminar sponsored jointly by the Institute of Chartered Financial Analysts and the Financial Analysts Research Foundation, held on September 18, 1974, in New York City.

The revised Graham formula factors in the current yield to maturity on AAA corporate bonds in the calculation of a company's intrinsic value:

Intrinsic value per share = EPS × (8.5 + 2g) × 4.4/y

Where

g = growth rate

y = yield on AAA corporate bonds

The effects of this formula on P/E ratios can be easily derived. If yields on AAA corporate bonds were to remain at 4.4 percent, then the original Graham model would remain intact. If yields on AAA corporate bonds increased to 6.6 percent, then P/E ratios would be reduced by 1/3 (4.4/6.6 = 2/3). If yields on AAA corporate bonds increased to 8.8 percent, then P/E ratios would be cut in half. In this last example, the future value of all companies would be reduced by 50 percent, all other things being equal.

For those who want to use Graham's amended model, some caution is warranted. The model requires that the user forecast interest rates well into the future. For an investor to rely on recent interest rates as an input to the model could be misleading. From 1965 until 1981, long-term interest rates rose gradually; this could cause investors to consistently input interest rates into the model that are too low. This would mean that the model would generally overestimate the future value of companies. In 1981, the situation reversed. From 1981 until about 2000, interest rates were generally declining. This would underestimate the future value of stocks. This could have tended to keep investors who relied on this formula from investing in one of the greatest bull markets in history.

The other risk to this model comes from growth-rate predictions. High long-term interest rates typically correlate with periods of high inflation. In an inflationary period, revenues and earnings growth may be increased because of inflation.

Our suggestion to investors: keep the effects of high interest rates in mind, but do not adjust P/E ratios downward unless you have a strong conviction that the investment environment is entering a long period of significantly rising interest rates.

CALCULATING TODAY'S VALUE

Notwithstanding the two flaws just listed, Graham's formula can be applied to all companies, both value and growth.

In order to calculate today's intrinsic value using Graham's formula, one must estimate the company's normalized current earnings per share and forecast the company's earnings growth rate into the future.

By analyzing easily available historical data on earnings and cash flow, investors should be able to determine an appropriate level of current earnings for each company under consideration. Generally, there is enough information readily available from the company and from other sources—including past, present, and projected earnings and cash flow figures—to come up with a reasonable estimate of current earnings for every public company.

In order to use the Graham model effectively, investors should convert current earnings per share into normalized earnings per share. To do this, one must adjust for where we are in the overall economic cycle and the company's industry cycle, and where the company is in its investment cycle. If the economy is in a recession, current earnings per share should be adjusted upward; in a boom period, they should be adjusted downward. If a company's industry is in a recession or a period of intense competition, current earnings per share should be adjusted upward; in a boom period for the industry, they should be adjusted downward. If a company is in the middle of a period of heavy investment for future growth, current earnings per share should be adjusted upward.

One must also forecast a growth rate in earnings for each company. We encourage investors to base a growth rate on normalized earnings. This will help to reduce the effects of the economic, industry, and individual company cycles. We like to think of the growth rate as the underlying long-term growth rate for the company. In his chapter on growth stocks, Graham explained that his formula is based on "the average annual growth rate expected over the next seven to ten years." For our purposes, we suggest that the investor use seven years; this time period is longer than a typical economic cycle, but brief enough so that the investor is accountable.

Growth versus Value

Calculating today's intrinsic value serves a different purpose for different types of stocks. For a value company, today's intrinsic value can provide a strong foundation for making a decision on whether or not to buy the stock. Its intrinsic value is unlikely to change much over the next seven years.

For a growth company, calculating today's intrinsic value is just the beginning of the process. Investing in growth companies requires that investors base their decision on the future value of the company. That's why today's intrinsic value is less relevant to the decision regarding growth stocks than it is to that regarding value companies. But that still does not diminish the importance of making the effort to calculate today's intrinsic value for growth companies. In the process of calculating the current intrinsic value, you should get a more thorough understanding of the company and its operations. Only by gaining a thorough understanding of the company's current operations can an investor begin to assess its future value.

The effort to understand a company today is an important factor in building a satisfactory margin of safety (which we discuss in Chapter 5). If you're unable to analyze a company's current operations with adequate precision, you should pass on the stock and look elsewhere.

Building a Seven-Year Forecast

When you are analyzing growth stocks, it is extremely important to build a reasonable seven-year forecast of every company under consideration.

At our firm, we underscore the importance of this step by building a detailed model for every company that is of interest to us. We begin the process of building a seven-year financial model by evaluating the company's income statement, cash flow statement, balance sheet, and management strength. We also look at the size of the company, the size of the industry, the potential for growth, and the potential profit margin. With that information, we build a detailed budget for the company. Our detailed budgets includes both revenue and earnings forecasts. We also develop a cash flow projection and build a balance sheet for each company.

Not every investor will have the time, resources, or ability to develop a forecast with the same detail as we do. But those who don't must be very careful to avoid excessively optimistic growth forecasts, which can sometimes lead to disastrous results for growth stock investors.

Because the future is always uncertain, investors may want to estimate a range of growth rates. If you believe that a company could grow at 10 percent per year, you may want to broaden the estimate of growth to 8 to 12 percent per year. This is appropriate, as long as you do not base your decision on the high end of the forecast.

What Happens after Seven Years?

Over time, even the fastest growth companies mature, and their growth rate slows. In order to use Graham's formula successfully, you need to slow the company's growth at some future point. We have chosen to do this after seven years for every one of our holdings. We have chosen to do this for three reasons. First, we think that developing a seven-year forecast is challenging enough. We have chosen to focus our analytical efforts on getting that forecast reasonably right. Second, over the long term, individual companies' earnings growth rates tend to converge at a sustainable level approaching long-term overall economic growth. Third, just as the pilot freezes a variable when executing an approach to landing, we have chosen to freeze this variable to make our analysis easier.

What growth rate do we use? Our empirical work has shown that most companies inevitably decline to a growth rate of around 7 percent per year. So we assign all of the stocks we analyze a 7 percent growth rate after seven years.

Using Graham's model, this means that we forecast a maximum P/E ratio of 22.5 times earnings for the earnings in Year 7 for each of our holdings.

CALCULATING FUTURE VALUE

Evaluation of growth companies requires the application of Graham's formula twice—an estimate of today's intrinsic value, and an estimate of a future intrinsic value. Because of the dynamic changes in the intrinsic value of growth companies, it is vital to project a future value for the company in order to determine a suitable price to pay for that stock in the current market.

For growth company investors, future intrinsic value provides investors with a key data point upon which to make a decision to buy, sell, or hold the stock.

Estimating a company's future value requires four steps:

1. Determine the company's normalized earnings per share.
2. Forecast the company's long-term earnings per share growth rate.
3. Estimate normalized earnings per share seven years from now.
4. Calculate the future intrinsic value using Graham's formula.

We have already discussed Steps 1 and 2.

In order to execute Step 3, investors should use current normalized earnings and grow them at the forecast rate for the next seven years. If Company A has normalized earnings of $1 per share and a forecast growth rate of 10 percent for the next seven years, then normalized earnings per share in seven years would be approximately $2 per share.

Step 4 follows from Step 3. Investors need to apply a capitalization rate to forecast earnings per share in Year 7. Since we use a forecast growth rate of 7 percent from Year 7 forward, we would apply a 22.5 P/E ratio to the earnings of Company A in Year 7. Thus the intrinsic value of Company A in Year 7 would be about $45 per share. This is how the formula would look:

Intrinsic value per share, Company A = [8.5 + (2 × 7)] × $2 per share

---

For investors who choose to use a range of projections, the following math will apply. Suppose an investor uses a forecast of 8 to 12 percent earnings growth for Company A over the next seven years. If the company has earnings per share today of $1, with an earnings growth rate of 8 percent, then earnings per share would grow to $1.71 per share in Year 7. If the company were to grow earnings per share at 12 percent per year, then earnings per share would grow to $2.21 per year in Year 7. Applying a 22.5 P/E multiple to both outcomes would yield an intrinsic value range of $38.47 to 49.72 per share.

Simpler Is Better

Why do we advocate the use of such a simple valuation model? Because the simplicity and essential soundness of the model are its greatest advantages. There has been a long-running battle among investors regarding the issue of complexity versus simplicity. As computing power becomes more ubiquitous and mathematical formulas become more precise, there is a natural temptation to make the formulas more complex.

The problem with complex formulas is that the investment world is not that precise. Earnings estimates are just that—estimates—and it's impossible to establish precise projections using estimates that are frequently inaccurate. In order to make good investment decisions, we need to have only an approximate idea of the intrinsic value of the company. To be fair, it can take time and experience to learn just how accurate a picture is required. But complex formulas are not the answer.

The other potentially fatal flaw with complex mathematical models is that they tend to be backward-looking. Models need historical data upon which to feed. Whether historical data will help make good investment decisions is anybody's guess; human analysis and input are required to determine which data are relevant.

We also think investors are well served by keeping their entire investment process simple. There are so many distractions in today's world that it is far too easy to lose sight of the few key factors necessary for investment success. As investors gain experience, they learn to ignore most of the events that are erroneously considered important when purchasing a stock. Most macroeconomic factors cannot be forecast with the necessary precision, nor can we understand the linkage between these factors and our stock holdings. Most investors are wasting valuable analytical time on events that they cannot know or that have little bearing on their decision to invest in a company.

Clarity of Focus

Once investors accept the idea that a simple model is better, they should be open to the advantages provided by a straightforward model like Graham's. Perhaps the most important benefit of Graham's valuation model is its ability

to provide the investor with clarity of focus by eliminating many of the allur-
ing but irrelevant variables involved in selecting a stock for purchase. Graham's
model forces the investor to focus on the specific factors required to make a
good investment decision: the quality and earning power of the underlying
business, earnings growth, quality of earnings growth, and future value. Such
outside factors as GDP growth, bond yields, and short-term economic conditions have little to do with the long-term prospects of an individual company.

A second major benefit of Graham's model is that by "freezing" many
important variables, incisive research and judgment can be applied to a few key
issues. Not only did Graham provide a valuation framework, but he also suggested a reasonable time frame (seven to ten years) in which to make decisions.

By using the Graham model, you can free yourself to focus on two
important parts of the process: understanding the company's operations and
building a reasonable seven-year budget.

GRAHAM'S GIFT TO GROWTH INVESTING

After a lifetime of espousing the virtues of value investing, Benjamin Graham
finally seemed to realize the power of growth stock investing late in his
career. The impetus for his change of heart might have been the performance of some of the great growth stocks of the 1950s, or it might have been
his success with GEICO.

Whatever the reason, Graham apparently felt strongly that the investing
world needed a way to analyze and value growth stocks. That was the gift he
gave us in Chapter 39 of the 1962 edition of *Security Analysis*.

That chapter is one of the most useful and straightforward treatises on
stock investing (growth or value) ever written. In it, Graham discusses the
leading theories of the day on growth stock valuation, examines the strengths
and weaknesses of each approach, and then lays out his own approach to
stock valuation.

Brilliant in its common sense and simplicity, it was a landmark chapter
in Graham's illustrious career before it inexplicably disappeared from future
editions of the book. The entire chapter is reprinted here.

Security Analysis (1962 Edition)

Chapter 39: *Newer Methods for Valuing Growth Stocks*

Historical Introduction

We have previously defined a growth stock as one which has increased its per-share earnings for some time in the past at faster than the average rate and is expected to maintain this advantage for some time in the future. (For our own convenience we have defined a true growth stock as one which is expected to grow at the annual rate of at least 7.2 percent—which would double earnings in ten years, if maintained—but others may set the minimum rate lower.) A good past record and an unusually promising future have, of course, always been a major attraction to investors as well as speculators. In the stock markets prior to the 1920's, expected growth was subordinated in importance, as an *investment* factor, to financial strength and stability of dividends. In the late 1920's, growth possibilities became the leading consideration for common-stock investors and speculators alike. These expectations were thought to justify the extremely high multipliers reached for the most favored issues. However, no serious efforts were then made by financial analysts to work out mathematical valuations for growth stocks.

The first detailed basis for such calculations appeared in 1931—after the crash—in S. E. Guild's book, *Stock Growth and Discount Tables*. This approach was developed into a full-blown theory and technique in J. B. William's work, *The Theory of Investment Value*, published in 1938. The book presented in detail the basic thesis that a common stock is worth the sum of all its future dividends, each discounted to its present value. Estimates of the rates of future growth must be used to develop the schedule of future dividends, and from them to calculate the total recent value.

In 1938 National Investor's Corporation was the first mutual fund to dedicate itself formally to the policy of buying growth stocks, identifying them as those which had increased their earnings from the top of one business cycle to the next and which could be expected to continue to do so. During the next 15 years companies with good growth records won increasing popularity, but little effort at precise valuations of growth stocks was made.

At the end of 1954 the present approach to growth valuation was initiated in an article by Clendenin and Van Cleave, entitled "Growth and Common Stock Values."[1] This supplied basic tables for finding the present values of future dividends, on varying assumptions as to rate and duration of growth, and also as to the discount factor. Since 1954 there has been a great outpouring of articles in the financial press—chiefly in the *Financial Analysts Journal*—on the subject of the mathematical valuation of growth stocks. The articles cover technical methods and formulas, applications to the Dow-Jones Industrial Average and to numerous individual issues, and also some critical appraisals of growth-stock theory and of market performance of growth stocks.

In this chapter we propose: (1) to discuss in as elementary form as possible the mathematical theory of growth-stock valuation as now practiced; (2) to present a few illustrations of the application of this theory, selected from the copious literature on the subject; (3) to state our views on the dependability of this approach, and even to offer a very simple substitute for its usually complicated mathematics.

The "Permanent-Growth-Rate" Method

An elementary-arithmetic formula for valuing future growth can easily be found if we assume that growth at a fixed rate will continue in the *indefinite future*. We need only subtract this fixed rate of growth from the investor's required annual return; the remainder will give us the capitalization rate for the current dividend.

This method can be illustrated by a valuation of DJIA made in a fairly early article on the subject by a leading theoretician in the field.[2] This study assumed a permanent growth rate of 4 percent for the DJIA and an over-all investor's return (or "discount rate") of 7 percent. On this basis the investor would require a current dividend yield of 3 percent, and this figure would determine the value of the DJIA. We will assume that the dividend will increase each year by 4 percent, and hence that the market price will increase also by 4 percent. Then in any year the investor will have a 3 percent dividend return and a 4 percent market appreciation—both on the starting value—or a total of 7 percent compounded annually. The required dividend return can be converted into an equivalent multiplier of earnings by assuming a standard payout rate. In this article the payout was taken at about two-thirds; hence the multiplier of earnings becomes $2/3$ of 33 or 22.[3]

It is important for the student to understand why this pleasingly simple method of valuing a common stock or group of stocks has to be replaced by more complicated methods, especially in the growth-stock field. It would work fairly plausibly for assumed growth rates up to, say, 5 percent. The latter figure produces a required dividend return of only 2 percent, or a multiplier of 33 for current earnings, if payout is two-thirds. But when the expected growth rate is set progressively higher, the resultant valuation of dividends or earnings increases very rapidly. A 6½ percent growth rate produces a multiplier of 200 for the dividend, and a growth rate of 7 percent or more makes the issue worth *infinity* if it pays any dividend. In other words, on the basis of this theory and method, no price would be too much to pay for such a common stock.[4]

A Different Method Needed

Since an expected growth rate of 7 percent is almost the *minimum* required to qualify an issue as a true "growth stock" in the estimation of many security analysts, it should be obvious that the above simplified method of valuation cannot be used in that area. If it were, every such growth stock would have infinite value. Both mathematics and prudence require that the period of high growth rate be limited to a finite—actually a fairly short—period of time. After that, the growth must be assumed either to stop entirely or to proceed at so modest a rate as to permit a fairly low multiplier of the later earnings.

The standard method now employed for the valuation of growth stocks follows this prescription. Typically it assumes growth at a relatively high rate—varying greatly between companies—for a period of ten years, more or less. The growth rate thereafter is taken so low that the earnings in the tenth or other "target" year may be valued by the simple method previously described. This target-year valuation is then discounted to present worth, as are the dividends to be received during the earlier period. The two components are then added to give the desired value.

Application of this method may be illustrated in making the following rather representative assumptions: (1) a discount rate, or required annual return of 7½ percent;[5] (2) an annual growth rate of about 7.2 percent for a ten-year period—i.e., a doubling of earnings and dividends in the decade; (3) a multiplier of 13½ for the tenth year's earnings. (This multiplier corresponds to an expected growth rate after the tenth year of 2½ percent, requiring a dividend return of 5 percent. It is adopted by Molodovsky as a "level of ignorance" with respect to later growth. We should prefer to call it a "level of conservatism.") Our last assumption would be (4) an average payout of 60 percent. (This may well be high for a company with good growth.)

The valuation per dollar of present earnings, based on such assumptions, works out as follows:

A. Present value of tenth year's market price: The tenth year's earnings will be $2, their market price 27, and its present value 48 percent of 27, or about $13.

B. Present value of next ten years' dividends: These will begin at 60 cents, increase to $1.20, average about 90 cents, aggregate about $9, and be subject to a present worth factor of some 70 percent—for an average waiting period of five years. The dividend component is thus worth presently about $6.30.

C. Total present value and multiplier: Components A and B add up to about $19.30, or a multiplier of 19.3 for the current earnings.

Valuation of DJIA in 1961 by This Method

In a 1961 article, Molodovsky selected 5 percent as the most plausible growth rate for DJIA in 1961–1970. This would result in a ten-year increase of 63 percent, raise earnings from a 1960 "normal" of, say, $35 to $57, and produce a 1970 expected price of 765, with a 1960 discounted value of 365. To this must be added 70 percent of the expected ten-year dividends aggregating about $300—or $210 net. The 1960 valuation of DJIA, calculated by this method, works out at some 575. (Molodovsky advanced it to 590 for 1961.)

Similarity with Calculation of Bond Yields

The student should recognize that the mathematical process employed above is identical with that used to determine the price of a bond corresponding to a given yield, and hence the yield indicated by a given price. The value, or proper price, of a bond is calculated by discounting each coupon payment and also the ultimate principal payment to their present worth, at a discount rate or required return equal to the designated yield. In growth-stock valuations the assumed market price in the target year corresponds to the repayment of the bond at par at maturity.

Mathematical Assumptions Made by Others

While the calculations used in the DJIA example may be viewed as fairly representative of the general method, a rather wide diversity must be noted in the specific assumptions, or "parameters," used by various writers. The original tables of Clendenin and Van Cleave carry the growth-period calculations out as far as 60 years. The periods actually assumed in calculations by financial writers have included 5 years (Bing), 10 years (Molodovsky and Buckley), 12 to 13 years (Bohmfalk), 20 years (Palmer and Burrell), and up to 30 years (Kennedy). The discount rate has also varied widely—from 5 percent (Burrell) to 9 percent (Bohmfalk).[6]

The Selection of Future Growth Rates

Most growth-stock valuers will use a uniform period for projecting future growth and a uniform discount or required-return rate, regardless of what issues they are considering. (Bohmfalk, exceptionally, divides his growth stocks into three quality classes, and varies the growth period between 12 and 13 years, and the discount rate between 8 and 9 percent, according to class.) But the expected rate of growth will of course vary from company to company. It is equally true that the rate assumed for a given company will vary from analyst to analyst.

It would appear that the growth rate for any company could be established objectivity if it were based entirely on past performance for an accepted period.

But all financial writers insist, entirely properly, that the past growth rate should be taken only as one factor in analyzing a company and cannot be followed mechanically in setting the growth rate for the future. Perhaps we should point out, as a cautionary observation, that even the past rate of growth appears to be calculated in different ways by different analysts.[7]

Multiplier Applied to "Normal Earnings"

The methods discussed produce a multiplier for a dollar of present earnings. It is applied not necessarily to the actual current or recent earnings, but to a figure presumed to be "normal"—i.e., to the current earnings as they would appear on a smoothed-out earnings curve. Thus the DJIA multipliers in 1960 and 1961 were generally applied to "trend-line" earnings which exceeded the actual figures for those years—assumed to be "subnormal."

Dividends vs. Earnings in the Formulas. A Simplification

The "modern" methods of growth-stock valuation represent a considerable departure from the basic concept of J. B. Williams that the present value of a common stock is the sum of the present worths of all future dividends to be expected from it. True, there is now typically a ten- to twenty-year dividend calculation, which forms part of the final value. But as the expected growth rate increases from company to company, the anticipated payout tends also to decrease, and the dividend component loses in importance against the target year's earnings.

Possible variations in the expected payout will not have a great effect on the final multiplier. Consequently the calculation process may be simplified by assuming a uniform payout for all companies of 60 percent in the next ten years. If T is the tenth-year figure attained by \$1 of present earnings growing at any assumed rate, the value of the ten-year dividends works out at about $2.1 + 2.1T$. The present value of the tenth-year market price works out at 48 percent of $13.5T$, or about $6.5T$. Hence the total value of \$1 of present earnings—or the final multiplier for the shares—would equal $8.6T + 2.1$.

Table 39-1 gives the value of T and the consequent multipliers for various assumed growth rates.

Growth Rate	Tenth-year earnings (T)	Multiplier of present earnings (8.6T + 2.1)
Table 39-1		
2.5%	$1.28	13.1x
4.0	1.48	14.8x
5.0	1.63	16.1x
6.0	1.79	17.5x
7.2	2.00	19.3x
8.0	2.16	20.8x
10.0	2.59	24.4x
12.0	3.11	28.8x
14.3	4.00	36.5x
17.5	5.00	45.1x
20.0	6.19	55.3x

These multipliers are a little low for the small growth rates, since they assume only a 60 percent payout. By this method the present value is calculated entirely from the current earnings and expected growth; the dividend disappears as a separately calculated factor. This anomaly may be accepted the more readily as one accepts also the rapidly decreasing importance of dividend payments in the growth-stock field.

An Apparent Paradox in Growth-Stock Valuations

Let us return to the Molodovsky assumptions, used as our model and taken as representative. His method requires that all stocks be presumed to sell a decade hence at 13.5 times their earnings in that year. (Similarly, Bohmfalk assumes that all the 100 growth stocks he valued in his article will sell at between 11 and 12½ times their earnings 12 to 13 years hence.) It is obvious, however, that the 1971 multipliers will vary greatly as between different companies, and that those which have had good actual growth during the 1960's will sell at much higher multipliers than those showing small improvement.

Why should not the valuers make the more realistic assumption that their issues will sell in the target year at a multiplier more or less proportionate to the assumed rate of growth? If a stock doubles its earnings in 10 years, and is presumed to be now worth 20 times its earnings, why should it not be expected to sell in 1971 as well at no less than 20 times its earnings? But if this assumption is made, the present value of the stock would have to be moved up to more than 20 times current earnings to avoid exceeding the 7½ percent required return. This would then suggest a higher multiplier than 20 for the 1971 earnings, and the adjustments would have to be repeated until the present value approaches infinity.

The mathematical fact is that for any stock presumed to give a combined dividend return and growth exceeding the discount rate the assumed multiplier in the target year *must* be lower than the derived current multiplier. Otherwise we should be back to the infinite valuation which made us discard the simple assumption of a combined perpetual growth rate and dividend return exceeding 7 or 7½ percent.

The objection to assuming a 13.5 multiplier ten years hence for earnings considered to grow at, say, a 10 percent rate in the decade can be overcome if the idea of conservatism and a safety factor are introduced into the discussion. A valuation of the Molodovsky type should be viewed not as that present price which will in fact produce an annual return of 7½ percent if the projected growth is realized, but rather as one which will produce a return *higher* than 7½ percent under such conditions. We consider it perfectly logical for the investor to require this mathematical result as compensation for the very large risk that the actual growth realized will prove less than the estimates.

Two Supplementary Calculations Recommended

To give this point a concrete expression for the investor, we suggest to analysts that their valuations of the kind we have been discussing be supplemented by either or both of two corollary calculations. The first would seek to approximate the true probable rate of return to the investor if the projected growth rate is realized. The simplest assumption for this purpose is that the shares will sell in 1971 at the same multiplier of their earnings as is applied by the valuer to the 1961 earnings. Since this will invariably exceed the 13.5 multiplier used in the first calculation, it will produce a rate of return above the basic 7½ percent. The difference will indicate either (1) the extra profit that may be expected from realization of the growth prediction, or (2) the amount of the safety factor embedded in the primary valuation. The second such calculation could determine, by a similar method, how much *below* the estimate the actual growth rate may fall and still produce the required 7½ percent return to the purchaser at the primary valuation.

Let us illustrate the derivation of these supplementary figures by using an issue with an expected 7.2 percent growth rate. Its current multiplier, shown in Table 39-1, worked out at 19.3—based on a 60 percent payout and a 13.5 multiplier in 1971. Assume now that the actual multiplier in 1971 will be the 19.3 found proper for 1961. This will add $11.60 to the 1971 value of a $1 of present earnings. By adroit manipulation of the compound-interest tables we can establish that, on the new basis of 1971 value, the rate of return realized by the purchaser at 19.3 times 1961 earnings will be about 10 percent rather than the basic 7½ percent. Similarly, even if the actual growth rate averaged only 5 percent, but the multiplier were maintained at 19.3, the investor at this price would still obtain his target yield of 7½ percent.

These calculations are by no means free of mathematical taint—partaking a bit of the bootstrap character—but they are not far off the mark, we think, in their implication that the original valuation formula includes a factor of safety of about one-third.

Uses of Growth-Stock Valuations

Obviously, the most direct and positive use of a set of growth-stock valuations made by any of the methods proposed would be for the selection of attractive (undervalued) issues and the identification of overvalued ones. The two techniques discussed above—those of Molodovsky and Bohmfalk—were applied in this manner in the respective studies. The former found an "investment value" for each of the stocks in the DJIA and compared it with the concurrent price. The February 1961 level of the unit as a whole (649) was found to be 10 percent above its investment value of 590; five of the components were selling between 75 percent and 95 percent of value, fifteen between 100 and 120 percent, and ten between 120 and 153 percent. These valuations, and the resultant indications of current cheapness or dearness in the market, depended both on the specific formula approach used by Molodovsky and on his choice of estimated annual growth rates. The latter varied between a nominal 1½ percent for United Aircraft to a maximum of 10 percent for Alcoa and Eastman Kodak.

Bohmfalk compares his valuations with current price in a different way. He calculates the growth rate implicit in the present price—i.e., that rate which, by his formulas would produce a value equal to the July 1960 price. This is done for 93 stocks classed into three quality groups. (He uses moderately different discount rates and growth periods for each group.) For the most part his projected growth rates are quite close to those implicit in the market price. (He takes 6½ percent for the DJIA which he found to be both its historic rate for 13 years past and the market-price rate.) But in two cases his rate is nearly three times the market rate; in one case the market rate is 40 percent above his own.

It may be interesting to compare the future growth selected by Molodovsky and Bohmfalk for the nine stocks appearing in both lists. We add the "historic" or 1946–1959 rate as found by Bohmfalk.

Table 39-2 indicates that historical growth rates play an important, though by no means determinative, part in the projection of future growth, and also that quite considerable differences of opinion on the rates to take for a given company may develop between highly competent analysts.

Table 39-2 Comparative Historical and Projected Earnings Growth Rates of Nine Stocks

	Historic	Bohmfalk's Projections	Molodovsky's Projections
Allied Chemical & Dye	7.5%	10.0%	6.0%
Alcoa	12.0	13.0	10.0
Du Pont	10.0*	10.0*	7.0
Eastman Kodak	9.5	11.5	10.0
General Electric	9.0	10.0	10.0
Goodyear	12.0	9.0	5.0
International Paper	4.5	8.5	3.5
Procter & Gamble	6.0	9.0	8.0
Union Carbide	9.0	9.5	5.0

Excluding General Motors

Other Uses of the Valuation Approach

A number of studies of the subject have been devoted to the various interrelationships between value (as a multiplier of current earnings or dividend), rate of growth, period of growth, and discount rate. If one starts with an actual or assumed dividend yield (or earnings multiplier) one can calculate alternatively (1) what rate of growth is necessary to produce a required overall return within a given number of years, (2) how many years' growth at various rates would be needed to produce the required return, and (3) what actual returns would follow from given rates of growth proceeding over given periods.[8] These presentations are undoubtedly of value to the analyst in making him aware of the quantitative implications as to growth rates and periods that must be read into the current market price for a growth stock.

Lessons from Past Experience

A study of actual investment results in groups of popular growth stocks will point up the need for substantial safety margin in calculating present values of such issues. We know, of course, that where high growth rates have been continued over long periods, investors have fared very well in such shares, even though they paid what seemed to be a very high multiplier of current earnings at the time. The outstanding example of such experience is International Business Machines. Its apparent high selling prices in the past have always turned out to be low in the light of subsequent growth of earnings and subsequent price advances. The 1961 multiplier of, say, 80 times current earnings could also prove to be an undervaluation if the rate of past growth is maintained sufficiently long in the future. Investors generally have been encouraged by the brilliant performance of IBM to think that almost any company with a good record of recent growth and with supposedly excellent prospects for its continuance can be safely bought at a correspondingly high multiplier.[9]

When growth-stock experience is viewed as a whole and not simply in the blinding light of IBM's achievements, quite a different picture emerges. One would have expected the general performance of growth stocks in the past two decades to have been decidedly superior to that of the market as a whole, if only because they have steadily increased in the market popularity, and thus have had an extra factor to aid their market prices. Available data would indicate that the facts are different from this plausible expectation. Let us refer to three studies or compilations on this point:

1. In an article on "The Investment Performance of Selected Growth Stock Portfolios," by T.E. Adderley and D.A. Hayes (*Financial Analysts Journal*, May 1957), the authors trace through annually to the end of 1955 the results of investment in each of the five growth-stock portfolios recommended in articles published in a financial magazine in 1939, 1940, 1941, 1945, and 1946. For each portfolio and each year the results, including and excluding dividends, were compared with the corresponding results of the DJIA. In the aggregate the performances ran surprisingly parallel. They may be summarized as follows:

Table 39-3 Overall Gains, Including Dividends Received		
Holding Period	**Recommended Portfolios**	**DJIA**
3 years	26%	22%
5 years	65	60
10 years	153	165

The average total gains for the varying periods (9 to 16 years) to the end of 1955 were 307 percent for the portfolios and 315 percent for the DJIA.

2. Bohmfalk's article gives an "Eleven-Year (1946–57) Record of Selected Growth Stocks," including 24 issues. Their annual results, compounded between 6 percent for Air Reduction and 25 percent for IBM. The author points out that the return averaged about 13 percent for the list—which compares with 13.4 percent shown in the same table for Standard & Poor's 425 industrials.

3. Wiesenberger's *Investment Companies 1961* has a separate analysis of the performance of "Growth-Appreciation Funds." Results for 1951–1960 are available for 20 funds, on a basis assuming reinvestment of all distributions from security profits and other capital sources. The range of total gain for the 10 years is from 392 percent down to 127 percent, with a mean of 289 percent. The corresponding figure for S&P's 500 Stock Composite Average is 322 percent.[10]

Comment: The results of these three studies point up the basic problems involved in attempting to select securities in the stock market primarily on the basis of the expected rate of future growth. We do not know the extent to which mathematical valuation methods entered into the results we have compared with the market averages. It is possible, though by no means certain, that perfected techniques of the sort described earlier in this chapter may produce a better comparative performance in future years. However we must express an ingrained distrust on our part, of the employment of refined mathematical calculations to arrive at valuations which at bottom are based on inherently inexact projections or "guesstimates" of performance for many years in the future.

Our Approach to Growth-Stock Valuation

The authors of this book, separately and together, in working on this problem in recent years have developed several methods and formulas. Let us describe briefly three of these approaches. Somewhat to our surprise, the multipliers produced for given growth rates showed only narrow differences under the respective techniques.

Our first method endeavored to apply to growth stocks the same basic treatment that we have recommended for common stocks generally, except that we eliminate the dividend factor in the valuation. This means that the value would be found by applying a suitable multiplier to the average earnings for the next seven years. For any expected growth rate this average would be about equal to the middle or fourth year's earnings. (Note that this does not reduce our contemplated growth period below seven years: the multiplier of the seventh-year figure.)

Our range of multipliers was established by two considerations. The first was a limitation of the seven-year growth rates to 20 percent per annum. This upper limit would envisage a 3½ fold expansion of earnings in seven years— certainly enough for any investment expectations. Our second step was to establish a similar maximum multiplier of 20 times the average or fourth year's earnings. This maximum was arbitrarily taken as 150 percent of the 13 multiplier assigned to large and sound companies of medium prospects, such as the DJIA group in the aggregate, for which we project future growth at a 3½ percent annual rate. These premises would suggest that the multipliers should advance proportionately from 13 to 20 as the expected growth rate rises from 3½ percent to 20 percent. The resultant table would work out as follows:

Table 39-4		
Expected Rate of Growth (for 7 years)	Multiplier of Average (fourth year earnings)	Multiplier of Current Earnings
3.5%	13x	15x
5.0	14x	17x
7.2	15x	20x
10.0	16x	23½x
12.0	17x	27x
14.3	18x	31x
17.0	19x	35½x
20.0	20x	41½x

This schedule bears an accidental similarity to the Molodovsky technique, in that all the multipliers of the projected *seventh-year* earnings would fall within the narrow range of 11½ to 12½. However, the student should recall that Molodovsky's and most other methods discussed above involve a calculation of dividend income and a discount factor, neither of which we allow for here.

Our second approach was developed independently by Charles Tatham and was published by his firm in 1961.[11] It is set forth in his book in his chapter on "Valuation of Public Utility Common Stocks" (Chapter 43).

Finally, our study of the various mathematical processes used by others led us to formulate two highly simplified methods of attaining approximately the same results as those produced by more complicated calculations. The first was our "8.6T plus 2.1" multiplier, developed directly out of the Molodovsky concept and previously discussed. The second is even simpler and reads as follows:

> Value = current "normal" earnings × (8.5 plus 2G), where G is the average
> annual growth rate expected for the next 7 to 10 years.

The specific figures in this formula are derived largely from the concept that a multiplier of 8.5 is appropriate for a company with zero expected growth, and a current multiplier of 13.5 is satisfactory for one with an expected 2½ percent growth. (The latter is a Molodovsky assumption.) In addition, the resulting multipliers for various other assumed rates appear to be as plausible as those worked out more laboriously by others.

A comparison of our four separate multipliers for various growth rates, together with the typical results of the Molodovsky method, is given [in Table 39-5].

It will be noted that our preferred, based on a 7-year projection of growth, yields current multipliers quite close to those from the other formulas for growth rates up to 10 percent. For higher rates our recommended multipliers are more conservative than the others. This follows in part from the great impact of the eighth- to tenth-year growth at such optimistic rates, and in part from our self-imposed limitation of 20 times fourth-year earnings. Since we have already expressed our lack of confidence in predictions of large percentage gains for many years in the future, we do not have to say more to defend our conservatism in this range.[12]

Table 39-5							
Expected Growth Rate	0%	2.5%	5%	7.2%	10%	14.3%	20%
Growth in 10 years		28.0%	63%	100.0%	159%	280.0%	519%
Multipliers by:							
• Molodovsky's method*	11.5x	13.5x	16.1x	18.9x	23.0x	31.2x	46.9x
• Tatham's table®				18	25		
• "8.6T + 2.1" formula	10.7	13.1	16.1	19.3	24.4	36.5	55.3
• "8.5 + 2G" formula	8.5	13.5	18.5	22.7	28.5	37.1	48.5
Our preferred method (7 year projection)	8.5	13.5	17	20	23.5	31	41.5

Molodovsky's method bases these rates on the assumption that the projected 10-year growth rates are the same are the same as the actual rates for the previous 5 years. ® From column for 7-year growth projections in Chap. 43, p. 591

Notes

1. *Journal of Finance*, December 1954
2. See N. Molodovsky, "An Appraisal of the Dow-Jones Average," *Commercial and Financial Chronicle*, Oct. 30, 1958.
3. Molodovsky here assumed a "long-term earnings level" of only $25 for the unit in 1959, against the actual figure of $34. His multiplier of 22 produced a valuation of 550. Later he was to change his method in significant ways, which we discuss below.
4. David Durand has commented on the parallel between this aspect of growth-stock valuation and the famous mathematical anomaly known as the "Petersburg Paradox." See his article in *Journal of Finance*, September 1957.
5. Molodovsky later adopted this rate in place of his earlier 7 percent, having found that 7½ percent per year was the average over-all realization by common-stock owners between 1871 and 1959. It was made up of a 5 percent average dividend return and a compounded annual growth rate of about 2½ percent in earnings, dividends, and market price.

6. See R. A. Bing, "Can We Improve Methods of Appraising Growth Stocks?" *Commercial & Financial Chronicle*, Sept. 13, 1956; "The Growth Stock Philosophy," by J. F. Bohmfalk, Jr., *Financial Analysts Journal*, November 1960; J. G. Buckley, "A Method of Evaluation Growth Stock," *Financial Analysts Journal*, March 1960; "A Mathematical Approach to Growth-stock Valuation," by O. K. Burrell, *Financial Analysts Journal*, May 1960; R. E. Kennedy, Jr., "Growth Stocks: Opportunity or Illusion," *Financial Analysts Journal*, March 1960; G. H. Palmer, "An Approach to Stock Valuation," *Financial Analysts Journal*, May 1956; and the various articles by Molodovsky.

7. Note that the ten-year past growth rate of Dow Chemical was set at 16 percent by Kennedy, 10 percent by Bohmfalk, and 6.3 percent by Buckley, all writing in 1960. See previous footnote.

8. An article by R. Ferguson in the May-June 1961 issue of *Financial Analysts Journal*, p. 29, contains an ingenious "nomograph," or arrangement of various figures in columns, which can be used for readily making a number of calculations of this type.

9. The difference between hindsight and foresight in growth-stock selection is well illustrated in this very instance of IBM. The SEC study of investment companies (to be published in 1962) shows that at the end of 1952 the 118 funds covered had only ½ of 1 percent of their common-stock holdings in IBM shares. This issue ranked twenty-third in a list of 30 largest holdings. These institutional investors were made cautious by the relatively high multiplier of IBM shares as far back as 1952. They were unable to forecast with sufficient confidence its coming superior performance so as to impel them to make a concentrated investment in its shares. While they participated to some degree in its later spectacular advance, this benefit was made relatively unimportant by the small size of their holdings.

10. No deduction from these performance results is made for sales load on mutual fund shares or commission cost on the S&P "portfolio." See also the third calculation in Appendix Note 10, p. 741.

11. *Price-Earnings Ratios and Earnings Growth*, Bache & Company, New York, Oct. 2, 1961.

12. The case for not paying extremely high multiples is most persuasive. In this regard, the student should read S. F. Nicholson, "Price-Earnings Ratios," *Financial Analysts Journal*, July-August 1960, pp. 43–45. In a study of 100 common stocks, principally industrial issues of investment quality, including many of the largest companies, over 11 selected time spans from 1939 to 1959, the author found that the stocks selling at the lowest multiples showed much more appreciation than the stocks selling at the highest multiples and that the individual issues which showed losses during these periods or which showed relatively little appreciation were predominantly in the high-multiple groups. A similar study of 29 chemical stocks produced comparable results. For example, "the 50 percent lowest price-earnings ratios averaged over 50 percent more appreciation than the 50 percent highest ratios." Among Nicholson's conclusions is the statement, "Many investors have apparently underestimated the importance of reasonable price-earnings relationships."

4

■ ■ ■

The Power of the Purchase Decision

Price is what you pay; value is what you get.
—WARREN BUFFETT

The relatively simple decision to purchase a car can help you understand a lot about purchasing a stock. When you decide to buy a car, there are two fundamental questions you must answer: what kind of car do you want, and how much do you want to pay?

If you are a typical buyer, you have done some research to identify the make and model you would like. If you are shopping for a new car, you have probably surfed the Web for prices and have a pretty good idea of how much you can squeeze the dealer. If you are looking for a used car, you have probably looked at the Blue Book and have a good idea of the prevailing prices for your desired car.

Let's say you have decided to buy a used car, a 2008 BMW 750 series sedan. You study the Blue Book prices and learn that the average price of that make and model for that year is about $75,000. Now that you have selected your car and learned its value, the next step is to make the purchase decision.

Price is the most important part of the purchase decision. If you could purchase the BMW for $75,000, that would be a fair price. Neither you nor the seller would have the advantage in the transaction. If you were lucky enough to buy the same car for $30,000, that would be a great purchase price. That's known as a buyer-advantaged transaction. If you were foolish enough to pay $100,000 for the car (the color was awesome!), that would be a very poor purchase decision. The advantage in that transaction would go to the seller.

Obviously, it's always best to purchase a car at a fair price or less. Clearly, we do not want to pay too much for the automobile.

The same holds true in the stock market. We would all like to pay fair price or less for the stocks we buy. In fact, we strongly believe that the buy discipline is the most important part of the stock investing process.

Ironically, when prospective customers invite us in to discuss our investment methodology, they are invariably far more interested in quizzing us on our "sell discipline" than on our "buy discipline." This is an unfortunate example of misguided focus, since the buy decision is far more important than the sell decision. Instead of planning an exit strategy when they buy a long-term asset such as a stock, investors should "seal the exits." Imagine that you are going to hold the stock for at least 30 years. That simple rule will change your discipline about purchasing a stock, and you will invest in better companies.

THE DIFFERENCE BETWEEN CARS AND STOCKS

Whether it is cars or stocks that you're buying, as Warren Buffett put it, "Price is what you pay; value is what you get." There are three very clear differences between the car market and the stock market.

First, the stock market is more volatile than the car market. Thus, the price of a company's stock can diverge widely from the actual value of the company itself. This is the key opportunity for investors.

Second, the stock market is more opaque and dynamic than the car market. It is more difficult to calculate what a company is worth. In fact, you may buy a company that is a BMW today, but that actually deteriorates into a Yugo tomorrow.

And finally, the stock market is open for business every business day. If you decide to sell a stock today, you can typically sell it today, and you will receive the proceeds in three business days. If you own a car and you decide to sell it, you must first find a buyer, and even then you have no assurance that you will receive your money in a timely manner.

The fact that the stock market is continuously open for business presents a wonderful—and often perplexing—issue for investors. Ben Graham addressed this unique feature of the stock market in *The Intelligent Investor.*

> Imagine that in some private business you own a small share that costs you $1,000. One of your partners, named Mr. Market, is very obliging indeed. Every day he tells you what he thinks your interest is worth and furthermore offers to either buy you out or to sell you an additional interest on that basis. Sometimes his idea of value appears plausible and is justified by business developments and prospects as you know them. Often, on the other hand, Mr. Market lets his enthusiasm or his fears run away with him, and the value he proposes to you seems to you a little short of silly.
>
> If you are a prudent investor or a sensible businessman, will you let Mr. Market's daily communication determine your view of the value of a $1,000 interest in the enterprise? Only in case you agree with him, or in case you want to trade with him. You may be happy to sell out to him when he quotes you a ridiculously high price, and equally happy to buy from him when the price is low. But the rest of the time you will be wiser to form your own ideas of the value of your holdings, based on full reports from the company about its operations and financial position.

The very fact that the stock market offers daily price quotations means that all of us have the chance to exorcise our fears at a moment's notice. Poof! If you do not like your stock, you can sell it in an instant. Over the last 20 years, the improvement in technology has made the direct cost of selling cheaper, even for the small investor.

This ability to sell a stock at a moment's notice is one of the greatest innovations in the history of capitalism. You can sell your stock positions every day to a faceless buyer at a very low transaction cost. What could be better?

The problem is that the daily price of your stock tends to divert your attention from the real value of the company. Through a fortuitous set of events, you are able to buy a stock for $10 per share when the real value of the company is $30 per share on the date of purchase. The stock quickly rises to $20 per share. You have doubled the value of your investment, yet the stock is still selling at a substantial discount to the real value of the company. Should you hold the stock, add to the position, or sell it at twice your cost?

Can you see how easily we can become diverted by the daily price changes in the market? The correct decision, in our view, would be to add to the position. The stock is still trading at a large discount to the real value of the company. Yet how many stock market investors have succumbed to the costly adage, "You never grow broke taking a profit."

How should an investor take advantage of the stock market without succumbing to its temptations? The answer is clear but not easy to do. An investor must take advantage of the volatility in stock prices at the time of purchase, and do so to a lesser extent at the time of sale. The rest of the time, however, the investor should ignore the market fluctuations and concentrate on the fundamental progress of the companies behind the stocks. The ability to do this requires discipline and preparation.

SETTING YOUR PURCHASE PRICE

Before you can decide on a price that you're willing to pay for a stock, you need to answer two questions:

- What's the company worth (based on Graham's formula)?
- What's your "hurdle rate"?

In Chapter 3, we laid out the framework for applying the Graham model to value growth companies. We contend that the dynamic nature of growth companies requires us to compute a future value of the company as well as a current value of the company. We choose to estimate a value seven years in the future.

If we were constructing a chart to estimate the value of Company A, it would look like Figure 4.1.

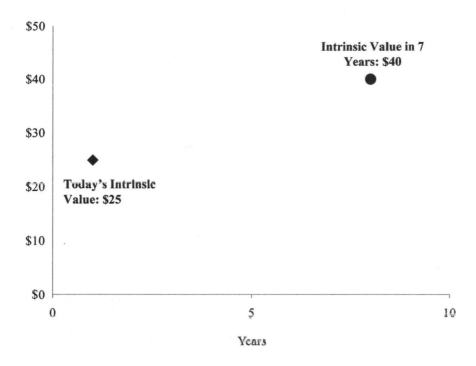

Figure 4.1 Intrinsic Value of Company A

The chart shows the intrinsic value of the stock today and its projected value in seven years.

As we wrote in Chapter 3, making the effort to calculate today's intrinsic value for a growth company is extremely important in order to gain an understanding of how the company operates. It is the future intrinsic value that is critical to our decision on whether to purchase the stock.

To avoid confusion in our discussion, we are going to leave out the intrinsic value today and include only the future intrinsic value. Let's assume that a company has a future intrinsic value (seven years from now) of $40 per share (see Figure 4.2). Assuming that the company pays no dividends, it is easy to calculate our expected return for different purchase prices.

The five charts in Figure 4.3 show the expected return for various purchase prices. Note how sensitive the expected return can be to different purchase prices.

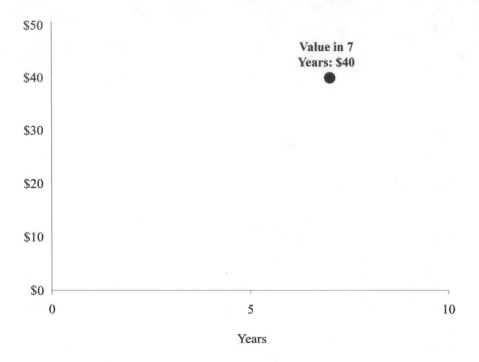

Figure 4.2 Future Value of Company A

Importance of the "Hurdle Rate"

The *hurdle rate* is the average compounded annual return that you hope to earn from your investments—or in this case, the compounded annual average return that you hope to earn from your stock portfolio. The hurdle rate is important for every investor in determining a purchase price for a specific stock that will meet the investor's investment objectives.

The hurdle rate can vary significantly from one investor to another depending on the investor's objectives. A conservative or short-term investor might be satisfied with a hurdle rate of 5 percent or less. More aggressive investors may have a hurdle rate of 8 or 10 percent. A select few investors with just the right temperament and investment savvy may shoot for a hurdle rate above 10 percent.

How do you settle on a hurdle rate? The two keys to setting a hurdle rate are your investment requirements and your ability to achieve those objectives.

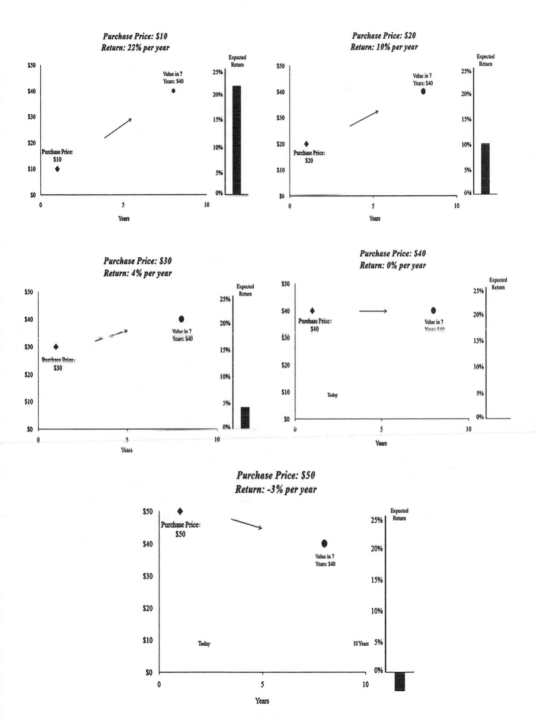

Figure 4.3 Return on Company A for Various Purchase Prices

In Chapter 2, we suggested that investors choose a target return of about 2 percent above their long-term desired return in order to compensate for cyclical market downturns. The target return and the hurdle rate are essentially the same thing. Once you've analyzed your cash flow and your retirement needs, for example, you might determine that you would need an 8 percent compounded return over the course of your investment lifetime to achieve your objectives. If you add 2 percent to that rate to compensate for cyclical market downturns, that would give you a long-term target return or hurdle rate of 10 percent.

The Difficulty of Outperforming the Market

An equally important and too often overlooked factor in setting a hurdle rate is the investor's ability to achieve those rates. Both Graham and Buffett have said that it is relatively easy to achieve reasonable returns from stocks but very difficult to achieve returns that exceed the market averages. In fact, less than 10 percent of all mutual fund managers are able to beat the market averages in any given year, and less than 2 percent beat the market over any 10-year period. But with the introduction of S&P 500 index funds, which seek to mirror the performance of the market, investors should be able to achieve returns in the range of 7 to 8 percent.

For investors who prefer to invest in individual stocks, we suggest a hurdle rate that is somewhat higher than the market return, perhaps 10 percent. We further suggest that the investor engage in a serious soul-searching exercise. Ask yourself if you have both the temperament and the resources to achieve these higher returns.

An investor who wants to hire an investment manager to achieve higher returns should understand that very few investment managers are able to outperform the market on a consistent basis. The vast majority underperform the market. To find a manager who can outperform the market, there are several important factors to consider in your screening process. Although the manager's track record is certainly an important

factor, there are several other factors that we consider even more important. You should interview the manager personally and gain a sense of her
competence, character, and courage. For those who are interested in
quantitative data, we believe that the portfolio turnover, employee
turnover, and client turnover can often be far more revealing than historical performance.

Do Not Change Your Hurdle Rate!

Once you set a hurdle rate, it's important that you stick with it, even though
changing market and economic conditions will often tempt you to make a
change. Unless your long-term objectives have changed, you need to ignore
the market conditions and maintain a nearly cultlike devotion to your
hurdle rate.

A steady hurdle rate is your primary guide in making your stock
purchase decisions.

Figure 4.4 demonstrates how an investor (Investor A) can use the
hurdle rate to make his stock purchase decisions. If the investor has a
hurdle rate of 5 percent, he can buy shares of Stock XYZ for a price of up
to $28.43 per share—which would have a calculated value in seven years of
$40 per share.

If he buys the stock at a price less than $28.43, he has entered a trans-
action that favors him, the buyer. If he pays a price greater than $28.43,
he has entered a transaction in which he has chosen to put himself at a
disadvantage as the buyer. (Our purchase decision is not an attempt to
take advantage of the seller, only to ensure that we are honoring our
hurdle rate.)

In the following example, Investor B has a higher hurdle rate (10 percent)
than Investor A. In order to achieve her higher hurdle rate with Stock XYZ,
she cannot pay more than $20.53 per share today. If she pays more than
$20.53, she has put herself at a disadvantageous position relative to her hurdle
rate. If she pays less than $20.53, she has enhanced her chances of earning her
hurdle rate. Figure 4.5 shows Investor B's situation.

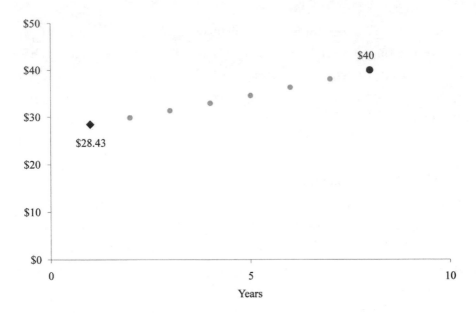

Figure 4.4 Investor A Hurdle Rate: 5 Percent

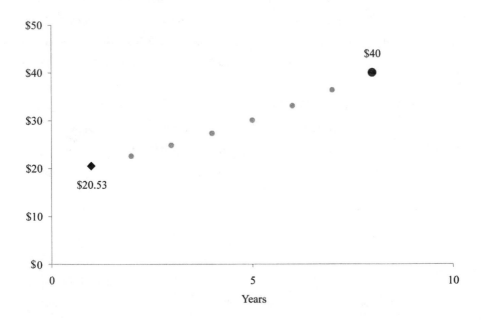

Figure 4.5 Investor B Hurdle Rate: 10 Percent

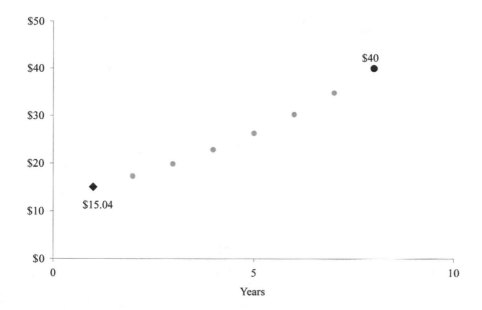

Figure 4.6 Investor C Hurdle Rate: 15 Percent

Investor C has an aggressive hurdle rate of 15 percent. He cannot pay more than $15.04 for the shares of the stock and still have a reasonable chance of earning a 15 percent hurdle rate. The chart in Figure 4.6 shows Investor C's situation.

The difficulty of earning high rates of return should be obvious from the three charts in Figures 4.4 to 4.6. Investor C has a much tougher set of circumstances. He will probably have to exercise above-average patience and certainly above-average discipline.

We cannot emphasize enough the importance of having a clear and unchanging hurdle rate. One of the unique characteristics of the public stock market is the ability to transact with an anonymous person on the other side of the trade. While you may be tempted to speculate as to why a seller chooses to sell at a given price, successful investing does not require that we know the motivation of the seller or the buyer on the other side of the transaction—only that the transaction makes sense for us. This means that we invest if we

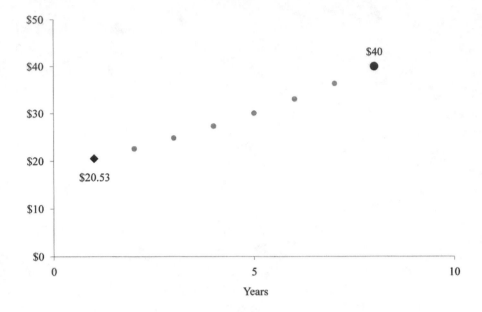

Figure 4.7 Investor B Hurdle Rate: 10 Percent

can reasonably value the company and we can buy the stock at a price that is likely to earn our hurdle rate.

Let's examine the insights we can gain by setting a constant hurdle rate.

In the following example, Investor B has established a hurdle rate of 10 percent. According to our example, Investor B could pay up to $20.53 per share, as Figure 4.7 illustrates.

We can now begin to look at different purchase prices for Investor B. If Investor B pays around $20 per share for Stock XYZ, that would be a "fair" price for the stock, earning her about 10 percent per year from the purchase. If she is able to buy the stock at a price below $20 per share, she has entered into a buyer-favored transaction. If the investor pays much more than $20 per share, that would be a buyer-disadvantaged transaction.

By establishing a set hurdle rate, you are able to make the purchase process a very simple, straightforward decision. If you can buy the stock at a price that will give you a return that is equal to or better than your hurdle rate, you can feel free to buy the stock. If you can't buy the stock at a price that will give you your hurdle rate or better, you don't buy the stock. It's a cut-and-dried decision.

Staying True to Your Purchase Price

Any investor who is seeking to purchase a stock needs to understand that there are three situations for the stock at any given moment:

- *Seller's advantage.* The stock is at a price level where the seller stands to sell the stock at a price that will not meet the buyer's hurdle rate. A disciplined investor will not be interested in buying the stock at this level.
- *Fair price.* The buyer can be satisfied with this transaction because he is getting a fair price on the purchase.
- *Buyer's advantage.* The stock price is at a level where the buyer can acquire the stock at a price that should yield a return above his hurdle rate.

Why would an investor buy a stock at a disadvantageous price? There are two primary reasons: (1) he doesn't know what the company is worth, and (2) either he hasn't set a hurdle rate or he violates that hurdle rate.

Unfortunately, staying true to your purchase price does not eliminate the chance that you may lose money on a specific stock investment. Occasionally a well-developed forecast of the future value of a stock is too high because of events that occur after purchase of the stock. This is the best argument for diversification, so that one stock does not fatally damage the portfolio returns.

VOLATILITY: THE GIFT THAT KEEPS ON GIVING

One of the enduring characteristics of the stock market has been its short-term volatility. Not only does the stock market vary by the day, month, or year, but individual stocks fluctuate widely as well. We do not choose to waste our analytical efforts on understanding why the stock market or individual stocks are priced at their current levels. We do care that this phenomenon repeats itself. This is crucial for those who want to earn returns well above 10 percent. We need the stock market to offer us growth stocks that are priced to earn our hurdle rate of 12 percent—and constant stock market volatility is the gift that gives us that opportunity.

Ben Graham has said that the stock market is a voting machine in the short run and a weighing machine in the long run. Put differently, the stock market is random over the short run and ruthlessly efficient over the long run.

There are many factors that cause the stock market to be a volatile short-term voting machine. When you understand those factors and their effect on the market, you will understand why the market's volatility is an endlessly repeating phenomenon.

The key ingredients in short-term volatility are human nature and physiology. We are all imperfect. We all suffer from biases related to our own experiences. We are subject to fear and greed. We are also influenced by physiological deficiencies. When our stock portfolios are doing well, a substance known as dopamine is triggered in our brains, creating the same reaction that is triggered by cocaine ingestion. When our portfolios are declining, our brain tells us that we are in mortal danger. Consider, then, that most investors fluctuate between a cocainelike high and mortal fear!

There are also a number of outside influences that affect the market and induce volatility. Let's examine the primary causes of stock market volatility.

Transaction-Driven Brokers

The brokerage industry, at its heart, is in the business of creating transactions. The retail broker typically works off a straight commission, based on client actions. These folks are among the most entrepreneurial of all! And they are exceedingly clever at getting customers to make changes. In recent years, the retail brokerage industry has attempted to shift toward a compensation structure based on assets under management. The problem, of course, is that the industry is attempting to change its spots. Today the management fees are so high that the clients cannot make progress. We predict the industry will inevitably revert back to what it does best—create transactions.

The rock stars of the brokerage industry are the investment bankers, who generate huge fees by creating transactions.

The framework used by the "analysts" who work for the retail brokerage industry is also designed to create transactions. The typical analyst report has a 12-month time frame. The buy or sell recommendation is typically based on whether the company will exceed or fall short of "consensus expectations" over the next 12 months. The phrases "target price" and "near-term catalyst" abound in these reports.

Investors should understand that there are at least two major flaws in the average report issued by a brokerage firm analyst. First, the report is applying a one-year time horizon to a long-lived asset. This makes little or no sense. Second, the reports base their recommendations on a data point that cannot be forecast with much accuracy: the next 12 months' earnings for a company.

The unpredictability of earnings over a 12-month time frame has been well documented over the years. A commonsense look at corporate income statements is all you need if you are to understand the difficulty of forecasting short-term earnings. For a typical corporation, pretax earnings are less than 10 percent of revenues. For an analyst to put together a reasonably accurate forecast, the analyst must not only estimate revenues correctly, but also forecast the myriad of expenses that the company is likely to report. In our view, it is far more manageable to construct a reasonable earnings forecast for the next several years than it is to make an accurate forecast for the next 12 months. Yet brokerage industry analysts continue to base their investment recommendations on these largely unreliable forecasts.

These forecasts manifest themselves in the frenzied trading activity and market response around brokerage industry recommendation changes.

Individual Company Announcements

Over the last 20 years, the timeliness and content of the information provided by U.S. companies has improved dramatically. Quarterly SEC filings of unaudited financial results are provided within 45 days after the end of the quarter. Audited annual financial statements are available within 90 days after the end of the fiscal year. Corporate compensation is regularly available through proxy statements. Investors have plenty of information to use in making good decisions on their stock holdings.

In their zeal to keep investors informed, many public companies have adopted quarterly earnings announcements and associated conference calls. The brokerage industry analysts must wait (breathlessly, I assume) to see whether, during the previous three months, the company has fallen short of, met, or exceeded their forecasted quarterly results. Today there is even a "whisper" number, which is supposed to reflect the earnings that the company is actually going to post, as opposed to the published brokerage industry estimates. Then the company gets on a quarterly conference call to talk about the "tone of business." The stock often reacts violently (plus or minus 10 percent in a single trading day) to a single data point.

For astute investors, the importance of these quarterly announcements is not in the heralding of future results. We have found little correlation between quarterly announcements and long-term stock performance. The real importance is that occasionally the market reaction to these announcements (especially if negative) gives astute investors the opportunity to purchase the stock at a price that meets or exceeds their hurdle rate.

Changes in National Economic Policy

There is a pendulum in long-term national economic policy, swinging back and forth between pro-growth and pro-distribution policies. Investors tend to overreact to these changes. If the change is toward greater distribution, investors tend to become more bearish toward stocks. If the change is toward growth, investors tend to be more bullish.

Short-term changes in the monetary policy of the Federal Open Market Committee (FOMC)—also known as "the Fed"—can be a source of volatility. If the Fed decides to ease monetary policy, the market often reacts positively; if the Fed tightens monetary policy, the market tends to react negatively.

Economic Crises

Major economic crises can be particularly scary events, but they represent the mother lode for investors who have the courage and knowledge of their individual stocks to take advantage of the crisis.

The stock market often reacts strongly to macroeconomic crises. Many investors suspend their forecast of future progress for their companies. During these events, many investors believe that the future value of their stocks has declined. We think that those investors who sell during these times are making a predictable and catastrophic mistake. The future value of a company is more dependent on its management decisions and its industry conditions than it is on the general economy. But the massive press coverage of economic problems tends to override our sensibilities. So we ignore what is important and focus on what is not.

In the case of most major crises, the crisis occurs at the end of the problem—not the beginning. The crisis actually initiates the process of repairing whatever problem created the crisis.

There is another, more serious risk associated with the aftermath of a macroeconomic crisis. Investors are diverted from their fundamental task of analyzing and identifying great investment opportunities when they attempt to analyze the repercussions of an economic crisis. Since you can't analyze the implications of an economic crisis effectively, why waste your time trying? In times of economic crisis, investors need to focus on their true objective, which is identifying and analyzing great stocks for their portfolio.

As stock market investors have learned, an economic crisis typically causes an almost universal decline in stock prices. For astute investors who can quell the butterflies in their stomach and concede that they cannot predict the outcome of the crisis, the crisis presents an outstanding opportunity to improve their investment position.

In 2008, major U.S. banks and other financial institutions around the world collapsed. Fannie Mae and Freddie Mac were put into receivership. Lehman Brothers and AIG collapsed, raising a very real possibility that the world's financial system would implode. No one could confidently predict whether the system would hold together.

The U.S. stock market responded by declining more than 50 percent from its peak in 2007. The stocks of many fine companies declined even more. Investors faced a very clear choice: focus on the economic travails (the resolution was unpredictable), or focus on the many fine companies whose stocks were selling at bargain-basement prices. At the market lows of 2008 and early 2009, stock market investors had very high odds of exceeding their hurdle rates. For astute investors, 2008 and 2009 represented a once-in-a-generation buying opportunity.

VOLATILITY FAVORS GROWTH STOCKS

One of the advantages of investing in growth stocks rather than value stocks is that growth stocks tend to be more volatile, providing more buying opportunities for well-prepared investors.

There are two reasons that growth stocks are more volatile—and both are based on simple mathematics.

In our stock investment strategy, growth stock purchase decisions are based on an estimate of the company's value seven years in the future. Value stock decisions are based on today's value. The dynamism of growth stocks means that estimates of future value tend to shift around more than estimates of today's value. A different way to think about this is to recognize that a primary component of a growth stock's value is its future growth rate (Graham's formula of 8.5 + 2G). For a value stock, the valuation is much less dependent upon future growth rates. Changing investor perceptions of growth will affect growth stocks more significantly.

A reduction in the forecast of growth rates has a dramatically greater effect on growth stocks than it does on value stocks, as the following examples demonstrate.

Value Company

A value stock with $1 of earnings drops from a 2 percent growth rate to a 1.5 percent growth rate—a decline of 25 percent in the growth rate. The following equations tell the story:

> Before the drop: 8.5 + [2 × 2 (growth) = 4] = 12.5 × $1 (earnings)
> = $12.50 intrinsic value
> After the 25 percent growth-rate drop: 8.5 + (2 × 1.5% = 3) = 11.5
> × $1 = $11.50

In this example of a slow-growth value stock, a 25 percent drop in the growth rate resulted in an 8 percent decline in the intrinsic value of the company—from $12.50 to $11.50.

Growth Company

A growth stock with $1 of earnings drops from a growth rate of 10 percent to a growth rate of 7.5 percent—also a 25 percent decline. The following equations illustrate how that 25 percent drop affects the value of the company:

> 8.5 + (2 × 10% = 20) = 28.5 × $1 = $28.50
> 8.5 + (2 × 7.5% = 15) = 23.5 × $1 = $23.50

In this growth stock example, a 25 percent drop in the growth rate of the company resulted in an 18 percent decline in the intrinsic value of the company, from $28.50 to $23.50.

What does that mean for growth stock investors?

The higher volatility associated with growth company stocks can work heavily to the advantage of the disciplined, long-term investor. You can count on repeated opportunities to purchase growth companies at prices that should earn a reasonable hurdle rate.

The history of growth companies suggests that stable growth is rare. More common is the situation in which the company experiences accelerations and decelerations in growth rates. Figure 4.8 shows a seven-year model; note the difference between steady-state growth and variable growth.

Stock prices tend to exhibit exaggerated responses to changes in growth rates, as Figure 4.9 illustrates.

Figure 4.10 shows the interaction between changes in growth rates and the typical reaction of stock prices.

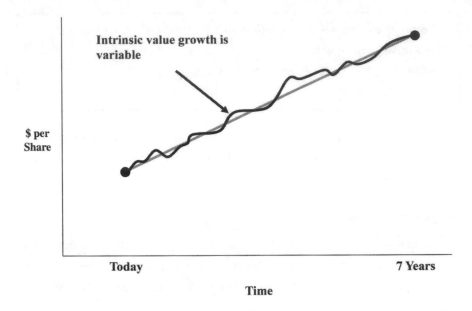

Figure 4.8 Intrinsic Value Growth Is Variable

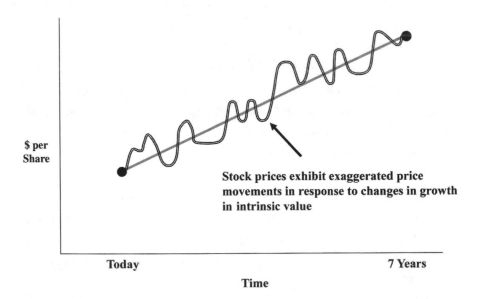

Figure 4.9 Stock Price Reacts to Intrinsic Value Growth

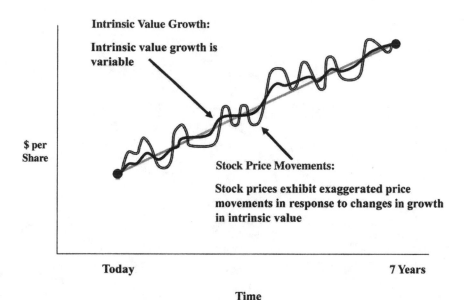

Figure 4.10 Interaction of Intrinsic Value Growth and Price Movement

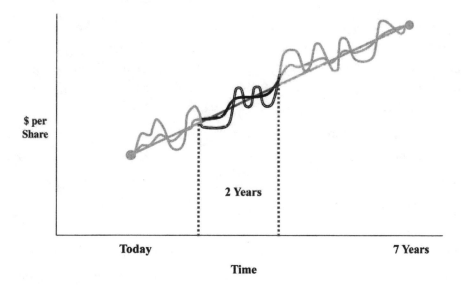

Figure 4.11 Exploiting Market Volatility

Reducing the seven-year chart to a two-year window gives us the range shown in Figure 4.11.

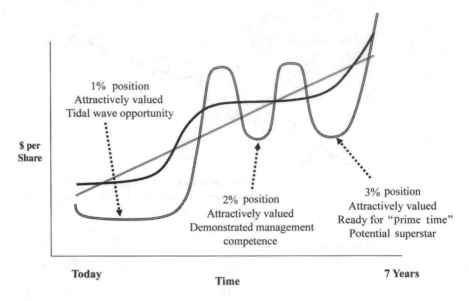

Figure 4.12 Exploiting Market Volatility in Purchasing

Figure 4.12 "zooms in" on the two-year period in which the stock can ideally be accumulated. This reflects our idealized methodology. We seek to build the position slowly. Ideally, we build to a 3 percent position in three increments. At each purchase point, we have gained incremental important knowledge, and the stock still offers an acceptable return.

All readers should understand that this is an ideal situation. The real world is much messier.

WHY RUSH TO BUY A STOCK?

The continuing volatility in the stock market offers the long-term investor additional opportunities to invest carefully. Rather than purchase a large position at a single point in time, there are several advantages to building up a position over months or years. Our firm typically spends up to three years in fully building a stock position.

Just as Rome was not built in a day, great companies and great stocks do not develop overnight. How you enter a stock position has a lot to do with how you exit the position. The practice of patiently building a position teaches the investor to be disciplined in holding the stock.

Although we can't quantify it, we suspect that you can gauge most investors' annual portfolio turnover rate by how they buy their stocks. If they purchase their positions all at once, we would guess that their portfolio turnover would be relatively high, and if they buy their stocks slowly, we would guess that their turnover rate would be relatively low.

There is a critical research function associated with purchasing a stock slowly. Even the most astute analysts can gain only cursory knowledge by reviewing all financial data and interviewing the company's management. The analyst is looking at a snapshot in time of the company. What the analyst cannot gain at first glance is knowledge of the management's ability to make real-time decisions.

Consider the initial investment in a stock as being like the early stages of a dating relationship. Everything is rosy. The investor has just discovered this company with a great business model and terrific future prospects. Management appears to have all the right answers. Then comes the hard part—the end of the honeymoon phase. The CFO leaves to "pursue personal interests." The company makes an acquisition that leaves you scratching your head. To make matters worse, management tries to defend that decision with reasons that make no sense to you.

Buying a stock slowly allows the investor to gain real-time experience with a management team before his position becomes too large.

Whirlwind courtships do occasionally lead to successful marriages, but your odds of a successful marriage generally increase if you spend at least a year or two getting to know the person. My wife has remarked on more than one occasion that to get to really know somebody, you need to know her through at least four seasons of a year. Investors who seek long-term holding periods— that is, to "marry" their stocks—should engage in a similar courtship.

Those investors who are willing to purchase a stock over several transactions can set up an interesting situation for themselves. Let's say you want to invest a total of 3 percent of your portfolio in Stock XYZ. Your initial purchase is a 1 percent position, and you plan to add two more 1 percent positions over the next two years.

By acquiring a position in a stock in that manner, you have set up a win-win situation for yourself. If XYZ doubles in price immediately after you make your purchase, you will probably wish you had bought more stock. No one ever bet enough on a winning horse. But the reality is, you've made money on your purchase. If XYZ declines after your purchase, you have the opportunity to learn more about the company and perhaps increase your position at a better price. Or you might take the opportunity to reevaluate the company and change your view of its prospects.

Although using this strategy can result in an opportunity cost, it can also save you from incurring a real cost. For instance, if your stock doubles after your initial 1 percent purchase, you may wish that you had bought more stock in order to have made more money on the stock. That's an opportunity cost. But while that viewpoint may be narrowly correct, it is misguided. An opportunity cost is not a real cost. No actual money has been lost—you've simply lost the opportunity to make more money. The real goal should be to avoid real losses—the money that is lost when you invest too much in a stock that later tanks. In fact, the fear of incurring an opportunity cost has probably caused investors more real losses than any other factor. Investing in a company slowly may cost you the opportunity to make more on the stock, but it can also help you avoid the real costs of losing money on the stock—which we contend is a much more important priority.

THE CISCO SAGA

In 2000, I suspected that Cisco Systems might be an overly popular stock when a prospective client told me that she had named her dog "Cisco." Since she was about the same age as me, I guessed that she might be referring to the old TV series *The Cisco Kid*. She corrected me, saying that she had named her dog after the stock because the stock had been so good to her.

Cisco was a textbook example of the importance of price in the purchase decision. The stock experienced extreme price fluctuations during the years from 2000 to 2002. In March of 2000, Cisco stock hit a new high of $82 per share. Two and a half years later, in October of 2002, it had plunged to just $8 per share, a decline of nearly 90 percent. What happened?

The answer does not lie in the fundamental progress of the company. Cisco continued to achieve excellent progress. Its revenue jumped 84 percent from 2000 to 2007, and its earnings jumped 77 percent during that period.

The fact is, the stock's collapse had far more to do with a dramatic over-valuation of the stock than it did with Cisco's fundamentals. The real story of Cisco's dramatic volatility was the market itself—not the company.

Investors who fell into the trap of buying Cisco stock at an inflated price or of later selling it at a price that was far below its intrinsic value could have avoided those mistakes by using Graham's formula to value Cisco stock. Based on Graham's valuation formula, using a 12 percent seven-year growth rate, the company would have been fairly priced at about $17 per share in 2000—about one-fifth its peak price of $82. By 2002, its intrinsic value, as determined by Graham's formula, would have climbed to about $20 a share—about two and a half times its price of $8 a share. Using Graham's formula would have helped you avoid buying the stock at its peak and could have helped you make a decision to buy the stock two years later, when it was trading at a bargain-basement price.

For a growth stock such as Cisco, it is important to look at a future estimated value of the company. You may recall that we use a seven-year estimated value for our companies. Under a seven-year forecast, Cisco would have projected earnings per share of $1.23 in fiscal 2007; the company actually reported $1.18 per share. To keep our estimates conservative, we would decay Cisco's growth rate to 7 percent per year beginning in 2007. Using this forecast growth rate of 7 percent in Graham's formula would yield a reasonable value of $28 per share in 2007. For those who are mathematically inclined, our forecast of $1.23 in fiscal 2007 earnings per share times a P/E multiple of 22.5 [8.5 + (2 × growth rate of 7%)] equals nearly $28 per share.

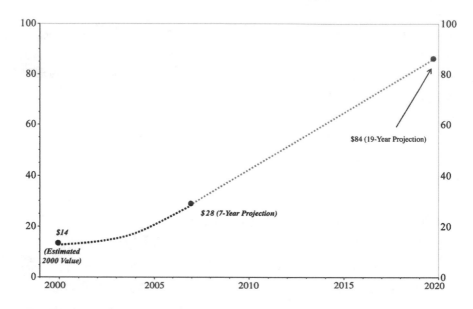

Figure 4.13 Cisco Systems: Intrinsic Value Progression
Source: FactSet.

Figure 4.13 shows the progression of intrinsic value for Cisco.

Figure 4.14 overlays Cisco's stock price activity on the company's intrinsic value. The reason for the Cisco stock collapse should be obvious. Cisco's common stock became dangerously overpriced in 2000 and severely undervalued in 2002. The reasonably astute investor who paid attention to the real value of Cisco as opposed to the common-stock price of Cisco could easily have avoided calamity and been offered the opportunity to buy a world-class growth company at a significant discount to future intrinsic value.

At the time of this writing (2011), Cisco remains a world-class growth company. The company has maintained its leadership position in the build-out of the information superhighway and has continued to increase its earnings and revenue at a robust pace.

The purchase decision is the single most important decision you will make with every stock you own. If an investor were allowed only one investment decision in the last century, we would assert that the best practical decision would have been the one described in Chapter 2: to equal-weight the

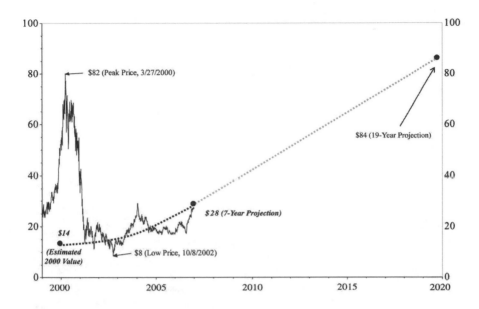

Figure 4.14 Cisco Systems: Historical Prices
Source: FactSet.

30 stocks in the Dow Jones Industrial Average in 1932. With the benefit of hindsight, the market bottom in 1932 clearly represented a historic buying opportunity. Even the least sophisticated investor could have made the decision to equal-weight the 30 stocks in the best-known index of the day.

The combined market cap of those original shares would have totaled about $5 billion. Today the value of those original Dow Jones stocks would be nearly $2 trillion—a gain of nearly 400 times. And that is without including the annual dividends from those companies, which, in and of themselves, now dwarf the original investment. It is unlikely that any trading decision you could point to would have ranked with that example—nor would any decision to sell a stock short.

The optimal portfolio would consist of growth companies with the stocks purchased at reasonable prices or less. If an investor is fortunate enough to pick the right stocks at the right price, the ideal scenario would be that those stocks would never become significantly overpriced, so you would never have to trade the portfolio. That's the power of the purchase decision.

5

...

Building a Margin of Safety for Growth Stocks

In the old legend the wise men finally boiled down the history of mortal affairs into the single phrase, "This too will pass." Confronted with a like challenge to distill the secret of sound investment into three words, we venture the motto, "margin of safety."

—Benjamin Graham

A margin of safety has been a critical element in two of my lifelong passions—flying and investing. If you ignore the margin of safety when you're investing, it could cost you your fortune; if you ignore it when you're flying, it could cost you your life.

I earned my private pilot's license in 1970 at a military flying club in Hawaii. After I learned that the federal government's GI bill would pay 90 percent of the cost of additional training, I embarked on a mission to obtain more licenses. Along the way, I earned a commercial license, instructor rating, instrument rating, instrument instructor rating, and a twin-engine license. I was happily enjoying my life as a father with minimal flying when one of my brothers bought an airplane. My family has always been very competitive, so I purchased an airplane, too. It was a beautiful Beechcraft Bonanza, a nonpressurized piston-engine aircraft. After several years of flying long, uncomfortable trips, I made the big leap to a Beechcraft King Air, a pressurized, turbine-driven, twin-engine aircraft. The insurance company scratched its head until it was nearly raw, but eventually allowed me to fly the plane. Two more King Airs followed. Each was bigger and faster than the earlier ones.

At first glance, owning an airplane is not an entirely rational decision. There is something about going higher, farther, and faster that causes a disciplined investor to rethink price-value relationships. Each knot of speed costs a lot more money and is worth every penny. So, in 2003 I purchased a light jet, a Beechcraft Premier I. Wow! The airplane typically accelerates from a standing start to 130 miles per hour in 15 seconds. On my first flight, I leveled off at low altitude, and before I could react, the airplane had accelerated to a speed of 325 knots, far above the speed limit (below 10,000 feet) of 250 knots. There are not yet traffic cops in the sky, so I managed to slow down this slippery beast without penalty.

I have been operating the aircraft safely for seven years. It is an incredibly useful piece of machinery, a time machine—45 minutes from Minneapolis to Chicago; 2 hours from Minneapolis to New York City. With this type of speed comes a lot of risk. At a cruising altitude of 41,000 feet, the aircraft is going through the air at over 500 miles per hour, or about 8 to 9 miles per minute. Have you ever been driving your car when a warning light came on? It often takes 30 seconds or more to understand the problem and react. In a jet, for each 30 seconds of analytical time, the aircraft has gone another 4 to 5 miles! Everything about flying a jet involves speed. How does one take advantage of the speed and still remain safe?

Ironically, the key to safe flying is the same as the key to successful investing: maintaining a margin of safety. From my perspective as an investor and a pilot, it is clear that the aviation community manages the margin of safety far better than the investment community. The reason is obvious: the cost of violating the margin of safety in flying is typically catastrophic, whereas the cost of violating the investment margin of safety involves one's pocketbook and one's pride.

Good pilots think obsessively about the margin of safety. Not too long ago, our planned flight pushed us against our margin of safety. My wife, Sue, and I (along with our chief pilot, Jim) were to fly from Minneapolis-St. Paul to Helena, Montana, with a stop in Brookings, South Dakota, to pick up my wife's sister, Chris. Brookings had suffered an ice storm. I called the airport to find out the status of the runways, and the airport was closed because of the ice. Jim and I began to consider other options. The two best choices were Watertown to the north and Sioux Falls to the south. Watertown had no control tower and would not issue a report on runway braking action. This is crucial for my aircraft because it does not have thrust reverse. Sioux Falls had both an operating control tower and airline service.

Chris called to say that she had a ride to Watertown. I could feel the margin of safety beginning to be squeezed too much for my taste. I told Chris that she had to find a way to get to Sioux Falls or we would not be able to pick her up. One could say that I traded one risk for another by denying my wife's sister. I felt I could always make up the relationship damage with flowers, but violating the margin of safety when flying is a very poor idea.

All's well that ends well. Chris found a ride to Sioux Falls and came to Montana with us.

Pilots make routine decisions day after day to ensure that their flights remain within their margin of safety. Operating an aircraft at the edge of the margin of safety does not mean that the flight will suffer harm; it is just not a good way to fly.

The margin of safety is as fundamental to managing our lives as it is to managing our portfolios. The point spread in sports offers a great example. If you are a Detroit Lions football fan, you are probably frustrated with the team's poor won–lost record for the past 25 years. True Lions fans expect their team to win every game. That is, they have given their team no point spread. Imagine if the Detroit Lions fans were rewarded for their team's futility by a point spread of 25 points per game. Betting on the Lions over a season in which you are given 25 points per game would be tantamount to having a huge margin of safety. Who would care whether the Lions won or lost; their fans could cry all the way to the bank.

Let's look at margin of safety differently. Most health professionals agree that the four keys to a long life are to drink moderately, avoid smoking, maintain a reasonable diet, and exercise regularly. If you follow these four guidelines, you have built a margin of safety for yourself, but are you guaranteed a long life? Of course not. If you smoke three packs a day, are you assured of dying young? Of course not. But if you do smoke three packs a day, you have reduced your margin of safety, thus reducing your odds of living a full life.

Automobile seat belts are another example of the margin of safety. Wearing a seat belt does not guarantee that you will survive a car crash unscathed. In fact, it doesn't even guarantee that you will actually suffer less damage than a person who is not wearing a seat belt. But the odds favor those wearing seat belts. They have a greater margin of safety.

Ben Graham is universally credited with introducing the concept of a margin of safety to the investment world. He learned the value of investing with safety in mind early in his career, when his investment portfolio was nearly wiped out by the crash of 1929. When discussing the concept in *The Intelligent Investor*, he wrote, "To have a true investment there must be present a true margin of safety. And a true margin of safety is one that can be demonstrated by figures, by persuasive reasoning, and by reference to a body of actual experience."

It's okay for investors to be slightly obsessive about their margin of safety because it is fundamental to effective investing. Margin of safety is critical to understanding proper diversification. Many investors are actually overly diversified, owning hundreds of companies through multiple mutual funds that are, themselves, overly diversified. What is the appropriate level of diversification? How many stocks should an investor own? The number varies by investor and is a function of the number of stocks for which the investor can calculate a satisfactory margin of safety. Simply adding one more stock to your portfolio for the sake of diversification actually contributes nothing to your margin of safety. Buying stocks without knowing the margin of safety can be tantamount to investment suicide. You need to determine a margin of safety for every investment you buy. If you can compute a margin of safety for only four stocks, then we suggest that you limit your portfolio to those four stocks and add in an S&P 500 index fund to provide diversification.

There is another vitally important link between the margin of safety when flying and the margin of safety when investing. Skilled and safe pilots obsessively evaluate the margin of safety before takeoff. Once you leave the ground in an aircraft, landing is assured. The only question is the form of the landing. The only way to avoid a landing is to decide not to take off in the first place. We believe the very best investors treat the purchase of a stock just like the best pilots view the next takeoff. They don't buy the stock until they can attain a margin of safety that helps assure a successful result.

The margin of safety is often defined as the difference between the intrinsic value of a stock and its market price. In other words, a stock that is trading significantly below its intrinsic value has a wide margin of safety, while a stock that is trading at or above its intrinsic value has no margin of safety. The more cheaply you can buy a stock relative to its intrinsic value, the bigger your margin of safety.

Graham himself focused heavily on price as a key determinant of margin of safety. He believed that even when purchasing the stock of a very mediocre company, if the margin of safety is great enough, the investor is likely to turn a profit. "It is our argument that a sufficiently low price can turn a security of mediocre quality into a sound investment opportunity—provided that the buyer is informed and experienced and that he practices adequate diversification," said Graham. "For if the price is low enough to create a substantial margin of safety, the security thereby meets our criterion of investment."

Graham also recognized that price alone is too narrow a definition of margin of safety. "The chief losses to investors come from the purchase of low-quality securities at times of favorable business conditions," Graham explained. "It is then that common stocks of obscure companies can be floated at prices far above the tangible investment, on the strength of two or three years of excellent growth. These securities do not offer an adequate margin of safety in any admissible sense of the term."

He recommended that to determine an accurate margin of safety based on a true valuation of the company, an investor needs to evaluate the performance of the company over a period of several years—"including preferably a period of subnormal business."

Graham also pointed out a key flaw in the use of margin of safety. "Even with a margin [of safety] in the investor's favor, an individual security may work out badly. For the margin guarantees only that he has a better chance for profit than for loss—not that loss is impossible."

STAYING WITHIN THE SAFETY ZONE

The margin of safety does not have clear boundaries. It is a safety zone. You need to continue to remind yourself that there will be no warning lights or "margin of safety" cops to tell you if you've violated the margin of safety. Self-discipline and a lifelong commitment to understanding and applying the concept of margin of safety are the keys to effective application of the margin of safety.

Most investors do not explicitly choose to violate the margin of safety. But they often unknowingly operate on the edge of the safety zone. There is enough ambiguity in the stock market—particularly over the short term— that many investors may enjoy some short-term success without remaining comfortably inside that safety zone.

The fact is, growth stock investing can sometimes reward investors who ignore the margin of safety. Just as a blind squirrel occasionally trips over an acorn in the forest, a growth stock investor may stumble across a great investment that carries his portfolio to great heights.

Margin of safety can vary by investor, depending upon the investor's experience, training, and temperament. The practice of flying by the use of instruments provides an important illustration. The first time a novice instrument pilot enters the clouds is an uncomfortable moment. The sounds are different; the forward visibility is diminished or gone. For the instructor pilot, the experience is routine. The difference is training and experience.

As a pilot gains experience, she begins to enjoy flying in the clouds. If she has the right equipment, it is actually safer than flying in the clear. Why? There are fewer other planes in the sky. Experienced pilots will tell you that the challenge of flying into a busy general aviation airport (i.e., one with lots of small planes and inexperienced pilots) on a sunny Saturday afternoon is greater than that of flying an instrument approach.

Most investors do not appreciate the importance of margin of safety. They do not commit themselves to learning how to handle the margin of safety in a variety of different investments. Perhaps Graham's greatest gift to his pupil, Warren Buffett, was the challenge to thoroughly learn and apply the concept of margin of safety.

Margin of Safety for Growth Stocks

Graham did a brilliant job of laying out the fundamental elements of setting a margin of safety for value stocks in *The Intelligent Investor*, but he conceded that setting a margin of safety for growth stocks requires a different approach. The difference relates to the dynamic changes in the intrinsic value of growth companies over extended periods of time.

Investment in value companies involves purchasing an asset with a relatively static value. The practice of investing in value companies tends to focus on price paid as a dominant variable in the margin of safety. This is appropriate. If you pay a low enough price for an investment with an essentially static value, you have stacked the investment odds in your favor.

But with a growth company, the future value of the company is far more important than the current value of the company. "The philosophy of investment in growth stocks parallels in part and in part contravenes the margin-of-safety principle," Graham explained. "The growth stock buyer relies on an expected earning power that is greater than the average shown in the past. Thus he may be said to substitute these expected earnings for the past record in calculating his margin of safety."

It is our contention that investors in growth companies can and must establish a margin of safety for each purchase. In doing so, they need to take into account that their purchase decision must be based, in part, on the future value of the company.

Keys to Building a Margin of Safety for Growth Stocks

Investors must follow three key rules for building a margin of safety when investing in growth companies:

1. Know what you own.
2. Develop reasonable estimates of future value.
3. Set a reasonable hurdle rate.

Know What You Own The first step in building a margin of safety is to research the company. This is true for both value and growth companies.

There is a plethora of literature available for anyone who is interested in learning how to analyze a company. While we can't delve in detail into the intricacies of stock analysis in this book, we can point you to the easiest way to gain an understanding of any publicly traded company: read the financial statements. Since the passing of the Safe Harbor Act in 1995, U.S. companies have been incented to provide timely and accurate financial statements in their 10-K, 10-Q, and proxy statements. The 10-K and 10-Q each provide three financial statements: income statement, cash flow statement, and balance sheet. There is plenty of information available in these three statements to allow an investor to thoroughly understand how the company operates. The proxy statement discusses management compensation. A brief examination of the proxy statement will offer great insights into how top management compensates itself.

For investors who are seeking a deeper understanding of the company, there are many more questions to pose. Has the company increased its earnings, revenue, and cash flow consistently over the long term? Is it in an industry that has long-term growth potential? Is the management team stable and experienced? Has management laid out its goals and milestones? Has it delivered on those milestones? Has it been successful in expanding its services or its product line? Has the company treated its shareholders fairly?

Recent changes in disclosure laws plus the ubiquitous Internet have given individual investors the ability to easily access and read transcripts of quarterly management conference calls and corporate presentations to institutional shareholders. These transcripts often give investors valuable clues into the mindset of top management. There is no excuse today for any investor, large or small, to be insufficiently informed on any publicly traded company.

We also suggest that investors be on the alert in their daily lives for unusual products or vendors. The retail sector offers such opportunities. If you find a retailer who seems to offer a consistently high-quality price-to-value relationship for its goods, maybe that retailer is doing something right. How about great restaurant chains? Innovative electronic products? If an investor knows something about the company's place in its markets, that investor is beginning to see the company and not just the stock.

Develop Reasonable Estimates of Future Value In order to determine a realistic margin of safety, it's important to develop a reasonable forecast for earnings and the future value of the company.

Ben Graham offered sage advice when he discussed his valuation model. He was not willing to forecast long-term revenue growth rates of above 20 percent per year. Consider that a company that is growing at a compound rate of 20 percent per year will double its revenues every 3½ years. Over seven years, the revenues will quadruple. The stress on the management team under these kinds of growth expectations is extreme. With a growth rate of 20 percent per year, only half of the company's employees will have been with the company for more than 3½ years. If the company experiences normal turnover, more than half the employees will be relatively new. The company must lease new space at a fast clip. On top of that, highly profitable growth rates often attract competitors.

Like Graham, we believe it is prudent to cap growth-rate estimates at 20 percent. Consider that the average company is likely to grow about as fast

as nominal GDP growth, perhaps 5 to 6 percent per year. Growth rates above
10 percent are fairly rare; growth rates of 20 percent or more are extremely
uncommon—and rarely last for more than a few years.

It's not unusual for investors to confuse a cyclical rebound in earnings
with a long-term growth rate. Often a company will enjoy a cyclical
rebound in earnings after a recessionary period. If the prior trough was deep
enough, a company may post short-term earnings growth of 100 percent or
more. Under those circumstances, we typically attempt to smooth out the
revenues and earnings over a long-term cycle to determine a more realistic
growth rate. This is called *normalizing the earnings*.

Investors must take great care in developing a long-term revenue forecast. From a purely mathematical standpoint, every stock is cheap if one
estimates a high enough growth rate. The estimated growth in earnings
and revenues should be defensible and achievable with high odds.

Figure 5.1 shows the range of possible outcomes from a typical growth
company.

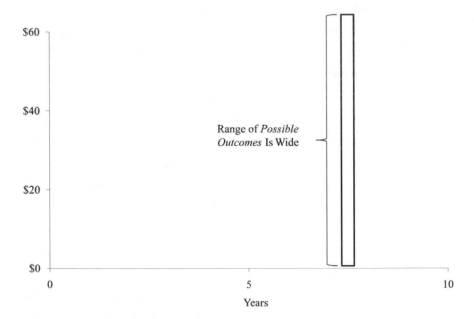

Figure 5.1 Margin of Safety: Develop a Reasonable Estimate of Future Value

Graham warned against optimistic forecasts. "For such favored issues the market has a tendency to set prices that will not be adequately protected by a *conservative* projection of future earnings," he explained. "A special degree of foresight and judgment will be needed in order that wise individual selections may overcome the hazards inherent in the customary market level of such issues as a whole."

Investors must also take great care when forecasting unsustainably high profit margins. A company might show very high profit margins today, but increasing competition may trim those margins. On the other hand, a company that is just emerging from a period of significant investment in research and development or new facilities might be poised for an extended improvement in profit margins.

Figure 5.2 illustrates that these forecasts result in a range of probable outcomes for the company.

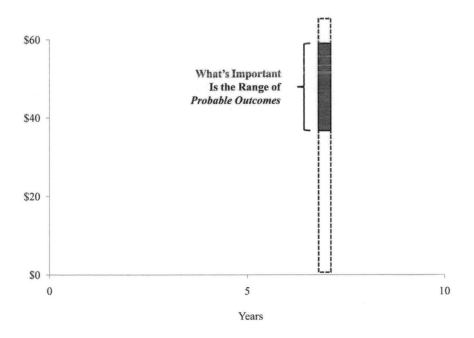

Figure 5.2 Margin of Safety: Develop a Reasonable Estimate of Future Value

Trees Do Not Grow to the Sky

All companies eventually mature. To us, that means that the growth rate in revenues and earnings must trend toward that of the average company. For growth company investors, it is important to "decay" the growth rates.

At our firm, we reduce the growth rates of every company to 7 percent or less after seven years. No exceptions. We recognize that this may seem arbitrary, but we do have supporting empirical evidence based on years of market experience, and we believe that the 7 percent cap is in line with nominal GDP growth. Using a 7 percent cap enables us to ensure that our forecasts are not too aggressive. We want to remain comfortably inside our margin of safety.

If we are lucky enough to own one or more of those rare companies that are able to sustain double-digit growth rates for long periods, then we are poised to benefit from that growth. In those cases, we were able to purchase the stocks at prices that we considered to be at or below fair prices based on a conservative forecast of future growth.

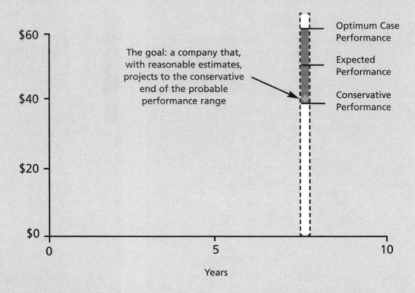

Figure 5.3 Margin of Safety: Develop a Reasonable Estimate of Future Value

Set a Reasonable Hurdle Rate If you have a sufficiently thorough under-standing of the company and have developed a conservative forecast of the company's growth, your hurdle rate becomes the third element in honoring your margin of safety. We have discussed hurdle rates in previous chapters. The hurdle rate is the target annual average compounded rate of return you want to earn from your investments.

If your goal is to achieve a 10 percent expected return, then you would purchase a stock only at a price that can provide you with a projected return of at least 10 percent. Figure 5.4 illustrates using a hurdle rate to determine an appropriate maximum purchase price.

It is perhaps easiest to explain the margin of safety when considering the purchase price of a stock. At our firm, we use a hurdle rate of 12 percent. When we evaluate a stock, we don't want to buy that stock unless we can buy it at a price that we believe is low enough to provide us with a 12 percent average annual return.

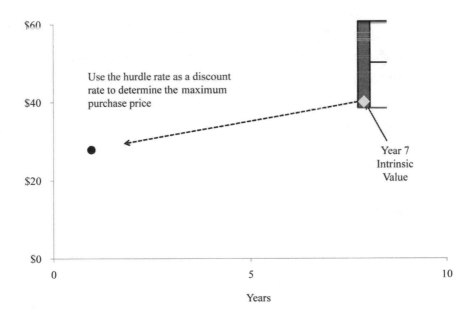

Figure 5.4 Margin of Safety: Determine the Maximum Purchase Price

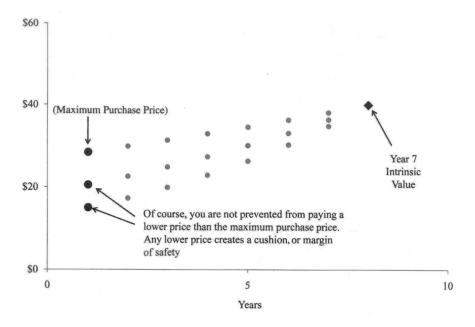

Figure 5.5 Margin of Safety: Pay a Fair Price or Less

If we buy Stock XYZ at a price that should yield an average return of 12 percent, we have established an adequate margin of safety. If we purchase the stock at a price that should yield an average annual compound return of 8 percent, we are still likely to make a long-term profit on the purchase, but we have eaten into our margin of safety. If we are fortunate enough to purchase the stock at a price that is likely to yield an average annual compound return of 15 percent, we have added to our margin of safety.

Figure 5.5 shows how we attempt to build in a margin of safety when we purchase a stock. Once we've placed a value on the stock and put together a reasonable seven-year projection, we try to buy the stock at a level that gives us an adequate margin of safety.

Figure 5.6 shows that the full margin of safety is a result of reasonable forecasts, determining a hurdle rate, and purchasing at a discount to the maximum appropriate purchase price.

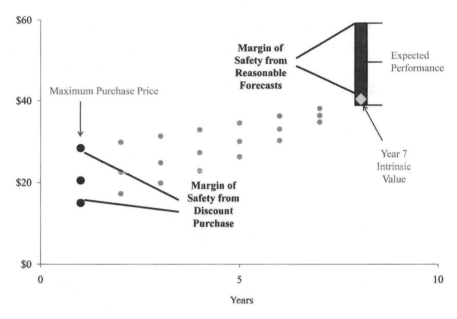

Figure 5.6 Margin of Safety: Combination of Reasonable Projections and Paying a Fair Price

The use of a hurdle rate tends to steer the investor away from a dangerous industry standard that is widely used today: relative performance. Once an investor starts on the slippery slope of relative performance, he has shifted the hurdle rate to a variable standard. If the investor's objective is to outperform a selected stock index or benchmark over the next three years, what is the expected return from that benchmark? Does the investor change the expected return for the benchmark each year?

Once you set a hurdle rate, it is vital that you stick with that hurdle rate through all types of economic or market cycles. Otherwise, if you tie your hurdle rate to a specific benchmark, you face a variety of problems. For instance, in a year in which the stock market is depressed for cyclical reasons, the expected return for the benchmark would be higher than usual. Investors who both honor the margin of safety and adhere to a relative performance standard would need a higher-than-average expected return in order to purchase a stock. We do not quarrel with tight standards in tough times. But the problem becomes deadly when the stock market is cyclically elevated, meaning that the forward return from the benchmark is lower than average. Investors who are adhering to a relative performance standard would have to reduce their hurdle rate when the market is elevated. In its simplest form, this approach can be described as loosening the standards as the market rises. This is a prescription for a high likelihood of loss of investor capital.

The concept of a shifting hurdle rate becomes more acute for an investment management firm, where clear communication is essential. A clearly stated, unchanging hurdle rate allows the analysts and portfolio managers to focus on the fundamental progress of the companies in the firm's portfolio.

Although money managers tend to be graded based on their relative performance versus the market, we prefer to operate on an absolute performance basis. We maintain the same hurdle rate regardless of the economic or market conditions. And while we believe that our hurdle rate of 12 percent is a very ambitious target, we know that if we can achieve a 12 percent return, our clients are very likely to retain us. We also believe that our ambitious hurdle rate should enable us to beat all benchmarks over long periods of time. We accept that in a runaway bull market, such as the late 1990s, we may underperform the benchmarks and lose customers. (In fact, that is precisely what happened during that period.) But our long-term performance through good markets and bad has served our clients very well.

GROWTH INVESTING IS LIKE FLYING A JET

A jet promises great speed; honoring the margin of safety creates the opportunity to harness that speed safely. Failure to honor the margin of safety can be catastrophic.

The same is true with growth stock investing. While failure to honor the margin of safety when investing in value companies can prove painful, failure to honor the margin of safety when investing in growth stocks can be catastrophic.

The performance history of the White Oak Select Growth Fund is an excellent example. While we do not mean to impugn the integrity or capability of any investment manager (or of anyone who invests in growth companies), White Oak's experience illustrates how intoxicating and dangerous investing in growth stocks can be. The mutual fund was founded on August 3, 1992. Oak Associates, headquartered in Akron, Ohio, has been the investment advisor during the fund's entire existence.

The fund was heavily invested in technology companies throughout the 1990s. Cisco Systems was its marquee holding. The fund emphasized its low turnover, which is especially appropriate for growth companies.

According to performance data published by FactSet, from the end of 1996 through August 31, 2000, the per-share performance of the fund was breathtaking. An investment of $10,000 in the fund at the end of 1996 would have grown to $36,890 by August 31, 2000. If a wealthy doctor had placed a million dollars from his retirement fund in White Oak at the end of 1996, he would have seen his portfolio grow to $3,689,000 as of August 31, 2000   and would be fantasizing about an early retirement.

The compound average annual return per share for White Oak was 42.7 percent per year from December 31, 1996 through August 31, 2000.

Unfortunately, the fund was crushed in the following two years. Between August 31, 2000, and September 30, 2002, the fund declined by 76.5 percent. In our hypothetical example, the doctor would have seen his $3,689,000 investment dwindle to a value of just $868,759, turning his retirement plans into a dimming memory.

The fund did recover somewhat in the general market recovery after 2002, increasing by 95.88 percent per share from September 30, 2002, through December 31, 2010. Thus, our doctor would have seen the value of his portfolio rebound to $1,701,725 by the end of 2010. This would have represented a gain of about 70 percent during his 14 years of investing in the fund, for an average annual compound return of just under 4 percent.

But what about those investors who purchased the fund at or near its peak value in 2000, lured by the incredible historical returns? According to a February 2001 article on CNNMoney.com, "The fund was up more than 25 percent through the end of October (2000)—before Nasdaq headed back into free-fall—and its asset base doubled to $6 billion as investors piled in."

It was a classic case of investors chasing "hot" returns—which is never a good idea. The results were all too predictable. In effect, investors "piled in" to White Oak just in time for the fund to experience a crushing decline. A $1 million investment in White Oak on August 31, 2000, would have declined to $235,000 at the low of September 30, 2002. Even by the end of 2010, the initial $1 million investment would be worth only $461,000. That is what we mean by catastrophic.

How do you think investors behaved after the severe decline in the fund's per-share value? A long-term investor might have concluded that the companies were still good and their stock prices had simply dropped. In fact, an astute investor might have added to her mutual fund shares. Unfortunately, the data suggest that investors did just the opposite—they abandoned the fund. From a peak of $6 billion in the fourth quarter of 2000, the fund dwindled to assets of about $300 million at the end of 2010, a decline of 95 percent. Since the per-share decline was 53.9 percent, that means that investors withdrew money from the mutual fund, rather than adding to it.

There are probably many lessons to be learned from this sad story. Let us focus on three of the most important lessons.

First, investing in growth stocks can bring extreme temptations. Fabulous results can lead to irrational purchasing; terrible times can lead to irrational selling. Investors in growth stocks must develop the self-discipline to deal with these temptations.

Second, we can only speculate as to what the fund manager was thinking with regard to the portfolio holdings during the entire period. We suspect the fund manager was facing the dilemma related to a major winning holding that we discussed in Chapter 2. In this case the winning stock was Cisco. Early investors in the fund were beneficiaries of the spectacular performance of Cisco from the early 1990s until 2000. By 2000, Cisco stock was extremely overvalued based on reasonable forecasts of its future prospects. As a first and obvious step, we think the fund manager could have closed the fund to new monies, including new investors. This would have prevented the purchase of Cisco at inflated prices. Second, he could have considered that the extreme overvaluation of Cisco had clearly reduced the margin of safety for that investment to the point where at least reducing the position would have been prudent.

And finally, the behavior of fund investors, by their collective decision to buy the fund at or near its peak and sell after it had bottomed out, made the situation even more catastrophic. Consider the outcome for investors who would have *sold* their holdings in late 2000 instead of buying and repurchased shares in the subsequent years. Instead of catastrophic losses, they would have enjoyed exceptional gains.

There is another overriding lesson to this story. All investors make bad decisions. Those investors who honor the margin of safety tend to keep their bad decisions from becoming catastrophic. If the fund manager had closed the fund to new monies or if the fund investors had not committed new money after the fund had appreciated in price, the losses would have been far less severe.

The concept of a margin of safety may have been Benjamin Graham's greatest gift to all investors. The margin of safety is vitally important—in life as well as in investing—and it's especially important to growth stock investors. It can help guide you in all phases of the investment process, helping you to invest in stocks at an acceptable price and avoid stocks that are priced too high. It can help keep your bad decisions from becoming disastrous, and it should be an essential part of the process for every investment decision you make. If a jet pilot can operate within a margin of safety, then you can too.

6

■ ■ ■

Characteristics of a "Great" Growth Company: Identifying Sustainable Competitive Advantage

If you don't have a competitive advantage, don't compete.
—Jack Welch

One mistake that investors often make is to assume that any company with rapid business growth is a great growth company. There is a difference. There's no question that growth is a critical component of long-term value creation, but focusing solely on the prospects for growth while ignoring the quality of the underlying business model can be a dangerous investment proposition. As Graham cautioned in *The Intelligent Investor,* "Obvious prospects for physical growth in a business do not translate into obvious profits for investors."

To make his case, Graham referred to the rapid growth in air traffic in the 1940s and 1950s. Air travel was arguably the Internet of its day, a disruptive technology that was powering rapid growth in demand. Virtually all major commercial airlines were aggressively expanding at the time. Industry revenue increased from $135 million to $2.9 billion between 1941 and 1960. Yet, despite industry growth that probably exceeded the most optimistic projections, profits were meager and were routinely wiped out by subsequent cycles of losses. This resulted in generally disastrous results for long-term investors in airline companies. Even when they are accompanied by rapid business growth, large operating losses are hardly the hallmark of greatness.

If sizable growth in the business is not enough to differentiate a great investment from an average or mediocre one, then what is? The airline example can shed more light on this question. Even though the airline industry had proved to be a largely unprofitable endeavor for long-term investors, a little upstart by the name of Southwest Airlines began to offer service in 1971 and shortly began to defy the industry trends. While the airline industry lost a staggering $39.6 billion between 1971 and 2009, Southwest generated $6.6 billion in profits. Long-term investors in the company were handsomely rewarded, with the stock up 4,674 percent since its IPO in June 1971.

This begs the question as to why Southwest Airlines was able to thrive during a period in which every other major carrier struggled. Clearly, the other airlines all benefited from the same tidal wave of opportunity. In fact, Southwest competed in the same industry under identical market conditions. Yet, the results for investors were dramatically different. We can boil down Southwest's superior financial results to one critical difference—the strength of the business model. Southwest's business model was highly defensible; the others' were not.

A defensible business model is the defining characteristic of a great growth company and the key to separating the big potential investment winners from the rest of the pack.

A DEFENSIBLE BUSINESS

From an investment perspective, the key characteristic of a company with a defensible business model is that the model enables the company to increase its intrinsic value at a much faster rate than companies with weak business models. Remember, growth in intrinsic value is the key driver of long-term investment returns because, over time, market values should converge with the real underlying value of the company.

To fully understand how a defensible business model enhances the value of a company, we need to revisit the definition of intrinsic value. The intrinsic value of a company is the net present value of all the future cash flows, discounted using a reasonable hurdle-rate return. It stands to reason, then, that anything that is capable of materially increasing the magnitude and sustainability of those cash flows would have a substantial impact on the value of the company. A defensible business model allows a company to do both.

It's easy to recognize a great growth company with a defensible business model after the fact, but as an investor, you need to be able to identify these companies before they become obvious to the market. Why are some business models defensible, while others are not? More important, how can you identify those businesses with defensible business models? If you can improve your ability to distinguish businesses with defensible businesses models, and be disciplined buyers of their stocks, you will greatly increase your odds of earning 10, 20, or even 100 times your initial investment. To do that, you need to better understand the fundamental characteristics that underpin a defensible business model. The first, and most important, attribute is sustainable competitive advantage.

SUSTAINABLE COMPETITIVE ADVANTAGE

At its most rudimentary level, a sustainable competitive advantage is a durable and unique set of capabilities and industry dynamics that give the company a superior chance of winning with customers. For instance, Southwest Airlines was able to institutionalize a demonstrably lower cost structure than its larger, more established rivals by exploiting second-tier airports, flying point-to-point routes, offering limited amenities, and purchasing only one model of aircraft. This, in turn, permitted Southwest to capture significant industry market share and generate attractive profits.

A sustainable competitive advantage has a variety of positive impacts on the business that foster long-term value creation. First and foremost, a competitive advantage is the key to protecting financial returns from the erosive impact of competition. Without a competitive advantage, the returns that the business earns will inevitably be competed down to average levels. Competitive advantage also allows the company to devote more time and effort to improving the existing value proposition for customers instead of squandering precious resources reacting to competitive assaults. Finally, long-term business planning is simplified and financial risk reduced as a result of the more stable future revenue stream that accompanies a competitive advantage.

Competitive advantage as an investment concept has substantial appeal, but its practical application has proved difficult for the average investor. The term was first popularized by Harvard professor Michael Porter in 1985 in his book *Competitive Advantage: Creating and Sustaining Superior Performance*. Warren Buffett has also weighed in on the importance of competitive advantage for investors. "The key to investing," said Buffett, "is not assessing how much an industry is going to affect society, or how much it will grow, but rather determining the competitive advantage of any given company, and above all, the durability of that advantage."

To maximize your chances of identifying competitive advantage in a potential investment, you need to understand the distinction between competitive *advantage* and competitive *strategy*.

A sustainable competitive advantage is structural in nature. It is not merely an endless series of tactical moves (such as price discounts or duplicable cost reductions) that allow a company to temporarily stay one step ahead of the competition, nor is it a unique long-term operating strategy. Sustainable competitive advantage is embedded in the underlying business model.

Competitive strategy, on the other hand, is a choice. It speaks to how a company elects to compete in the marketplace. For instance, certain firms in an industry might strive to be the low-cost producer, while others may adopt a strategy geared toward offering premium products and services to a select group of clients. Still others may choose to emphasize distribution or technological capabilities that benefit customers. The permutations of competitive strategy are limitless; the expression of competitive advantage is not.

Since a sustainable competitive advantage is structural in nature, once it has been firmly established in the marketplace, it exists independent of future strategy choices. This is not to say that strategy choices no longer matter. They are important because a competitive advantage can clearly be enhanced or eroded by a successful or ill-advised strategy choice. As investors, we are interested in the choice of strategy to the extent that it is consistent or inconsistent with a company's underlying competitive advantage.

Strategy experts may be quick to point out that a well-defined and well-executed business strategy may allow a company to carve out a competitive advantage where one did not previously exist, as was the case with Southwest Airlines. However, predicting which companies will develop a *future* competitive advantage is far more difficult than identifying those companies that *currently* have a sustainable competitive advantage. The former is a discussion that is beyond the scope of this book. The latter is something that the average investor can accomplish with reasonable accuracy, given the right framework and a decent amount of intellectual effort.

In our research, we try to uncover companies with a sustainable competitive advantage that will enable the company to grow profitably for many years. In our experience, competitive advantage takes one of two forms: *barriers* that keep potential competitors out of the market, or *handcuffs* on customers that make them reluctant to switch to an alternative supplier.

Competitive Barriers

Competitive barriers are essentially hurdles that competitors must clear just to get into the game. At a minimum, effective competitive barriers severely impede a competitor's ability to offer a similar product or service to potential customers. In many cases, these barriers create near monopolies by shutting would-be competitors out of the market altogether. There are many signs that may indicate that a company is benefiting from high barriers to competition, including a limited number of competitors, rarity of new entrants into the market, high and stable market share, and significant power afforded to a regulatory authority to determine product or service requirements.

Competitive barriers can be regulatory, asset, or scale-based.

Regulatory Barriers Regulatory barriers are laws and regulations or uniform standards created by self-regulatory bodies that impede the ability of competitors to enter a market. There is nothing like having Uncle Sam or other powerful self-interested organizations with broad regulatory authority telling would-be competitors to kindly stay out. Regulatory barriers can be direct or indirect. Direct regulatory barriers include intellectual property laws, fees, licensing requirements, and capitalization requirements. Indirect regulatory barriers include subsidies, targeted tax breaks, and government favoritism, such as protection from lawsuits.

Regulatory hurdles offer some of the most formidable barriers to competition. However, they can also be among the most arbitrary competitive advantages, given that they are dependent on the often fickle and politicized decisions of a small group of regulators. Investors must be careful to gauge the potential for regulatory barriers to survive changes in political attitudes.

Among the best-known regulatory barriers are those that exist in the health-care industry for pharmaceutical and medical device products. The U.S. Food and Drug Administration (FDA) requires companies to demonstrate a satisfactory level of safety and efficacy before a product can be marketed to physicians or consumers. For pharmaceutical companies, the approval process for a promising new drug can often take 10 years or more and cost hundreds of millions of dollars. It involves long and expensive clinical trials that must follow stringent protocols. In addition, only a small percentage of the drugs that enter clinical trials are ultimately approved, both because of the uncertainty surrounding the performance of unknown chemical and biologic agents and because of the stringent standards enforced by the FDA. Few companies have the financial wherewithal and regulatory expertise to withstand such a process. In exchange for enduring the significant investment in time and money required for FDA approval, the pharmaceutical companies are rewarded with a period of marketing exclusivity to allow them time to recoup their costs plus a profit.

To illustrate the power of this regulatory barrier, one need look no further than the blockbuster antidepressant drug Prozac. Prozac (fluoxetine), developed and manufactured by Eli Lilly, was approved by the FDA in 1987. It was a top-selling drug that became a household name in the early 1990s. Eli Lilly's annual sales of Prozac reached an estimated peak of $2.8 billion, thanks in large part to the regulatory barrier provided by the FDA. In August 2001, that competitive barrier was removed when Barr received FDA approval to sell generic fluoxetine. Sales of Prozac plummeted. As illustrated in Figure 6.1, two years after the approval of generic fluoxetine, Prozac sales had plummeted 77 percent from their peak.

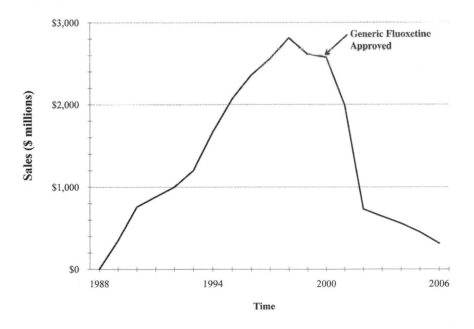

Figure 6.1 Sales of Prozac, 1988–2006

A lesser-known type of regulatory barrier is one erected by a private standards body. The next time you are in your living room, take a look at the front of your digital television set or Blu-ray player. You will probably see a laundry list of branded technologies that have been incorporated into that particular consumer electronics device. What you may not realize is that a number of those technologies are required to be in those devices, because they have been mandated by a private standards body. For instance, standards mandate that all DVD and Blu-ray disc players must contain Dolby audio processing technology. This is a powerful competitive advantage for Dolby, because when device manufacturers are already paying to include one mandatory sound technology, the prospects for additional sound technology companies to attain broad adoption are substantially reduced. That is exactly what we have seen, as Dolby and a smaller sound technology company by the name of DTS have essentially created a sound duopoly. Dolby and DTS account for the vast majority of advanced sound technology on professionally produced video and consumer electronics devices. Dolby's technology has been featured in nearly five billion devices to date. We see clear evidence of Dolby's competitive position in its impressive financial results (see Table 6.1) and in the continued proliferation of devices incorporating Dolby technology.

Another common regulatory barrier to competition is a patent. Patents can protect a company's technology, manufacturing processes, or in some cases even certain business processes from imitation. Many companies trumpet the size of their patent portfolios. In reality, most patents are of little practical value. A small percentage of patents, however, provide significant barriers to competition. An example of a company building barriers around a valuable patent portfolio is Gentex Corporation.

Gentex designs and manufacturers electro-optical products, which combine photoelectric sensing devices with related electronic circuitry to produce such products as auto-dimming automobile mirrors, dimmable aircraft windows, and fire alarms. The company's flagship product is its electrochromatic auto-dimming mirrors, which were first introduced in 1987. These

Table 6.1 Select Dolby Operating Metrics ($ in millions, except per share numbers)									
For the Year Ended:	09/01	09/02	09/03	09/04	09/05	09/06	09/07	09/08	09/09	09/10
Revenue	$125	$162	$217	$289	$338	$392	$482	$640	$720	$923
Operating profit	$10	$1	$48	$68	$84	$130	$187	$287	$364	$429
Operating margin	7.9%	0.3%	21.9%	23.5%	25.6%	33.1%	38.8%	44.8%	50.5%	46.5%
Normalized EPS	$0.07	$0.00	$0.35	$0.46	$0.50	$0.73	$1.03	$1.56	$1.97	$2.33
Return on invested capital	N/A	N/A	N/A	52.9%	52.0%	64.2%	60.8%	36.7%	35.9%	40.9%

mirrors use proprietary, patented technology to detect light from rearward-approaching vehicles and darken the surface of the rearview mirror to reduce glare. In total, Gentex has 321 U.S. and 208 foreign patents related to electrochromatic technology, automotive rearview mirrors, microphones, displays, and sensor technology. The patent barriers combined with cumulative knowledge and a proven track record with the original equipment manufacturers (OEMs) has resulted in steady growth in rearview mirror sales to the auto manufacturers and a dominant market share within vehicle models offering automatic-dimming mirrors. The company estimates that it controlled more than 83 percent of the auto-dimming mirror market in 2009. See Table 6.2 for financial information on Gentex.

While many regulatory barriers come in the form of codified standards or rules that provide explicit barriers to competition, there are more subtle forms of regulatory barriers. Subsidies, such as ethanol mandates; preferred tax treatment, such as tax breaks for utilizing and investing in sources of alternative energy; and protection from lawsuits all represent regulatory barriers that may not explicitly deny access to the competitive playing field, but that can provide barriers in the form of a significant cost or time advantage that deters would-be competitors.

Cabela's, Inc., is a specialty retailer that has benefited from indirect regulatory barriers. It offers a vast array of hunting, camping, and fishing equipment to consumers through catalogs and the Internet, as well as through its expanding network of retail stores. Its extensive, proprietary inventory combined with its unique décor, featuring large aquariums and mounted animals from across the world, make its stores a destination site for outdoor enthusiasts. In fact, the company's cavernous stores typically attract more than 4 million people per year. To put this in perspective, the top-drawing team in Major League Baseball had total attendance of approximately 3.7 million fans over the course of an 81-game home schedule for the 2010 season. This type of drawing power makes Cabela's a coveted retail business for municipalities that are seeking to spur economic growth and development. Consequently, a number of local municipalities have provided

Table 6.2 Select Gentex Operating Metrics ($ in millions, except per share amounts)

For the Year Ended:	12/01	12/02	12/03	12/04	12/05	12/06	12/07	12/08	12/09	12/10
Revenue	$310	$395	$469	$506	$536	$572	$654	$624	$545	$816
Operating profit	$82	$115	$147	$150	$136	$126	$139	$91	$93	$191
Operating margin	26.4%	29.1%	31.3%	29.7%	25.4%	22.1%	21.2%	14.6%	17.1%	23.4%
Normalized EPS	$0.34	$0.47	$0.59	$0.60	$0.54	$0.53	$0.60	$0.40	$0.42	$0.85
Return on invested capital	19.3%	22.8%	27.7%	33.0%	27.6%	22.5%	22.2%	14.4%	16.0%	28.8%
Auto-dimming mirror shipments (millions)	7.2	8.8	10.3	11.6	12.6	13.4	15.2	14.3	11.7	16.8

preferred tax treatment as well as targeted investment in roads and other public infrastructure to lure Cabela's to their taxing jurisdiction. These incentives can significantly reduce the up-front cost of investing as well as ongoing operating costs. A portion of these benefits is captured in the company's balance sheet in an asset called "economic development bonds," which is shown in Table 6.3.

Unfortunately, even with the advantage of competitive barriers, companies like Cabela's are not immune to the fallout from their own misguided management decisions. Cabela's decision to open several mega-sized stores that proved too big for the respective markets, as well as sloppy inventory management, cut into the company's profits from 2007 to 2009. These missteps were compounded by the severe recession in 2008 and 2009, which hit retail particularly hard. However, this does not diminish the advantage provided by the indirect regulatory barriers. In fact, since 2009, the company has recognized its errors and rectified its strategy. The firm has become more effective at sizing its new stores for their respective markets and has vastly improved its inventory management capabilities. As a result, return on invested capital began to recover in 2010.

Asset Barriers Asset barriers are barriers to competition that are created by a company's having preferred or sole access to proprietary assets. These may be hard assets, such as diamonds, or intellectual property, such as software code, that is unique to the company and would take considerable time, effort, and money to replicate (assuming that a reasonable substitute can be developed at all). In contrast to regulatory barriers, proprietary assets do not require a regulatory or standards body to erect barriers to competition. They are barriers in and of themselves.

Asset barriers to competition generally stem from favorable access to hard assets, geographic location, or proprietary intellectual property.

A competitive advantage built on favorable access to hard assets is probably the easiest asset barrier for investors to gauge. For instance, coal companies have an asset barrier in the form of their ownership of the mineral rights to

Table 6.3 Select Cabela's Operating Metrics ($ in millions, except per share amounts)

For the Year Ended:	12/01	12/02	12/03	12/04	12/05	12/06	12/07	12/08	12/09	12/10
Revenue	$1,078	$1,225	$1,392	$1,556	$1,800	$2,064	$2,350	$2,553	$2,632	$2,663
Operating profit	$62	$76	$85	$97	$115	$144	$151	$141	$93	$187
Operating margin	5.7%	6.2%	6.1%	6.2%	6.4%	7.0%	6.4%	5.5%	3.5%	7.0%
Normalized EPS	$0.72	$0.89	$0.96	$0.96	$1.08	$1.35	$1.40	$1.31	$0.86	$1.62
Return on invested capital	N/A	N/A	16.6%	14.2%	10.3%	10.4%	8.5%	7.1%	6.6%	9.5%
Economic development bonds	$29	$56	$72	$145	$146	$117	$98	$113	$109	$104

large reserves of coal. A handful of companies own the vast majority of such mineral rights in the United States. Ownership of large deposits of coal is a valuable asset in an economy where roughly 45 percent of electricity generation still comes from coal-fired plants. Although the value of those mineral assets and the potency of the competitive barrier can be undermined by cheaper forms of electricity generation, the replacement of our current coal-generating infrastructure would likely require considerable time, effort, and capital.

Geographic location is also a relatively straightforward form of competitive advantage. For instance, a waste management company that owns the only landfill in a local geographic area has a near monopoly position. The competitive barriers are high, since the process of establishing a new landfill is lengthy and costly. In addition, the existing landfill operator is unlikely to sit idly by when a new entrant emerges. It can use its current scale to respond with aggressive pricing tactics, virtually guaranteeing substantial start-up losses as the new entrant looks to attract trash haulers and build volumes. Of course, local trash haulers are free to haul their loads to more geographically dispersed landfills, but the economics of such a decision may prove untenable, given the cost of hauling heavy loads long distances.

Proprietary intellectual property (IP) can provide equally formidable barriers to competition, but it often is more difficult to assess. Barriers formed by proprietary intellectual property can come from a variety of sources, including internally developed technology, databases of unique information, cumulative knowledge or learning curve advantages, capital (usually to fund start-up losses), and proprietary processes.

For example, CoStar Group has accumulated more than 400 different pieces of information on approximately 3.7 million commercial real estate properties in major markets in the United States, the United Kingdom, and France. Individual data points include building characteristics, historical sales and lease data, income and expense history, tenants, and lease expirations. The company has methodically assembled this proprietary database over the past 20 years, providing an asset barrier to competition that would probably take many years and hundreds of millions of dollars to replicate. The barriers presented by such a database are illustrated by the company's high client retention rate (exceeding 90 percent in most years) as well as by its long-term improvements in return on invested capital in the face of continued aggressive reinvestment in new markets and products (see Table 6.4).

Another example of a company with asset barriers is Varian Medical Systems, the leading provider of radiation therapy systems used in the treatment of cancer. Varian's competitive barriers are twofold: proprietary IP and a robust feedback loop with customers. Varian's technological expertise, combined with a clear understanding of its customers' operating realities, has allowed it to develop a superior clinical value proposition with advanced technical features, seamless system integration, ease of use, and quality customer service delivered at competitive prices. As a result, Varian has been able to dominate its niche with an estimated 60 percent share of the overall radiation treatment systems market. See Table 6.5 for financial information on Varian.

Scale-Based Barriers Scale-based barriers refer to the proverbial "low-cost producer" position in the market, attained as a result of the efficiencies associated with increased size. These efficiencies can come from a variety of sources, including purchasing, manufacturing, research and development, sales and marketing, managerial specialization, and financing costs. Scale barriers generally require significant time and money to replicate. Absolute size does not determine scale barriers. It is the size relative to the competition and the relevant market opportunity that matters. As a result, scale advantages may be limited by local market dynamics. This is particularly true in retail endeavors, where marketing and distribution scale are generally achieved on a local level. Remember, Sears and Kmart were once considerably larger than Walmart and possessed superior scale on a national level. But Walmart had developed scale advantages where it counts, on the local and regional level. Consequently, Walmart was able to leverage its distribution and advertising costs more effectively and create scale barriers to entry in those local markets.

Significant scale advantages combined with great execution can present virtually impenetrable barriers to competition. For instance, UPS and FedEx

Table 6.4 Select CoStar Group Operating Metrics (Properties in Database) ($ in millions, except per share amounts)

For the Year Ended:	12/01	12/02	12/03	12/04	12/05	12/06	12/07	12/08	12/09	12/10
Revenue	$73	$79	$95	$112	$134	$159	$193	$212	$210	$226
Operating profit	($23)	($6)	$0	$7	$7	$14	$18	$40	$32	$30
Operating margin	−31.3%	−7.0%	0.0%	6.0%	5.5%	8.9%	9.3%	18.7%	15.2%	13.2%
Normalized EPS	($0.91)	($0.22)	$0.00	$0.22	$0.24	$0.46	$0.58	$1.27	$1.00	$0.90
Return on invested capital	−19.7%	−5.5%	0.0%	5.7%	4.8%	9.9%	11.2%	21.7%	17.0%	11.4%
Properties in database (millions)	0.95	1.03	1.50	1.60	1.80	2.10	2.70	3.20	3.60	4.00

Table 6.5 Select Varian Medical Systems Operating Metrics ($ n millions, except per share amounts)

For the Year Ended:	9/01	9/02	9/03	9/04	9/05	9/06	9/07	9/08	9/09	9/10
Revenue	$774	$873	$1,042	$1,236	$1,383	$1,598	$1,755	$2,070	$2,214	$2,357
Operating profit	$105	$145	$198	$257	$305	$309	$339	$419	$474	$534
Operating margin	13.6%	16.6%	19.0%	20.8%	22.1%	19.4%	19.3%	20.3%	21.4%	22.7%
Normalized EPS	$0.48	$0.65	$0.87	$1.13	$1.38	$1.43	$1.62	$2.05	$2.37	$2.69
Return on invested capital	26.6%	32.8%	38.8%	50.3%	53.9%	46.8%	36.7%	40.5%	39.7%	42.3%

have developed an unassailable duopoly in the priority package delivery business in the United States. Their massive scale and distribution density allow them to earn handsome profits, while would-be competitors have largely abandoned the market. DHL attempted to crack that market in 2003 when it acquired Airborne Express. DHL was no underresourced start-up. It was a major player globally, and it invested aggressively on top of its acquisition to establish a complete domestic delivery network. Just five years later, DHL abandoned its domestic service effort because of large operating losses and an inability to wrestle meaningful market share away from UPS and FedEx. The scale and execution advantages enjoyed by UPS and FedEx were too much for DHL to overcome. See Table 6.6 for financial information on UPS and Table 6.7 for financial information on FedEx.

Customer Captivity

Even when the barriers to entry for new competitors are low, companies can still create a competitive advantage by developing a captive customer base. In this case, the competitive advantage stems not from barring competitors from the market outright, but rather from building customer loyalty to discourage them from switching to competitive offerings. The degree of customer captivity is a function of the costs that a customer must incur to switch to a competitive or substitute product. In other words, if the switching costs are high relative to the expected value to be gained from the new product or service, customers will be reluctant to swap suppliers. Additionally, even when competitors can establish a demonstrably superior value proposition, they still may be forced to spend heavily on marketing to overcome the inertia of existing customer loyalties.

Common signs that a company is benefiting from high levels of customer captivity include low customer turnover and high customer retention, persistent pricing power, brand loyalty, successful brand extensions, and strong consumer routine or habit. Each of these has the beneficial impact of increasing the magnitude and certainty of financial returns in the business.

Table 6.6 Select UPS Operating Metrics ($ in millions, except per share amounts)

For the Year Ended:	12/01	12/02	12/03	12/04	12/05	12/06	12/07	12/08	12/09	12/10
Revenue	$30,321	$31,272	$33,485	$36,582	$42,581	$47,547	$49,692	$51,486	$45,297	$49,545
Operating profit	$3,962	$4,096	$4,473	$4,989	$5,143	$6,635	$578	$5,382	$3,801	$5,874
Operating margin	13.1%	13.1%	13.4%	13.6%	14.4%	14.0%	1.2%	10.5%	8.4%	11.9%
Normalized EPS	$2.16	$2.26	$2.46	$2.74	$3.44	$3.81	$0.34	$3.29	$2.37	$3.66
Return on invested capital	20.8%	19.0%	19.9%	21.2%	23.6%	23.0%	2.0%	17.4%	16.0%	31.6%
Packages delivered (millions per day)	13.5	13.0	13.0	14.1	14.7	15.6	15.8	15.5	15.1	15.6

Table 6.7 Select FedEx Operating Metrics ($ in millions, except per share amounts)

For the Year Ended:	5/02	5/03	5/04	5/05	5/06	5/07	5/08	5/09	5/10	5/11
Revenue	$20,607	$22,478	$24,710	$29,363	$32,294	$35,214	$37,953	$35,497	$34,734	$39,304
Operating profit	$1,321	$1,471	$1,440	$2,471	$3,014	$3,276	$2,075	$747	$1,998	$2,378
Operating margin	6.4%	6.5%	5.8%	8.4%	9.3%	9.3%	5.5%	2.1%	5.8%	6.1%
Normalized EPS	$2.72	$3.03	$2.96	$5.03	$6.08	$6.58	$4.16	$1.50	$3.98	$4.69
Return on invested capital	10.2%	10.9%	9.4%	14.0%	15.8%	15.3%	8.9%	3.1%	8.8%	10.2%
Packages delivered										
(millions per day)	4.8	5.3	5.5	5.9	6.1	6.5	6.9	6.8	7.0	7.0

Since all forms of customer captivity are based on switching costs of one form or another, we will use the two terms interchangeably. While the switching costs that underpin customer captivity can take many forms, broadly speaking, these costs fall into two categories: the tangible or "hard" costs and the intangible or "soft" costs of switching.

Hard Switching Costs Hard switching costs are the easily quantifiable portion of the cost of switching, such as equipment costs, installation costs, start-up costs, and retraining costs. Measuring the impact on customer captivity from hard switching costs is relatively straightforward—the more money it costs to switch to a competitive product, the more likely it is that a customer will remain captive.

For example, what would it cost XYZ Corporation to rip out its Oracle database and install a competitor's product? The hard switching costs are significant and include the cost of the new software and any upgraded hardware, the cost to reformat the information and port it from the old database to the new one, and the cost of retraining the workforce. The hard switching costs most likely will run into the tens of millions of dollars for larger corporations.

On the opposite end of the spectrum from database providers are sellers of general commodity products, such as paper clips. The hard cost of switching paper clip vendors is probably quite low for the vast majority of customers. It requires no changes in infrastructure, no new software or hardware, and no costs of retraining.

However, there is more to customer captivity than the hard switching costs. While rational customers will always carefully estimate the hard costs of switching to a competitive or substitute product or service, in the end it is often the soft switching costs that determine the real level of customer captivity.

For instance, in our database example, it is obvious that the hard costs of switching are high, but perhaps there are real cost savings or potential productivity benefits that could more than offset those hard switching costs over time. But customers must also consider the significant soft switching costs, which include the cost of lower productivity until users become fully proficient with the new database and the potential for business disruption caused by corrupted or lost information during the data porting process. These costs are real, but they are much more difficult to quantify.

Soft Switching Costs Soft switching costs refer to the intangible, difficult-to-quantify costs of switching. These costs include the cognitive effort and time involved in evaluating the value proposition of the new product or service and the uncertainty in capturing the potential for financial, business, or psychological risk.

Soft switching costs are also heavily influenced by the specific reference point of the buyer. For instance, a bank that handles millions of dollars of cash on a daily basis is likely to place more value on the reliability and thoroughness of a new security system than a retailer of mattresses that handles little cash and has no easily portable inventory.

Even if the hard costs of switching are negligible, the soft switching costs can still provide a barrier that is sufficient to keep customers from fleeing to the competition. For instance, consider the bank or credit union where you choose to keep your checking account. What would it cost you to switch that account to another institution? The monetary (hard) cost of switching is quite low. You would probably need to buy some new checks, perhaps pay a nominal account closing fee, and consider the value of an hour or two of your time to fill out the new account paperwork and reenter your electronic bill payment information. In fact, it is likely that the new institution will provide you with some monetary incentive to switch that would offset the hard costs. Yet, in spite of these relatively nominal hard switching costs, checking account customers rarely switch financial institutions. In this case, the soft switching costs—the inconvenience of evaluating the alternatives and filling out the necessary paperwork, the hassle of reentering online bill payment information, and other such issues—tend to far outweigh the perceived benefit of switching for the average account holder. That is why financial institutions see modest turnover in core checking account customers.

Brand loyalty is another classic example of the power of soft switching costs on customer captivity. Consider the high level of customer captivity at Intuit Inc. Intuit has a stable of well-regarded software products and services for consumers and small businesses that are marketed primarily under the Quicken, TurboTax, and QuickBooks brands. While Intuit's software solutions are functionally robust, reliable, and easy to use, competitors offer solutions with many of the same traits. Yet, Intuit has managed to maintain a dominant market share in its core small business accounting, consumer finance, and tax preparation software markets primarily because of the high soft costs of switching software providers.

Intuit's flagship product is QuickBooks, which is the leading accounting software for small businesses and their accountants. The hard switching costs are relatively low; the entry-level accounting package from a leading competitor currently lists at $199.99, while a more robust option is listed at $2,995 for five user licenses. This is unlikely to break the bank for the majority of small businesses. However, financial accounting is a mission-critical application for any business, and more so for small businesses. Many small business owners depend on accurate day-to-day cash flows and expense management. An accounting misstep can entail substantial financial risk and potentially even threaten the viability of the business. Consequently, Intuit customers are not easily swayed to switch to a new, unfamiliar product. Just ask Microsoft.

Microsoft has invested heavily in an attempt to invade Intuit's coveted small business market as well as its leadership position in personal finance software. It is safe to say that Microsoft is not lacking in investable cash or talented software engineers to attack Intuit's stronghold. Microsoft's cash balance of $41.3 billion dwarfs Intuit's annual revenues of $3.5 billion. Yet, Intuit estimates that its QuickBooks accounting software has a commanding 85 percent plus share of the market, and its Quicken personal finance software an even more dominant 95 percent market share. The high levels of customer captivity have repelled Microsoft's efforts to wrestle away meaningful market share for many years. We see strong evidence of this durable competitive advantage in the company's long-term financial returns (see Table 6.8).

Table 6.8 Select Intuit Operating Metrics ($ in millions, except per share amounts)

For the Year Ended:	07/01	07/02	07/03	07/04	07/05	07/06	07/07	07/08	07/09	07/10
Revenue	$1,096	$1,312	$1,597	$1,802	$1,993	$2,293	$2,673	$2,993	$3,109	$3,455
Operating profit	($81)	$51	$339	$419	$529	$566	$669	$696	$683	$863
Operating margin	−7.4%	3.8%	21.2%	23.3%	26.5%	24.7%	25.0%	23.3%	22.0%	25.0%
Normalized EPS	($0.12)	$0.07	$0.50	$0.66	$0.88	$0.98	$1.18	$1.28	$1.29	$1.66
Return on invested capital	−9.1%	4.6%	23.6%	31.3%	43.5%	56.0%	39.6%	21.7%	18.5%	24.6%

Network Economics Network economics is a rare, but powerful, type of switching cost in which each incremental customer increases the overall value of the network. The increased value not only attracts new customers, but also increases the cost of switching for the existing participants on the network. This is not to be confused with a network effect, which refers to the increase in the size of the network, but not to the "economic value" to the participants in the network. For instance, MySpace demonstrated a phenomenal network effect as it grew rapidly from just 2 million accounts in 2005 to more than 200 million accounts just three years later. However, the company now is reportedly suffering from a decline in revenues and profits and may be forced to lay off workers. That downturn suggests that the company's business model lacked the network economics necessary to hold customers captive. MySpace has been displaced by Facebook as the social network of choice, with more than 500 million Facebook users worldwide. Is the Facebook business model differentiated enough to establish the high levels of customer captivity necessary to sustain true network economics? Only time will tell.

Arm Holdings is a little-known technology company that serves as a compelling example of network economics at work. Although you may not have heard of Arm Holdings, chances are that you use products every day that incorporate the company's intellectual property. In 2010, approximately 6.1 billion products were shipped with semiconductor chips based on Arm's proprietary technology. This included cellular phones, tablets, netbooks, e-readers, hard disk drives, printers, and automobiles, to name just a few. However, Arm does not make the chips; rather, it licenses its proprietary intellectual property to hundreds of semiconductor manufacturers, who pay Arm a license fee for access to the chip design (or core) and/or a royalty for each chip manufactured. Arm has created a vast ecosystem around its IP that includes not just the semiconductor designers, but also device manufacturers, foundries, and software developers such as Microsoft (Windows), Google (Android), Apple (Apple OS), and Nokia (Symbian). Each new entrant to the Arm ecosystem increases the overall value of the network by broadening customer choice and functionality when deploying Arm-based solutions. Additionally, third-party developers are tied up on the Arm architecture, rather than on competitors'. Arm's competitive advantage has helped it achieve steady growth in the number of licensees and products containing Arm's proprietary technology. See Table 6.9 for financial information on Arm.

Common Signs of Competitive Advantage

The following list summarizes the key metrics and some other potential indicators of an underlying structural advantage in business. The list is meant to be a guideline, not a replacement for rigorous analysis of the individual companies and industry structures. Furthermore, as Yogi Berra warned, "The future ain't what it used to be." So even if the statistics suggest that a competitive advantage exists, the investors must make a reasonable assessment of the continued durability of that competitive advantage.

Potential Signs of Competitive Advantage

- High and stable market share
- Steady market share gains
- Low frequency of exit or entrance of industry competitors
- Persistent pricing power
- Materially higher operating margins than direct competitors
- Loyal customers and low customer churn
- High repeat purchases
- Brand transferability to new categories
- Strong consumer routine or habit
- Long product cycles
- Robust domain expertise
- Proprietary manufacturing or business processes

There is one final key metric that we have yet to discuss—return on invested capital. Analyzing a company's return on invested capital can help you ascertain whether or not the company truly does possess a sustainable competitive advantage.

Table 6.9 Select Arm Holdings Operating Metrics [$ in millions, except per American Depositary Share (ADS) amounts]

For the Year Ended:	12/01	12/02	12/03	12/04	12/05	12/06	12/07	12/08	12/09	12/10
Revenue	$213	$243	$229	$294	$399	$515	$516	$430	$493	$637
Operating profit	$67	$66	$31	$60	$82	$96	$79	$86	$74	$167
Operating margin	31.5%	27.4%	13.5%	20.6%	20.6%	18.7%	15.3%	20.1%	15.0%	26.3%
Normalized earnings per ADS	$0.12	$0.12	$0.06	$0.11	$0.11	$0.13	$0.11	$0.13	$0.11	$0.23
Return on invested capital	156.6%	97.5%	48.5%	34.6%	14.3%	12.9%	11.3%	11.0%	7.4%	16.9%
Number of products with Arm IP (millions)	420	455	732	1,272	1,562	2,390	2,894	3,981	3,866	6,100

RETURN ON INVESTED CAPITAL

Return on invested capital (ROIC) is a key gauge for determining how effective a company is at earning a return on the shareholder capital entrusted to it. It is directly related to the strength and sustainability of a company's competitive advantage.

ROIC is calculated by dividing the normalized operating earnings of the business by the average amount of stakeholder capital deployed over the period being measured. (Normalized operating earnings are what the company should earn in a "normal" operating environment, adjusted for nonoperating items such as interest expense/income or contributions from minority interests in other businesses.) Average invested capital represents the average capital invested by all financial stakeholders (both equity and debt holders).

$$\text{Return on invested capital (ROIC)} = \frac{\text{normalized operating earnings (after tax)}}{\text{average capital invested in operations of business}}$$

For instance, if a company generated $10 million in normalized operating earnings over the course of a year on an average capital base of $100 million, the return on invested capital would be 10 percent:

$$\text{Return on invested capital (ROIC)} = \frac{\$10,000,000}{\$100,000,000} = 10\%$$

Companies that are capable of sustaining a superior ROIC can increase their intrinsic value at an accelerated rate. To illustrate this point, let's look at examples of three companies with $100 million of capital invested in the business. Company A earns a modest 7 percent return on invested capital. Company B earns an attractive 15 percent return on invested capital. Finally, Company C has a highly defensible business model and earns a superior 25 percent ROIC. For simplicity, we will assume that each company has ample opportunities to reinvest the profits generated by the business at the same ROIC.

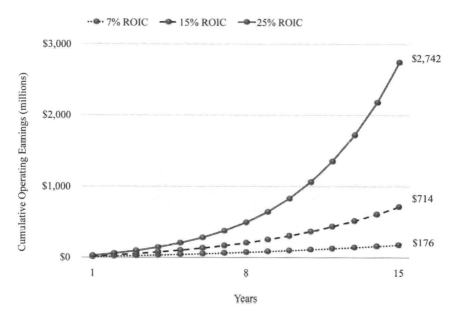

Cumulative Operating Earnings in Millions

··●· 7% ROIC ─●─ 15% ROIC ─●─25% ROIC

Figure 6.2 ROIC and the Power of Compounding

As outlined in Figure 6.2, over 15 years, Company A will have gener
ated a respectable, but unspectacular $176 million in cumulative earnings
(1.8 times the original $100 million of capital invested in the business).
Look what happens to the earnings for the higher-ROIC companies.
Company B will have earned $714 million (more than seven times the
original investment), and Company C will have generated a staggering
$2.7 billion—27 times the original investment! The more defensible the
business model, the more likely it is that the company will be able to
generate and sustain a superior ROIC.

Since these profits accrue to shareholders, they should ultimately be
discounted in the price of the stock. If that is true, we should see a strong
correlation between return on invested capital and long-term investment
returns. Evidence of this relationship can be seen in Figure 6.3, which
compares the return on invested capital to total returns over the 15-year

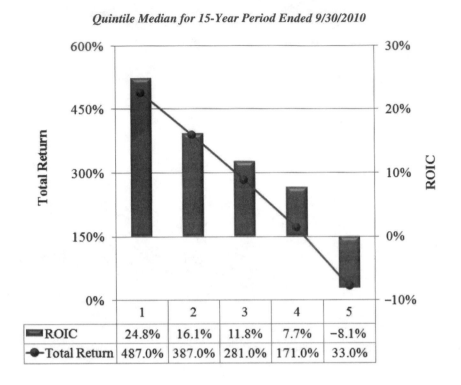

Quintile Median for 15-Year Period Ended 9/30/2010

	1	2	3	4	5
ROIC	24.8%	16.1%	11.8%	7.7%	−8.1%
Total Return	487.0%	387.0%	281.0%	171.0%	33.0%

Figure 6.3 Total Return versus Return on Invested Capital

period ending September 30, 2010. The data represent the median ROIC and total return to shareholders for each quintile, sorted by ROIC. We recognize that these empirical data are just a snapshot in time. However, examinations of other long-term investment periods paint a similar picture. That is, the correlation between the ROIC and investment returns in stocks is meaningful and persistent.

DANGEROUS COMPETITIVE ADVANTAGE MYTHS

The dirty little secret surrounding sustainable competitive advantage is that few companies actually possess one. True competitive barriers or high levels of customer captivity are rare. Many companies talk a good game, but when it comes right down to it, the rhetoric does not stand up to the unrelenting competitive pressures. To further complicate matters, the assertions of competitive advantage tend to be loudest when they are best supported by positive near-term financial performance (just listen to management or read the analysts' research reports), such as when a hot new product or a fleeting tactical advantage results in a temporary surge in the key financial metrics.

Fortunately for investors, the errors in assessing competitive advantage typically revolve around the same set of flawed indicators—a hot new product, "celebrity" CEOs, and efficient execution. We must confess that we have fallen prey to each of these seductive myths in the past, wounding both our pride and our pocketbooks. Our pain is your gain, if we can help you avoid some of the same expensive lessons with a few examples.

- In 2003, Crocs, Inc., a small shoe manufacturer based in Colorado, began selling an innovative sandal made of moldable and durable resin called Crosslite. Demand for the shoe exploded, and the company sold millions of pairs in just the first few years, generating $847 million in revenues at the peak in 2007. The Crocs brand became synonymous with the unique space-age shoes. But then something happened. Other shoe manufacturers began to offer shoes that were strikingly similar to Crocs, some at lower prices. Revenues declined to $646 million over the next two years, and the company lost a combined $227 million in 2008 and 2009 after generating net operating profits of $168 million just one year earlier. The company had a hot product (and for a while a hot stock), but the brand was not strong enough to capture consumer purchases in the face of me-too competition. In other words, initial sales were prolific, but customer captivity was low. *A hot new product is not a sustainable competitive advantage.*

- In the mid-1990s, the household products company Sunbeam Corp. had fallen on hard times. In July 1996, Sunbeam hired a high-profile corporate turnaround specialist by the name of Al Dunlap. The market celebrated Dunlap's arrival at Sunbeam, and the stock surged after his appointment. Initial financial results improved as Dunlap ruthlessly slashed costs. However, those encouraging early results were followed by a massive loss. According to an account published in the June 1998 issue of *BusinessWeek*, Dunlap had embarked on an aggressive campaign to boost revenue and earnings via a series of questionable sales practices. But his attempts to stuff the channel with merchandise soon caught up with him. Sunbeam's business performance collapsed along with the stock price. Al was unceremoniously fired by the board just shy of a year after he had been brought in to save the company. Sunbeam never fully recovered. The financial media's fascination with celebrity CEOs such as Al Dunlap has spawned a widely held belief that any company can develop a competitive advantage provided it has a CEO with a reputation for success at the helm. We have seen celebrity CEOs come and go, with little effect on the long-term promise of the companies they led. *A smart and charismatic CEO is not a sustainable competitive advantage.*

- Consider your local grocery store. If it is like most grocery stores, it is clean, the produce is fresh, and it nearly always carries what you need at a reasonable price. The management team and the workforce probably execute very well on delivering value to you and the other customers. In fact, the grocery store you frequent may even be slightly better than the local competition on most days. But is that enough to prevent a customer from shopping at a crosstown rival? Unlikely. Just ask all the food retailers that have fallen victim to Walmart's expansion into the grocery business over the past decade. *Efficient execution is not a sustainable competitive advantage.*

Like most myths, these competitive advantage myths are all based on elements of the truth. A hot new product may not be a competitive advantage, but a business structure and culture that promote ongoing innovation, such as Apple's, can lead to a powerful competitive advantage. Similarly, a company may not be able to sustain competitive advantage purely through executional efficiency or the individual will of a smart and charismatic CEO, but both operational excellence and good leadership are critical in establishing and enhancing a competitive advantage.

DISSIPATING COMPETITIVE ADVANTAGE

One last point that investors must consider regarding competitive advantage is that competitive advantage is not forever. Investors need to be vigilant for changes that suggest that a competitive advantage is waning. In some cases it is obvious, as massive structural changes in the industry, changes in regulatory or political regimes, or disruptive technology rapidly undermine an existing competitive advantage. A classic example of this would be the impact that affordable digital cameras had on the advantages enjoyed by the traditional photo film manufacturers such as Eastman Kodak Co.

More likely, though, the loss of competitive advantage is far less dramatic. Ironically, our experience suggests that the most dangerous enemy of a sustainable competitive advantage is not the competition, it is neglect or strategic distraction on the part of management. In the majority of the instances where we have seen companies surrender a competitive advantage, they have typically squandered it over a period of years. This is why a commitment to protect and nurture a competitive advantage—a dedication to operational excellence—is critical to long-term investors and a vital attribute of a great growth company.

OPERATIONAL EXCELLENCE

The irony of great growth companies is that they do not obsess about being the biggest; rather, they obsess about being the absolute best. Consequently, they maintain a dogged focus on consistent, high-quality business execution. This commitment to operational excellence not only reinforces, but also typically enhances any underlying structural advantages in the business. In fact, we would contend that it is extremely difficult to maintain a defensible business model for an extended period of time (structural competitive advantage notwithstanding) without an ability to execute the business strategy at a high level day in and day out.

While great people and sound processes are the fundamental building blocks for sustained operational efficiency, culture is the foundation upon which those blocks are laid. Much like a competitive advantage, sustainable operational excellence is embedded in the culture, a culture of excellence. As a result, a culture of excellence transcends any one manager, or even the broader leadership group. It is part of the corporate DNA of great growth companies, emanating from the CEO right down through the ranks of the frontline employees.

Assessing the strength of a company's culture as it relates to operational excellence is a tricky proposition even for seasoned investors. The problem is that corporate culture is a near-ethereal aspect of a great growth company, and it does not lend itself to traditional financial or industry analysis. Yet, it is critical to long-term operating success. How, then, does an investor gauge a company's culture and its ability to sustain great operating performance? Operating history can be a good guide, but there is no foolproof way to assess the likelihood that a company's current high level of operational efficiency can be sustained. However, we believe that investors can enhance their prospects of owning companies with sustained operational excellence by focusing on the following criteria, which are indicative of a true culture of excellence.

Clarity of Mission

Great growth companies that have sustained operational excellence over a period of many years have demonstrated striking clarity of mission. They have a clear understanding of their capabilities. They do not delude themselves into chasing growth chimeras that are beyond their core competencies, even when the market opportunity is substantial. Nor do they express remorse over making attractive long-term investments, even if this means that their short-term financial performance may suffer. Investors will observe that great growth companies exhibit a high level of consistency in their strategic rhetoric and corporate actions. For this reason, investors should be extremely wary of companies that claim to have a tight operational focus, then inadvertently choose to "diversify" into areas that are not consistent with their business mission and core competencies.

Relentless Pursuit of Perfection

Operational excellence is not an end point; it is an ongoing process—a continual process of self-improvement. Companies with high levels of operational efficiency are constantly asking questions: How can we be more efficient? How can we add more value to the customer without driving up costs? The answer to these questions is often small refinements to the process that over time can add up to sizable execution gains. For this reason, great executors find themselves in the counterintuitive position of emphasizing process over outcomes. They realize that they need to break the process down in order to understand where gains can be made. Additionally, great executors recognize that if the process is sound, the outcomes will be satisfactory far more often than not. This will often materialize in dialogue with investors as management chooses to emphasize the importance of seemingly inconsequential process improvements.

Freedom within a Framework

One might think that great operating companies would employ rigid operating protocols to ensure that performance does not drift outside certain tolerances. Actually, the opposite is true. Great operating companies provide employees with a significant amount of latitude. However, this inherent trust and individual job flexibility fall within a clear operating framework that is designed to maximize the value proposition to customers. Consequently, there is a high level of personal accountability that accompanies this freedom. This combination of freedom and responsibility is appealing to talented, self-motivated individuals, which makes these companies magnets for the most coveted employees. In-depth conversations with management and employees can provide insight into the level of trust afforded to employees, but this is probably not practical for the average investor. We suggest that investors examine the level of employee turnover as an alternative gauge, given that employees who are provided with broad latitude to execute and grow are likely to stick around.

Coaching against the Game

Companies with a penchant for operational excellence typically measure results against an absolute standard of excellence. This operating philosophy is similar to a concept in competitive team sports known as "coaching against the game." The late John Wooden, the legendary basketball coach at UCLA, epitomized this philosophy. Coach Wooden had little interest in what the opposition might do. He rarely scouted the competition. Instead, he would routinely drill his players on the basic fundamentals: passing, dribbling, rebounding, defensive positioning, and so on. His goal was to maximize the potential of his team—a worthy absolute standard of excellence. This standard is higher than an industry standard because the goal of great companies (or teams) is not simply to be better than average—the goal is to be the best by a wide margin. To measure progress on this front, great operating companies generally focus on a handful of key fundamental metrics to measure business progress. Management routinely reports on these key metrics in discourse with the investment community.

Rigorous Intellectual Honesty

John Adams once observed, "Facts are stubborn things." In other words, the facts do not change just because you choose to ignore them. Great companies embrace this wisdom. Accordingly, they seek to uncover the relevant facts and then address the facts of their situation head on. This means that they must foster open communication across the organization and a culture that permits employees to risk speaking candidly without fear of retribution. Investors can generally get a sense of the level of intellectual honesty by gauging the level of management's candor in discussing corporate successes and failures.

Infectious Passion

A striking characteristic of the leaders and employees at great growth companies is that they almost uniformly have an infectious passion for the business and the corporate mission. While human nature suggests that personal financial success is almost always a driver, it seems to be secondary to the concept of delivering a consistently superior value proposition for the customer.

Servant Leaders

Average or even good businesses rarely develop into great ones without great leadership to shape the culture. There is a leadership saying generally attributed to longtime Coca-Cola CEO Bob Woodruff that captures the prevailing attitude of great business leaders: "There is no limit to what a man can achieve provided he doesn't care who gets the credit." Great leaders are rarely interested in personal accolades. In our experience, leaders who have overseen the successful development and growth of sustainable business franchises are generally authentic, humble, and fiercely passionate servants to their company and its employees. Accordingly, great leaders focus much of their efforts on developing people and being a standard bearer for the company's corporate identity. Unfortunately for investors, like a great culture, great leaders do not wear signs that indicate their superior leadership capabilities. Great leaders cannot be picked out of a lineup; investors must assess their leadership capabilities over time.

Identifying these indicators of cultural excellence, regrettably, is not as straightforward as measuring a company's financial progress. But it is critical that investors carefully assess a company's ability to sustain operational excellence. The combination of operational excellence and sustained competitive advantage lays the foundation for a truly defensible business model. There is, however, one other aspect of a great growth company that is essential in generating outsized growth in intrinsic value and superior returns for investors—a large addressable market.

TIDAL WAVES OF OPPORTUNITY

A big market opportunity may not be the most important factor in distinguishing a great company from a mundane one, but it is a critical determinant of long-term investment returns. The tidal wave of demand offered by an attractive, growing market can drive substantial growth for the business. When it is accompanied by a defensible business model, this growth should translate into substantial gains in intrinsic value for investors. Consequently, the ultimate market potential of a company's products and services needs to be carefully weighed when targeting companies for investment.

The mathematical advantages of big markets are glaringly obvious. All other things being equal, a $10 *billion* market offers more potential for growth than a $10 *million* market. Most investors intuitively understand that capturing even a small slice of an enormous market can drive considerably more growth than being the dominant player in a tiny market. It stands to reason, then, that capturing a big piece of a big market is an even better investment proposition! These are the situations that we seek as investors.

While each industry or market has its own unique set of demand factors that drive development and growth, there are five broad forces that tend to underpin most big market opportunities: broad shifts in lifestyle and social trends, demographics, government intervention, product innovation, and disruptive technology.

Broad Shifts in Lifestyle and Social Trends

Broad changes in lifestyle and social trends tend to be tectonic shifts that give investors ample time to anticipate the development of the significant new markets they often create. One lifestyle trend that has evolved over the past two decades is the increasing popularity of video games. For many years, video games were largely the domain of hard-core gamers—a narrow demographic comprised largely of teenage boys. Today, gaming spans demographic boundaries. For instance, a large portion of the market today consists of casual gamers who may play an occasional game of Scrabble on their smartphone or construct virtual buildings in the online social game Cityville.

According to AppData.com, Cityville currently has more than 95 million active players. It is this growing level of social acceptance across multiple demographic groups that points to an expanding market opportunity for the video game industry.

Other examples of broad shifts in lifestyle or social trends that have contributed to the growth of huge new markets include the rise of do-it-yourself home improvement in the 1990s, the growth of online social networking in the past decade, and the proliferation of environmentally friendly consumer products in recent years.

Demographics

The baby boom generation represents a classic example of the power of demographics. Baby boomers have been instrumental in the introduction and growth of a variety of huge, lucrative market opportunities. One example of this is the growth in the mutual fund industry. From 1985 to 2009, as the baby boomers began to save in earnest for retirement, mutual fund assets increased from $495 billion to $11.1 trillion (2010 *Investment Company Fact Book*, p. 124). Granted, the shift away from defined-benefit pension plans and to defined-contribution plans or 401(k)s combined with the regulatory and marketing prowess of the big mutual fund companies created the perfect vehicle for capturing the boomers' retirement dollars. But the sheer number of boomers and the reality of their approaching retirement drove the dramatic growth. The aging of the baby boom generation has also had an impact on the demand for a broad range of other consumer, financial, and medical products and services. Now that the boomers are entering retirement, what new market opportunities will emerge? And what opportunities will emerge from the Millennial generation, which rivals the boomers in sheer numbers?

Government Intervention

Government intervention in the economy can create large market opportunities. To be clear, a market that depends on government intervention should be met with a healthy dose of skepticism. It is open to manipulation by politicians, regulators, and powerful special interest groups, which can lead to unhealthy market distortions. That said, the potential for government action to create huge, unexploited market opportunities is real, and, provided the underlying demand is not manufactured along with the regulations that create the market, the opportunity for investors can be real as well.

For instance, the for-profit postsecondary education industry depends largely on federal financing of education (as do most state and private colleges). However, independent of the government-led funding mechanism, there is a strong organic demand for postsecondary education. Consequently, the market for for-profit schools has represented fertile ground for investors over the past couple of decades, mushrooming to revenues of $15.4 billion in 2009. The ethanol industry is another example of government intervention creating a large market. Currently at 10.6 billion gallons consumed annually (according to the Renewable Fuels Association), the ethanol industry has experienced a sevenfold increase from a decade earlier. However, unlike the demand for post-secondary education, demand for ethanol is largely a product of government fiat—a function of federal and state mandates. Most independent research suggests that if ethanol were required to stand on its own merits, it would be an economic failure. Investors must understand the source of the demand in all markets, but they need to be particularly careful in markets that are driven by government intervention.

Other examples of regulatory authority creating market opportunities include designated rating agencies for financial instruments, mortgage finance conduits (Fannie Mae, Freddie Mac, FHA), and hazardous waste handling and disposal.

Product Innovation

Most industries that have demonstrated a long period of sustained growth have benefited from product innovations. Product innovations can be evolutionary or revolutionary, but most innovations are of the evolutionary variety. That is, they represent stair-step improvements in existing product offerings, not giant leaps forward. These types of innovations are an important factor in stimulating incremental demand and sustaining growth in many industries, but they are particularly important in more mature markets. For instance, Nike's continual technical innovations in athletic shoes and apparel have helped to expand the market and sustain growth for both Nike and the overall category.

While evolutionary product innovations are common, revolutionary product innovations are rare, but powerful. They are fertile ground for investors, because revolutionary product innovations are radical improvements that transform the market and tend to shift the entire demand curve. Generally the increase in demand is demonstrated by a marked increase in customer penetration or a newfound ability to command premium pricing. We saw this in the market for digital music sales. Apple's product innovations—the marriage of a sleek device (the iPod) with access to broad content (iTunes)—resulted in a significant increase in penetration rates for consumers purchasing digital music. In the year prior to the launch of the iPod (2001), digital music sales accounted for a negligible component of total music sales. According to IFPI, global digital music sales reached $4.6 billion in 2010 and accounted for 29 percent of record company revenue.

Disruptive Technology

Disruptive technology is a particularly virulent form of product innovation that spurs the development of entirely new markets and, in the process, upsets old business models. The net effect is to effectively dislodge existing customers and put them up for grabs.

A powerful example of disruptive technology spawning vast new market opportunities is the Internet. In the roughly 15 years since the Internet has been commercialized, it has undermined numerous long-established markets (such as newspapers and music distribution) and created multiple new markets (such as online advertising, e-commerce, and software as a service). The current poster child for surfing a tidal wave of Internet demand growth generated by the Web is Google. Google did not exist 15 years ago (it was founded in 1998), yet in its first 12 years, the company generated a cumulative $113 billion in revenues and $37 billion in operating profits while amassing a cash war chest of nearly $35 billion. An investor buying Google stock on the IPO in 2004 would have realized a gain of 606 percent through January 31, 2010.

The Internet search engine market that Google has come to dominate is just one of many enormous market opportunities unleashed by the disruptive power of the Web. Table 6.10 highlights several major markets powered by the rapid growth in the Internet and the companies that emerged to capitalize on those new demand opportunities. The sizable markets listed in Table 6.10 were virtually nonexistent 15 to 20 years ago.

The point is not to belabor the power of the Internet in shaping new markets, but rather to highlight how disruptive technology can unlock vast new growth opportunities for well-managed companies. We have seen this pattern of innovation repeated time and time again. The Internet is today what automobiles were in the early part of the twentieth century, plastics in the 1930s and 1940s, airlines in the 1950s and 1960s, and personal computers in the 1980s and 1990s. If you are concerned that we may be nearing the end of innovation, consider the observation of Charles H. Duell, former commissioner of the U.S. Patent Office. Duell insisted that "everything that can be invented has been invented." He made that comment in 1899. You can bet that every time the pundits claim that we are approaching the limits of human ingenuity, another disruptive new technology is about to be launched and a number of entrepreneurial growth companies are preparing to capitalize on it.

But disruptive product innovations in sexy new markets are not the only source of opportunity for great growth companies. Large existing markets can also offer fertile opportunities for resourceful companies. This is true even when the markets are slow-growing or centered on more mundane endeavors. For instance, there have been no market-transforming technology innovations in medical waste collection in the past 20 years. Yet, a company by the name of Stericycle has grown from a regional player in this large and once highly fragmented market to the dominant national provider. Investors in Stericycle stock have benefited handsomely along the way, with a total return of 3399 percent over the past 15 years.

Table 6-10 The Power of Disruptive Technology—the Internet

Market	Estimated Market Size	Representative Companies
Internet advertising (search and display)	$26–39 billion	Google, Yahoo, AOL
Online payment networks	$5 billion	PayPal (owned by eBay), Google Checkout, Amazon
Social networking	$3 billion	Facebook (private), MySpace (owned by News Corp.), Twitter (private), LinkedIn
E-commerce	$176 billion	Amazon, eBay, traditional retailers moving online
Electronic securities trading	$4 billion	E*TRADE, Schwab, TD Ameritrade, Scottrade (private)
Distributed computing and content delivery networks (CDNs)	$5 billion	Akamai, Limelight Networks, Level 3
Digital music and video distribution	$7 billion	iTunes/Apple, Netflix, Rovi
Infrastructure as a service (IaaS)/data centers	$2 billion	Equinix, Savvis, Rackspace, AT&T, Verizon/Terremark
Ethernet exchange	$1 billion	Neutral Tandem, Equinix, CENX (private)
Software as a service (SaaS)	$10 billion	Salesforce.com, Ultimate Software

AVOIDING "BAD" GROWTH

Investing in growth companies would be a lot easier if all business growth were created equal, but, unfortunately, it is not. Investors must be wary of "bad" growth. By bad growth, we mean growth in a business that is likely to produce an unattractive return on the capital invested to generate that growth. For instance, although all the major airlines were able to achieve substantial growth of their business, Southwest Airlines was the only carrier that was able to generate a level of return on invested capital that justified the rapid reinvestment in the business. Bad growth often stems from a "growth for growth's sake" mentality that results in costly acquired growth or misguided attempts to diversify the business. Investors should be wary of growth initiatives that depend on the integration of sizable acquired businesses or that stray from a company's core mission.

THE LINEAR GROWTH TRAP

Investors can also get tripped up by the linearity trap. Growth is linear only in theoretical financial models. In the real world, growth will generally ebb and flow. For instance, growth may slow as a company reaches capacity in an existing manufacturing plant. New capacity must be brought on line, and new people must be hired and trained. Similarly, a software company may see many new business deals hit in one quarter, only to see a lull in customer decision making in the next quarter. All the while, the same underlying secular growth trends remain intact. Additionally, investors must be careful not to confuse cyclical and secular growth when assessing long-term market potential. Many growth investors have been singed by chasing cyclical upticks in market demand that they believed to be secular growth trends. The point is that secular growth can often appear cyclical at individual companies, and vice versa, so investors must be careful to distinguish between the two by diligently assessing the underlying drivers of the growth.

PRECISION INDECISION

Projecting market potential for growth companies can be an intimidating exercise for the average investor, particularly since the markets in question may still be developing. Developing or rapidly expanding markets can foster a greater sense of uncertainty about the long-term prospects. However, it is typically not the uncertainty of the markets, but rather the quest for precision that creates the primary forecasting difficulty. Investors must recognize that when companies are poised to benefit from a tidal wave of opportunity, precision is impossible and, dare we say, unnecessary. That statement may sound heretical, particularly in the age of sophisticated quant models, but it is true. As Warren Buffett pointed out, "It is better to be approximately right, than precisely wrong." In other words, investors need merely to make a reasonable assessment of the market opportunity and the potential for the targeted company to capture share. Demands for precision can have the perverse impact of steering investors to companies in mature industries that have little prospect for gains in intrinsic value, while avoiding investments in attractive growth companies.

SERVING THE BEST INTERESTS OF SHAREHOLDERS

Once you've found a company that possesses all the key characteristics of a great growth company—sustainable competitive advantage, operational excellence, and a large addressable market—there's still one more question that must be answered before you can seriously consider investing in the stock: "Who will get to keep the value created?"

GOOD STEWARDSHIP

Though business is a conduit through which the shareholders own the assets, the corporate structure does not guarantee that the returns earned on those assets will accrue proportionally to the shareholders. Even if managers have executed superbly and generated significant gains in earnings and cash flow, poor corporate stewardship can result in the dissipation of large portions of this shareholder wealth. Too often, corporate assets are either diverted to the management and the board or squandered on various value-destroying initiatives. That's why it is critical that investors carefully consider the commitment of the corporate decision makers to being good stewards of shareholder assets.

Good stewards recognize that corporate assets are not there for their personal benefit. They understand that they are caretakers of the assets for the real owners of the business, the shareholders. Warren Buffett captured the essence of good corporate stewardship when he outlined his expectations for corporate managers at Berkshire Hathaway: "Run the business like (1) you own 100 percent of it, (2) it is the only asset in the world that you and your family will ever have, and (3) you cannot sell or merge it for at least a century."

Unfortunately, most managers operate under a set of less idealized assumptions than those found at Berkshire Hathaway. Although that can complicate your job as an investor, there are ways to detect whether or not a company's managers and board members are committed to serving the best interest of their shareholders. You can often gauge that commitment by examining their decision-making framework, incentive systems, capital policies, and level of transparency.

Long-Term Decision Making

Good corporate stewards think and act like long-term owners of the business. They gear both their strategic and their tactical decisions toward maximizing the long-term intrinsic value of the business, even if this means forgoing lucrative short-term financial rewards or incurring the displeasure of the short-term-oriented analysts on Wall Street. But shareholders who are in it for the long run should covet a management team that is willing to sacrifice near-term earnings to make prudent investments that will enhance the company's long-term competitive position. Managers with a healthy long-term perspective are more willing to make prudent long-term investments such as investing in R&D to drive product innovation, retooling manufacturing facilities to maintain an efficiency advantage over the competition, or investing in incremental distribution infrastructure to increase market penetration. In contrast, a management team that obsesses over quarterly earnings or other short-term financial metrics probably has motivations other than maximizing long-term shareholder value.

FactSet Corp. serves as a prime example of a company that has made bold, yet prudent investments to maximize long-term intrinsic value in spite of the obvious adverse impact on short-term earnings. When excesses within the housing and financial markets resulted in a near meltdown of the global financial system, FactSet's customers in the financial sector were hit particularly hard. Some of them (like Lehman and Bear Stearns) collapsed, while many others were forced to lay off significant numbers of employees to remain solvent. But instead of cutting costs to get through the economic crisis, FactSet continued to invest in people and IT infrastructure to support a promising new fundamental research product and strengthen its existing value proposition to its customers. FactSet management believed that the improvements would increase business with its existing customers while enticing new customers to switch from the competition. This initiative put pressure on near-term earnings, particularly in light of the cyclical pressure on its customers, but the management team was confident in the long-term potential returns. As its end markets began to recover, it was clear that FactSet was in a much stronger competitive position because of its proactive investments in new and innovative products and customer support. Shareholders have benefited, and should continue to benefit, from this focus on maximizing the long-term value of the company.

Structural Alignment with Long-Term Shareholders

Good stewards embrace incentive compensation systems that structurally align their financial interests with those of the long-term shareholders. Poor stewards tend to prefer short-term incentives that contribute to their own personal financial benefit. Undoubtedly, no incentive system can guarantee alignment with shareholders' interests; true stewardship stems from a deep commitment on the part of the management and the board. However, a properly designed incentive plan can help steer managers in the right direction by reducing the inherent conflict between maximizing the long-term value of the company and pursuing short-term financial gratification. Equally important, proper alignment of incentives will ensure that good corporate stewards are justly rewarded when they execute well on behalf of the long-term shareholders.

Investors need to exercise a fair amount of judgment when they are evaluating the myriad of incentive plans in use at corporations across the United States. There is no perfect incentive system—only degrees of alignment. A shareholder-friendly incentive plan will reinforce management behavior that maximizes the long-term intrinsic value of the business. At a minimum, a well-designed incentive system should be heavily tilted toward long-term fundamental performance objectives and shy away from benchmarks that are heavily laden with short-term financial rewards. Management should also be able to clearly articulate why the chosen fundamental metrics are the key drivers of their long-term objectives. You can get a good picture of the company's compensation structure in its proxy (which is filed with the SEC).

Here are some of the key attributes to look for in a company's incentive compensation plan:

- *Reasonable base salaries.* There is no absolute threshold for what constitutes a reasonable or unreasonable base salary, but the more proxies an investor examines, the easier it becomes to identify companies with excessive base salaries. Investors must also consider the business context. In other words, some businesses are more readily influenced by manager decisions than others. For example, the CEO of a small, rapidly growing professional services business will arguably have more potential to influence long-term outcomes than the CEO of a multinational oil company. Ironically, the salaries often suggest otherwise.
- *Financial payouts tied to long-term performance metrics.* The vast majority of a manager's compensation should be tied to the achievement of challenging fundamental performance objectives. The exact metrics will vary from company to company and from manager to manager, but they should be tied directly to the individual manager's sphere of influence.

Additionally, good stewards will be able to substantiate the relationship to long-term growth in intrinsic value. Good stewards will usually embrace performance metrics that incorporate both a return on capital and a growth component.

- *No special perquisites.* Special perquisites indicate a sense of entitlement on the part of management that is not consistent with good corporate stewardship. In the instances where senior managers are provided with certain perquisites, they should be consistent with the benefits that are offered broadly to all employees. Common abuses may include contributions to an executive-only retirement program, tax true-ups on option and restricted stock grants, paid financial advisory services, spousal travel reimbursement, car allowances, and club membership dues.

- *Incentives that encourage stock ownership.* Material equity ownership in the company should help align management with shareholders, both figuratively and literally. However, investors must be careful to understand the nature of the equity participation. Not all equity incentives are created equal. Look for discounted share repurchase programs where managers must invest their own hard-earned capital alongside outside shareholders, or restricted stock and options that vest only if long-term fundamental performance hurdles are attained. Look out for excessive use of time-based stock options. They are structurally flawed incentive vehicles that can sometimes reward management for suboptimal performance. Warren Buffett once referred to time-based stock options as "royalties paid on the passage of time."

You should also consider alignment in a broader sense than just incentive compensation. More specifically, try to ascertain if the corporate governance policies adopted by the board and outlined in the corporate bylaws actually protect the interests of shareholders or if they are designed to protect the entrenched interests of the management team and the board. The list of corporate policies is far too long and varied to cover in its entirety, but shareholders should question any policy where the intent is to diminish shareholder rights. This may include classified boards, poison pills, unreasonable limits on shareholders' ability to act by written consent or call special meetings, and dual-class capital structures that give certain shareholders preferred voting rights.

Capital Discipline

Good corporate stewards demonstrate capital discipline. By capital discipline, we are referring to the intelligence and restraint exercised by the management and the board when investing shareholders' capital. Over the years, we have owned a number of seemingly great growth companies that have generated significant gains in earnings and cash flow, only to see much of it frittered away through severe lapses in capital discipline.

Good stewards recognize that the assets of the firm belong to the shareholders and that they have an implied responsibility to invest those assets wisely. Consequently, good stewards will have a disciplined capital allocation process. Specifically, any investment will be expected to generate an adequate risk-adjusted return under a set of reasonable assumptions. At many growth companies, you should expect a return rate in the neighborhood of 15 percent.

Every bit as important as management's hurdle rate is its willingness to openly discuss the company's capital allocation process. It should be able to clearly articulate the strategic rationale and key financial assumptions underpinning its capital projects.

As investors consider a company's capital discipline, they must understand that a management team has three basic options for investing shareholders' capital: (1) reinvesting in the core business, (2) investing in other businesses, or (3) investing in its own shares through share repurchase plans.

Any capital that cannot be profitably invested in one of these three options should be returned to the rightful owners, the shareholders. But before we delve deeper into the issue of returning capital to shareholders, let's examine how good stewards approach each one of the three options for investing shareholders' capital.

Reinvesting in the Core Business All other things being equal, we would prefer a company that reinvests in its core business because that's the area that offers the highest risk–adjusted return and the greatest potential to enhance long-term intrinsic value. However, even when they are reinvesting in the core business, good stewards will carefully consider the return on each incremental dollar of investment. Nothing is taken for granted. If the long-term potential return of a capital project is judged to be substandard, those investments should be avoided.

Reinvesting in the core business can take many forms. It may mean adding more engineers in product development, launching a new brand-building campaign, increasing training for customer support personnel, or installing a new business intelligence platform. Gauging the return potential of any of those initiatives might be difficult, but management should be able to articulate the rationale for such spending and the impact it is expected to have on long-term intrinsic value growth.

Investing in Other Businesses Investing in other businesses through acquisitions, joint ventures, minority investments, or other means can sometimes increase the company's intrinsic value. But there has been a persistent tendency on the part of corporate managers to overpay for and inflate the expected financial contribution from acquired entities. In fact, a growing body of empirical evidence and experience suggests that most corporate acquisitions actually destroy shareholder value for a number of reasons, including hubris, a penchant for blind empire building, misaligned financial incentives, analytical sloppiness, or poor judgment.

Successful investments in outside businesses tend to be modest in size, leverage existing core competencies, and incorporate a large cushion in the purchase price to account for uncertainties.

Share Repurchases The third option for investing shareholders' capital is to purchase the company's own stock in the open market. These share repurchases should be treated like any other investment of shareholders' capital. Management needs to consider the long-term expected return on the capital deployed. Unfortunately, there has been a tendency in recent years to place share repurchases in a separate category. Many companies engage in share repurchases irrespective of the long-term implied return on those purchases. Often they justify the purchases as a vehicle to soak up equity dilution from stock option grants. This is nothing more than a disguised wealth transfer from outside shareholders to insiders and, hence, is a poor example of corporate stewardship. Let us be clear on this issue: investing capital in one's own corporate equity does not absolve management from the responsibility of assessing the return potential.

In some cases, companies are aggressive in their share repurchases and are seeking to materially shrink the share count. Granted, a shrinking share count is preferable to dilution; however, the reduction in share count tells an investor nothing about the return generated on the capital invested in the repurchased shares. Investors benefit from share repurchases only if the expected return on the repurchased shares is adequate. If the expected return on the capital used to repurchase those shares is inferior, the appeal of a shrinking share count is entirely cosmetic. Good stewards understand this and will be able to articulate the return expectations of all capital investments, including investments in their own shares.

Returning Capital to Shareholders

For all great growth companies, there comes a day when they are generating far more cash than they can prudently reinvest in the business. Good stewards recognize that generated cash flow that exceeds the needs of the business (aka, excess capital) should be returned to the shareholders. Good stewards will also articulate an explicit policy for returning excess capital to shareholders.

The Downside to Share Repurchases When considering how to return capital to shareholders, there is one trap that even well-intentioned managers and intelligent investors fall into—considering share repurchases to be a "return" of capital.

Contrary to the popular perception, share repurchases are *not* a return of capital. Even if the shares are purchased at attractive prices, shareholders will receive a return of capital only if they decide to sell their shares—which, of course, defeats the purpose of investing in the company in the first place.

Doling Out Dividends The only true return of shareholders' capital is a dividend. Dividends treat all shareholders equally. They also encourage managers to own large amounts of stock because they are actively participating in the ongoing cash flow–generating ability of the business. Dividends are an underutilized tool for increasing alignment.

Yet, despite the arguments for paying a dividend, many great growth companies have declined to offer dividends for a variety of reasons. Perhaps the most common is the perception that paying a dividend is a tacit acknowledgment that the company has exhausted its growth opportunities. Ignoring for a moment the fact that good managers do not gear their business strategy or their capital decisions to appease Wall Street, this belief has been empirically invalidated. A study by Robert Arnott and Cliff Asness (published in the *Financial Analysts Journal,* January 2003) demonstrated that dividend-paying companies actually grow future earnings at a faster rate than non-dividend-paying companies.

According to Arnott and Asness, "The historical evidence strongly suggests that expected future earnings growth is fastest when current payout ratios are high and slowest when payout ratios are low. Our evidence thus contradicts the views of many who believe that substantial reinvestment of retained earnings will fuel faster future earnings growth. Rather, it is consistent with anecdotal tales about managers signaling their earnings expectations through dividends or engaging, at times, in inefficient empire building."

For growth companies with excess capital, nothing demonstrates their regard for their shareholders and their commitment to good stewardship better than a generous quarterly dividend.

The Accretion Canard

When justifying the investment of capital in an acquisition or a share repurchase, management teams often refer to a financial engineering concept that is commonly called *accretion*. Accretion refers to the boost to earnings per share that comes from investing capital that is currently earning a low return (such as cash on the balance sheet) into an asset with a higher return (such as an acquired business). On the surface, it seems to make financial sense. What's not to like about an investment that earns a higher return and increases earnings per share?

The answer, as it turns out, is quite a lot. A claim of accretion is a specious argument for making an investment. Accretion sounds good on the surface, but it does not tell us whether the investment is a prudent use of shareholders' capital. An investment can be nicely accretive to earnings and still earn a subpar return for shareholders.

For instance, assume that Company A has $100 million of cash on its balance sheet earning 1 percent in a money market fund, which comes to $1 million per year. The management team decides to use that $100 million to acquire Company Z, which is expected to earn $3 million after tax. The acquisition will be accretive to earnings because the $3 million in acquired earnings is greater than the $1 million in interest income that the company was earning on the cash. However, if you consider the acquisition in the context of the return on the capital invested, it is a paltry 3 percent. Shareholders would be better served if the company simply returned the capital to them in the form of a dividend. After all, it is the shareholders' money, and it is likely that most investors would be able to find alternative investments that would pay more than a 3 percent return. Yet, accretion is regularly used to justify the investment of shareholders' capital in projects with subpar returns.

Poor Stewardship in Practice

If you invest in a growth company that has all the operational elements of a great company, including a dominant position in a growing industry and double-digit earnings and revenue growth, you should be able to expect a solid return on your investment. But a lack of commitment to the basic precepts of good stewardship can sometimes separate a company's shareholders from the payout that they seemingly deserve.

Shareholders of Adobe Systems know that story all too well. Adobe is perhaps most broadly known for the ubiquitous PDF files that have become the de facto standard for electronic documents, but its business franchise runs much deeper. The company designs software that helps customers create, deliver, and optimize content across multiple operating systems, media, and mobile devices. Its flagship Creative Suite software product has been the industry standard for more than 20 years, providing Adobe with a defensible business model and a highly captive customer base.

That's why Adobe's long-term shareholders may still be wondering what has happened to their share of the spoils. Despite the fact that Adobe's revenues increased 128 percent and normalized earnings per share increased 62 percent from 2004 to 2010, Adobe's share price actually declined 8 percent, and the company paid no dividends to shareholders. What gives?

Although Adobe management has done an admirable job of defending and growing the core business, the management and board have made a number of questionable investments of shareholders' capital during this six-year period. These "investments" include $5.2 billion to acquire two businesses and $6.8 billion to repurchase shares, for a total of $12.0 billion. To be fair to Adobe management, the acquisitions were of exciting businesses with dynamic growth prospects, but the prices paid appear to have been too high to offer acceptable returns on capital. Additionally, the company's share count has declined in recent years because of the share repurchases, but overall, much of the capital used to purchase Adobe shares has gone to prevent dilution from stock issued for acquisitions and stock option grants, with little regard for the return on the capital used to repurchase those shares. The net effect of these investments is that, according to FactSet, the company's corporate return on invested capital declined from a robust 36 percent in 2005 to just 12 percent in 2010, dragged down by poor capital discipline.

All in all, the evidence suggests a fundamental lack of commitment to good corporate stewardship, resulting in an erosion in the company's earnings multiple. If Adobe management had instead simply returned the capital spent on acquisitions and share repurchases in the form of a dividend, shareholders would have received roughly $21 per share in dividends. That's a pretty good return on a stock that could have been purchased five years ago for around $30 per share.

Transparency

Good stewards have nothing to hide; they are transparent in all noncompetitive aspects of their business, including business strategy and incentive compensation plans. This allows shareholders to properly evaluate both the company's execution and its alignment. Many managers eschew transparency on the grounds that it will put them at a competitive disadvantage. Most of those arguments are simply flimsy defensives designed to obfuscate practices that are unfriendly to shareholders.

TIME WELL SPENT

A good corporate marketing team with the right spin can make any company sound like the next great growth stock. But truly great companies with a sustainable competitive advantage, a defensible business model, and a commitment to good stewardship are very rare. We often analyze at least 20 companies before we find one that possesses this powerful combination of attributes. But the reward for uncovering those special gems can be substantial. As famed fund manager and author Peter Lynch once put it, "You only need a few good stocks in your lifetime. I mean how many times do you need a stock to go up tenfold to make a lot of money? Not a lot."

7

. . .

Down in the Trenches: Putting the Principles into Action

*Patience and tenacity of purpose are worth more
than twice their weight of cleverness.*
—THOMAS HENRY HUXLEY

Occasionally, inclement weather forces pilots to remain on the ground. This has created an important learning environment. The term for this unique pastime is *hangar flying*, which consists of pilots sitting around and swapping flying stories. If the group is lucky, one or more of the pilots will have a great deal of experience and will be willing to share some stories. This is an important source of learning for the less experienced pilots.

The aviation community has elevated hangar flying to a special weeklong event that attracts some of the greatest pilots on earth—and beyond. I am referring to the annual Experimental Aircraft Association (EAA) fly-in held in Oshkosh, Wisconsin. More than a million people a year ground themselves and spend their days examining all the latest equipment and the newest homebuilt aircraft while swapping stories of their aviation experiences.

It is not possible to adequately capture the dynamic spirit of the EAA fly-in. But to give you an idea, my first visit featured three former astronauts, including Frank Borman, who was the commander of *Apollo 8*, the first mission to fly around the moon. The astronauts, who talked about their early flying days in J–3 Cubs, were among many outstanding seminar speakers. Others, including my brother Jay, an experienced pilot and engineering professor at the University of Wisconsin, shared their wisdom and experience on every aspect of flying and building aircraft. But the seminars were just part of the experience. Add to that the constant buzzing of aircraft and the daily air shows, and you can understand why the EAA fly-ins have been the greatest hangar flying events I have ever experienced.

It is in the spirit of the EAA fly-in that we want to offer you a hangar flying experience. In this chapter, we are going to discuss several of our investment experiences—both good and bad—with some of the stocks we've purchased over the past few years. The aim of these unvarnished accounts is to chronicle the process we followed in making our buying decisions.

We hope that these stories will be instructive in helping you build your store of knowledge and motivating you to venture into the investment world to gain your own experience, using the strategies introduced in this book.

APPLE INC.

Today, Apple Inc. is considered to be one of the most innovative and successful technology companies on earth. Not only does it boast sales of more than $75 billion a year, but its market capitalization of more than $300 billion makes Apple the second-largest publicly traded company in the world.

But when we first began to analyze Apple in the late 1990s, it had the reputation of being an over-the-hill computer maker with a declining market share and an uncertain future. In May 1998, when we made our first purchase of Apple stock, the company's annual sales had fallen to $5.9 billion, down from a peak of $11.1 billion in 1995. With Apple's unit sales at just 2.7 million and its share of the personal computer market dwindling below 4 percent, it looked as if the newly introduced Windows 98 and Windows NT would enable Microsoft to dominate the computing world forever.

However, there was one compelling development that had captured our attention during the previous year. Apple had acquired a software company called NeXT, and that purchase brought the return of its cofounder, Steve Jobs, who assumed the mantle of interim CEO.

The consensus view shared by Wall Street and many investors at the time was, "Why would anyone want to own an antiquated personal computer company with a 4 percent share when you could own a market leader like Dell, Compaq, or Hewlett-Packard?" However, we were intrigued both by the initial turnaround that Jobs had begun to implement and by some of the inherent competitive advantages that the company still possessed. Still, our determination to buy the stock in 1998 and build a position in the company over the next four years was met with great skepticism by many of our clients, exacerbated by Apple's tepid performance in the first few years after we began building a position in the stock. But our confidence in the company and our determination to remain patient with our investment in the face of criticism ultimately paid off in a way that far exceeded even our most optimistic expectations.

What were the factors that led us to invest in Apple at a time when most of Wall Street was shunning the faltering computer maker? Outlined here is a summary of the factors we identified that we believed would give Apple high odds of reemerging as a great growth company.

Visionary Leader

Steve Jobs had always been known as a creative visionary, and when he retook the reins at Apple, he articulated his vision for Apple as a company that excelled at designing easy-to-use consumer devices that leveraged the Internet, not just computers. Jobs understood the transformational power of the Web and the paradigm shift that was beginning to take shape. No longer would the PC be viewed as just a computational or word processing device; it would also be viewed as a communication device or "digital hub" within the home, connected to the Web and capable of processing multiple forms of media.

The Internet

The Internet was clearly emerging as a huge structural change in the industry. Ironically, changes of this magnitude tend to favor companies with *low* market share. The low-market-share company can often respond more nimbly than its more entrenched competitors. The Internet also helped lower a huge barrier that had become a thorn in Apple's side: the operating system. In particular, 94 percent of existing PCs were using the Windows operating system. Macintosh computers did not "play well" with Windows-based PCs. Applications designed for Windows could not run on Macs, and vice versa. The Internet, however, helped level the playing field. As users migrated more and more to the Web, the type of operating system they used became much less relevant as long as they had a Web browser.

Strong Brand Name and Loyal Customer Base

The Apple brand was one of the most recognized brands in the world, and despite all the troubles the company had recently experienced, Apple still boasted an extremely loyal and fanatical installed base of 22 million Macintosh users.

Intellectual Property Rights

Apple was one of only a few computer companies in the world that owned the intellectual property rights to both its hardware and its software. This provided a platform for innovation and differentiation in the face of commodity-like PCs. It also allowed Apple to capture the full value of its computers and made Apple's gross margins noticeably higher than those of its competitors.

Simplified Product Line

One of Jobs's first key initiatives upon his return was to simplify the company's product line. He eliminated 15 of 19 product offerings, including printers and the Newton personal digital assistant. The company would now focus on four key offerings: a professional desktop computer and notebook computer targeted toward content creators and other professionals, along with desktop and notebook computers targeted at the consumer/educational market. The powerful G3 family of desktop computers for professionals boasted speeds twice as fast as its Pentium II competitor. Since its introduction in the fall of 1997, the G3 line had helped propel the company back to profitability. This was followed by the introduction in May 1998 of the portable Powerbook G3 for professionals, which was equally well received.

Business Model Transformation

Apple's previous business model had been focused on manufacturing computers with the intention of selling them, but the business model that Jobs preferred was one similar to Dell's—selling the computers first, and then building them. After Apple simplified its product line, the next challenge was to transform the business model to eliminate the sloppy inventory management practices that had haunted the company in the past and pushed it to the brink of bankruptcy in 1996. Jobs brought in Tim Cook from Compaq to help facilitate this transformation.

Prior to Cook's arrival, Apple had been carrying as much as five weeks of inventory in its plants and was turning inventory only 10 times per year, compared to 40 times for Dell. Much of this could be attributed to problems with supply chain management. Managers did a poor job of matching production to demand because they were relying on sales forecasts that were way off. As a result, the company either would miss potential sales because it could not meet demand or would be stuck with massive amounts of excess inventory that had to be written off at staggering costs.

From his experience at Compaq, Cook knew that one of the most important metrics in the PC manufacturing business was how fast a company could turn its inventory. He was adamant about changing this debilitating cycle at Apple and set out to remake the company's inefficient, bloated supply chain while streamlining its ineffective production process.

To accomplish this goal, Apple decided to exit the manufacturing business. It closed several plants and laid off thousands of workers. The company outsourced the majority of its manufacturing and assembly to contract manufacturers with economies of scale and demonstrated expertise in supply chain management. The results were game-changing. Instead of building thousands of computers in advance based on suspect sales forecasts, Apple was able to project sales weekly and adjust production on a daily basis. This resulted in an 82 percent reduction in total inventories, freeing up more than $350 million in working capital. Inventory turns surged to more than 60 times, not just matching but surpassing Dell to make it one of the most efficient PC manufacturers in the world.

Another important change to Apple's business model was announced by Steve Jobs in November 1997: Apple would now begin selling computers direct, both by phone and on the Internet through Apple's new online store. The online Apple store was an instant success; within a week, it was the third-largest e-commerce site on the Web.

Improved Financial Condition

During the initial phase of our research on Apple in early 1998, the company's financial condition had improved markedly as a result of many of the factors just mentioned. The G3 product line was flying off the shelves. At Macworld in January 1998, Jobs announced that the company had recorded its first profitable quarter in more than a year. In April 1998, Jobs announced another profitable quarter, more than doubling Wall Street estimates. This return to profitability, coupled with the monies freed up through improved inventory management, yielded a much stronger balance sheet as well. At the end of the March 1998 quarter, Apple had more than $1.8 billion in cash on its balance sheet versus long-term debt of $950 million. The company's market capitalization was around $3.5 billion. It was obvious to us that the business momentum at Apple was turning. Although the consensus on Wall Street was still extremely negative on Apple's long-term prospects, we were champing at the bit to make our initial purchase.

Buying the Stock The final element of our fundamental research was to utilize our Graham valuation framework to estimate the intrinsic value of Apple. Because of the significant changes that were underway and the company's recent return to profitability, it was particularly important to utilize "normalized" financial assumptions. We used normalized annual revenues of $5.8 billion after adjusting for product line eliminations. Although Apple's turnaround had led to a dramatic acceleration in earnings, we felt it was prudent to use a normalized seven-year growth rate of 10 percent. A reasonable estimate of a normalized operating margin at the time was 10 percent, yielding normalized earnings per share of $0.52 on a split-adjusted basis.

When we applied the Graham valuation formula {[8.5 + (2 × growth)] × earnings per share}, we used 10 percent as the growth rate and $0.52 as the normalized earnings per share:

$$[8.5 + (2 \times 10\%)] \times 0.52 = \$14.82$$

Our valuation of $14.82 represented a 112 percent premium compared to the company's (split-adjusted) stock price at the time of roughly $7 per share. So far, so good. The next step was to calculate a projected value for the company seven years out. In order to determine future intrinsic value, we projected growth of normalized earnings per share at 10 percent for the next seven years and then applied a decayed terminal growth rate of 7 percent to the Graham model. Under these assumptions, Apple would earn $1.01 per share in the seventh year. Applying the 7 percent terminal growth rate, the valuation equation for the intrinsic value seven years out would look like this:

$$[8.5 + (2 \times 7\%)] \times \$1.01 = \$22.73$$

Comparing this intrinsic value of $22.73 to the split-adjusted stock price of Apple at the time ($7) produced a seven-year compound annual expected return for someone purchasing the stock of 18.3 percent, well in excess of our 12 percent hurdle rate. This attractive expected return, along with a major announcement from Apple, prompted us to begin purchasing shares on behalf of our clients on May 6, 1998. The important company announcement unveiled the company's new product strategy for consumers and professionals. It featured two lines of portables and two lines of desktops, and an entirely new Mac computer model. The new model, which featured a radical new design, was called the iMac—an "Internet-age computer for the rest of us." Upon the completion of our initial purchase of Apple, our average cost was $7.60 (see Figure 7.1).

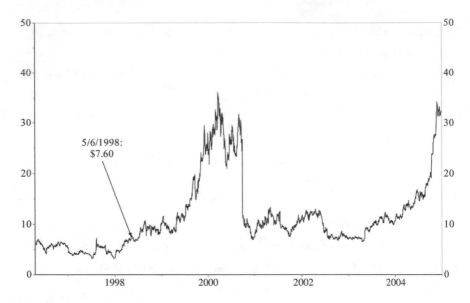

Figure 7.1 DGI Purchases: Apple Computer, May 6, 1998

Source: FactSet.

Age of the iMac With its striking blue, translucent, triangle-shaped chassis, the iMac garnered most of the design awards in 1998. It featured easy Internet access and Pentium-toasting PowerPC G3 performance. "We designed iMac to deliver the things consumers care about most—the excitement of the Internet and the simplicity of the Mac," explained Jobs. "Today we brought romance and innovation back into the industry. iMac reminds everyone of what Apple stands for. iMac is a complete Internet-age computer right out of the box."

The iMac was targeted at the consumer and education market and featured an amazing all-in-one design that was twice as fast as the fastest Wintel PC targeted for the home, and at half the price in some cases. Later that month, at the Macworld developers conference, Jobs demonstrated the simplicity of the iMac by showing a video contrasting an eight-year-old boy and his dog assigned the task of setting up an iMac and getting on to the Internet and a middle-aged man assigned the same task, but with an HP personal computer. It took the boy only 8 minutes to get the iMac set up and begin surfing the Web, while it took the man 28 minutes to complete the same task!

The announcement of the iMac also caused a wave of interest from the all-important software developer community. Over the two months following the iMac announcement, software developers announced nearly 200 new and upgraded Mac application titles.

Then in July 1998, Apple announced its third consecutive profitable quarter, generating $101 million in net income and again beating Wall Street estimates. Apple stock responded positively to the results, but it again became volatile as the skeptics rang in.

We capitalized on the skepticism and volatility offered by Mr. Market and added to the position on August 5, 1998, at an average cost of $8.70. As illustrated in the price chart in Figure 7.2, Apple stock continued to soar as the company's fundamental progress accelerated. The iMac was the best-selling computer in the nation for most of the fall of 1998, and it drove Apple sales well beyond most Wall Street predictions.

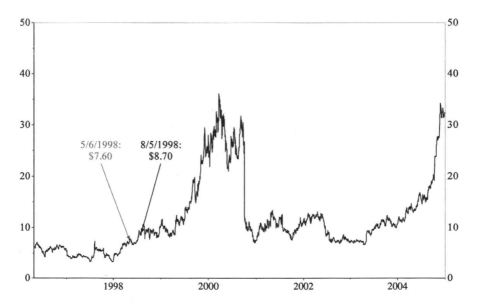

Figure 7.2 DGI Purchases: Apple Computer, August 5, 1998

Source: FactSet.

In October 1998, Apple continued its pattern of exceeding estimates and announced another profitable quarter, wrapping up a full year of profitability. This trend persisted in 1999, with Apple often exceeding the average industry unit growth by two to four times. Gross profit margins were at four-year highs approaching 30 percent, and year-over-year profit growth was surging. This, coupled with world-class asset management (low-single-digit inventory days) resulted in significant operating cash flow generation, further strengthening Apple's balance sheet.

In July 1999, Apple posted a net profit of more than $200 million thanks to the continued success of the iMac. A significant financial highlight of the quarter was an ending cash balance of $3.1 billion, the successful conversion of $661 million of debt into stock, and an ending inventory balance of one day! The company's market capitalization at the time was roughly $8.5 billion.

At Macworld New York in July 1999, Apple launched the final important piece of the Apple product family, the portable iBook. Looking nothing like its drab Wintel competitors, the iBook boasted a clamshell-like design with a variety of two-tone color options. Like the iMac, it captured nearly all the design awards for 1999.

Over the next 12 months, sales and earnings continued to reach new heights, as did Apple's stock price and market capitalization, reaching $35 per share split-adjusted and $23 billion, respectively (see Figure 7.2). More new products were announced, including the Power Mac G4 Cube in July of 2000. The Power Mac G4 Cube system delivered the performance of a Power Mac G4 in an eight-inch cube. The G4 Cube was designed to appeal to both professional users and high-end consumer users who were seeking more power coupled with a small design. The Cube was a revolutionary new product launch similar to that of the iMac, but it ended up flopping relative to expectations.

With seven consecutive quarters of profits and operating cash flow generation, Apple entered the second half of 2000 with a war chest of a balance sheet—$3.8 billion in cash and short-term investments and only $300 million in long-term debt. That war chest would soon be needed, as the tide was about to turn.

The High-Tech Collapse In the fall of 2000, a worldwide business slowdown began to affect not only PC industry sales, but also shipments of Apple computers. This, along with disappointing education market sales and a slower uptake of the G4 Cube, caused Apple to preannounce a major shortfall in anticipated September quarter sales and earnings. This announcement came after the market closed on Thursday, September 28, 2000. On Friday, September 29, 2000, Apple's stock price dropped 52 percent! Our hearts were in our throats as we watched Mr. Market cough up shares at half the value of the prior day. Although we were surprised and disappointed, we thought the stock price reaction was extreme and concluded that Mr. Market was overly depressed. We felt that the business slowdown at Apple was temporary and that our margin of safety was not meaningfully diminished. Therefore, we capitalized on the sharp price decrease and added to our position, this time at an average cost of $13.90, less than twice the net cash per share on Apple's balance sheet. (See Figure 7.3.)

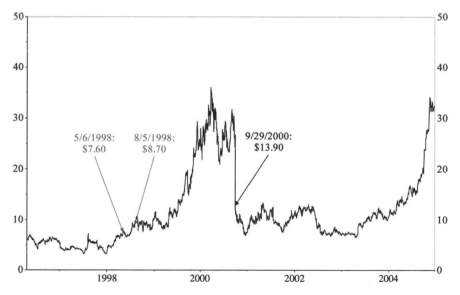

Figure 7.3 DGI Purchases: Apple Computer, September 29, 2000

Source: FactSet.

Given the sharp drop in Apple's stock price, we felt that it was prudent to formally update our client base in writing. On October 3, 2000, we sent a letter to our clients updating them on the recent events surrounding the sharp drop in Apple's stock price, why we believed it happened, and our assessment of the situation. Figure 7.4 contains the actual letter we sent.

In the days that followed, Apple traded even lower as Wall Street jumped off the Apple bandwagon and investors continued to liquidate shares. In conjunction with the official release of the September quarter results, Jobs announced that channel inventories were way too high and that the company would slash prices to remedy the problem. This action would cause a further dampening of Apple's financial results but would clear the decks as the company headed into 2001. In January 2001, the company reported its first quarterly loss in more than three years.

The year 2001 proved to be a pivotal year for Apple. Despite the technology industry slowdown, the September 11 terrorist attacks, and the ensuing economic recession, Jobs pushed a torrid pace of innovation in order to position the company for the next decade. He reiterated his vision of the personal computer becoming a "digital hub" for capturing, storing, editing, and sharing digital content, including photos, audio, and video.

The company launched Mac OS X, the most significant overhaul of the Mac operating system since its introduction in 1984. This was followed by the launch of a key software application, a "digital jukebox" called iTunes. In the spring of 2001, Apple debuted the Apple Store, opening its first two retail store locations, one in Virginia and one in California. Over the course of the next few months, there were significant redesigns of the iMac, iBook, PowerBook, and PowerMac, along with the cancellation of the disappointing G4 Cube.

Despite Jobs's efforts, the stock continued to flounder. While Wall Street was still taking a wait-and-see approach, we did the math and made one final purchase of Apple stock on October 11, 2001, at an average cost of $8.81 (split-adjusted). (See Figure 7.5.)

APPLE COMPUTER

October 3, 2000

Given the recent events affecting the stock price of Apple Computer, we wanted to update you on what happened, why we believe it happened, and most importantly, our assessment of the situation.

What Happened?

On September 28, 2000, Apple Computer announced that earnings for its quarter ending September 30, 2000 would be substantially below Wall Street analysts expectations due to slower than expected sales in the month of September. The company stated that sales for the quarter would be between $1.85 and $1.90 billion and earnings per diluted share, before investment gains, would be between $.30 and $.33. Wall Street estimates called for roughly $2.0 billion in sales and $.45 in diluted earnings per share before investment gains.

Why?

Management of Apple cited three reasons for the shortfall: (1) lower than expected September sales due to a business slowdown in all geographies, (2) lower education sales, especially in the September peak selling season, and (3) a slow start for the company's new Power Mac G4 Cube. In addition, the company stated that it will be providing lower growth targets for next quarter (Dec.) and the next Fiscal year (Sept. 2001).

How did the stock react?

The stock dropped from $53.50 to $25.75 (-52%) on Friday, September 29, 2000.

What was our assessment of the situation?

Although we were surprised and disappointed with the news on Apple, we felt the subsequent price decline was an extreme overreaction. Why? Apple Computer is a leading personal computer company with one of the strongest brand names in the world. It is one of the only computer companies in the world that owns the intellectual property rights to both its hardware and software designs. Its products offer innovative designs that stress ease of use for the customer. Apple has recently redesigned four of its five product offerings and has a dynamic new product pipeline that should drive earnings in 2001 and beyond. We felt the business slowdown was short-term in nature and that the downside risk to the stock was minimal.

Financially, Apple has about $14 per share of cash and marketable securities, nominal debt, generates strong operating cash flow, and operationally is one of the best run companies in the computer industry. It is rare to be able to purchase tech companies of this size at such a low valuation.

Figure 7.4 Letter on Apple Computer

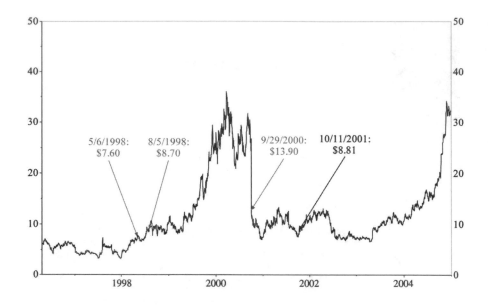

Figure 7.5 DGI Purchases: Apple Computer, October 11, 2001

Source: FactSet.

What did we see in Apple that most of Wall Street overlooked? The dazzling parade of innovative new products certainly caught our attention, but it was the strength of the balance sheet and the discounted stock price based on Graham's formula that compelled us to buy more shares. Apple's market value at the time was $6.2 billion. Subtracting the $4.2 billion in cash on the balance sheet, we were paying a "net" market price for the stock of *$2.85 per share*. With normalized earnings per share at the time of $0.78, we were essentially buying the stock at a P/E ratio of less than 4! Based on Graham's formula, our $8.81 purchase price offered a staggering seven-year annual expected return of 24.2 percent! When applying the formula, we assumed that the company would grow normalized earnings of $0.78 at 10 percent for seven years and then 7 percent thereafter. Based on that, the projected earnings per share in seven years would be $1.52—and the intrinsic value of Apple stock would be $34.20. To that, we added back Apple's $6 per share of cash on the balance sheet to come up with a final intrinsic value of $40.20.

That was nearly five times the $8.81 we paid and a seven-year projected average annual return of 24.2 percent. Here's the equation:

$$[8.5 + (2 \times 7\%)] \times \$1.52 = \$34.20 + \$6 \text{ per share cash on the balance sheet} = \$40.20$$

After our final purchase of Apple in October 2001, the company continued to pursue an aggressive path of product redesign and new product introductions. With the introduction of the iPod on October 23, 2001, 12 days after our final purchase, Apple sowed one of the seeds of its eventual success. The iPod signaled a significant and important departure from the company's Mac business. Initially, the iPod delivered solid but unspectacular sales.

In spite of Apple's efforts, the economic recession and a shrinking industry caused the company's sales to stagnate. For the better part of the next two years, Apple's quarterly revenues hovered around $1.5 billion, generating minimal profits. Not surprisingly, Apple's stock price was range-bound as well, trading between $7 and $12 over the same period. With the introduction of the iTunes Music Store in early 2003, however, iPod sales began to soar. Later that year, a Windows version of iTunes was released, and the iPod soon became the fastest-selling music player in history. On April 17, 2003, a full *18 months* after our final purchase, Apple's stock price hit a low of $6.36. After a four-year period of carefully and opportunistically building our position, we found ourselves well below our average cost in Apple and more than 50 percent below one of our purchase points.

Not surprisingly, some of our clients were growing restless and were not afraid to express their displeasure with our investment in Apple. Again and again, we would hear, "Why own this antiquated PC company with a 4 percent share of the market?!" We would respond with our belief that Apple was in the process of making the transition to "a consumer electronics company that makes clever devices that hang off the end of the Web." We requested their continued patience with our investment in Apple.

The Worm Finally Turns In 2003, the financial picture began to improve for Apple. The iPod/iTunes revolution triggered a "halo effect" and spurred the sales of newly designed Mac computers. Revenues began to grow rapidly again, reaching $8.3 billion in 2004 and surpassing the previous peak of $8.0 billion in 2000. Apple's financial rebirth began to be reflected in its stock price. Between early 2003 and 2006, the price of Apple stock increased more than 12 times, from just over $6 to $80.

Our seven-year financial projections for Apple were beginning to appear unduly conservative. Apple's trailing 12-month revenues in December 2005 had already surpassed our *2008* sales projection of $15.5 billion. Operating margins for the company had increased from 4 percent in 2004 to almost 13 percent in 2006 as a result of higher sales and a mix shift away from computers toward higher-margin consumer electronics. Earnings per share surged from $0.36 to $2.36 over the same period.

Apple's remarkable financial progress stirred many internal debates about the company's longer-term sales potential. In 2006, we looked for a comparable consumer electronics company to serve as a reality check for our seven-year sales forecast for Apple. At the time, we were using normalized revenues for Apple of $19.0 billion. Applying our 12 percent annual revenue growth assumption resulted in $42.0 billion in revenues for Year 7 (2013).

The consumer electronics company that we chose to compare Apple to was Sony. We looked back at Sony's historical sales to determine an appropriate time frame for comparison purposes. We chose to use 1990, given that Sony had generated $18.2 billion in sales that year. By 1995, Sony's sales had grown to $45.9 billion. This confirmed for us that our 2013 projection of $42.0 billion in sales for Apple was reasonable. Our assumptions again proved conservative, as Apple registered sales of *$76.2 billion* in calendar 2010! From 2006 on, Apple continued to capture consumer mindshare and market share with the introduction of additional new devices. The company was no longer known as Apple Computer, Inc., given that the computer was no longer the singular focus of the company.

In January 2007, Apple Inc. revolutionized the mobile phone market with the introduction of the iPhone. Within 15 months of the iPhone's official release, Jobs announced that Apple had become the third-largest mobile handset supplier in the world! Three new versions of the iPhone were introduced over the following three years, and by March 2011, more than 100 million iPhones had been sold worldwide.

The successful launch of the iPhone was followed by the April 2010 release of the iPad, Apple's new tablet device. More than 3 million iPads were sold in the first 80 days and 14.8 million by December 2010, more than all other tablet PCs combined.

As Figure 7.6 illustrates, the stock price of Apple eclipsed $360 in February 2011. With a market capitalization of over $300 billion, Apple is now the second-largest company in the world. Since our initial purchase of Apple in May 1998, the stock has experienced a price increase of more than

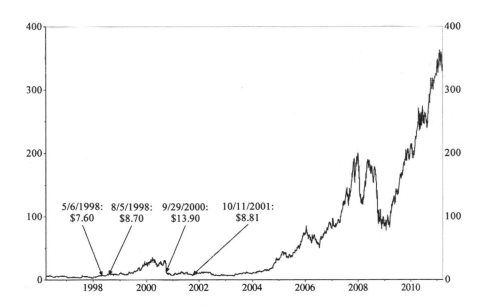

Figure 7.6 DGI Purchases: Apple Computer
Source: FactSet.

45 times! The road to that return was long and rocky. It required extreme patience and resolve in order to endure the years of underperformance and the persistent doubts of our clients. But when we looked at the balance sheet, the intrinsic value, and the wave of exciting new products that Apple was launching, it was a simple decision. Little did we know how wrong we were—the growth of the company and the stock far exceeded even our wildest expectations.

POLO RALPH LAUREN

When he founded Polo Ralph Lauren Corp. in 1967, Ralph Lauren introduced a line of men's ties that were distinctly different from the current styles. In the four and a half decades that followed, Lauren has taken a distinctly different approach to both his expanding line of apparel and his management style that has made the company one of the most successful clothing manufacturers in the world.

Success came quickly for Lauren. Two years after founding the company, he opened his first designer boutique for men inside Manhattan's Bloomingdale's and began winning men's fashion awards. He introduced the familiar Polo pony and the first women's line in 1971. The company hit it big in 1974 when Paramount Studios asked Ralph Lauren to design clothing for the actors in *The Great Gatsby*.

By 1991, the company was earning more than $50 million on sales of more than $800 million. Beyond its core men and women's clothing business, Ralph Lauren's Home Collection, which began in 1983 as a pioneering concept of extending a clothing fashion toward home furnishings, was emerging as a powerful new growth engine. Its distribution and sales strategy included department stores, specialty stores, shops-within-shops, Ralph Lauren stores, licensing, and outlet stores.

On June 17, 1997, the company completed an initial public offering with the sale of 11.17 million shares at $26. The initial market capitalization was $2.6 billion. Net income for the fiscal year ended March 28, 1998, was $120 million, or $1.20 per share, on sales of nearly $1.5 billion.

The ensuing seven years brought compounded revenue growth that exceeded 12 percent, but stock performance was nonexistent. Earnings growth trailed revenue growth as the company positioned itself for long-term sustainability.

It turns out that Ralph Lauren's philosophy for his clothing line also applied to his concept for building the business behind the product. In 1970, Ralph Lauren was quoted as saying, "I'm not a fashion person. I'm anti-fashion. I don't like to be part of that world. It's too transient. I have never been influenced by it. I'm interested in longevity, timelessness, style—not fashion."

The Ralph Lauren brand is widely recognized throughout the world. The dominant position it enjoys in the United States has been extendable to its relatively small footprint internationally. Witness the growth in the company's European business from nothing 10 years ago to more than $1 billion in revenues today.

The company divides its business into three primary segments: wholesale, retail, and licensing. The wholesale segment distributes its brands primarily to major department and specialty stores located throughout the United States, Canada, Europe, and Asia.

Its retail segment sells directly to consumers through full-price and factory retail stores located throughout the United States, Canada, Europe, South America, and Asia, and through other channels, including e-commerce. Its licensing segment sells the trademark rights to unrelated third parties for use in connection with the manufacture and sale of designated products, such as apparel, eyewear, and fragrances, in specified geographical areas for specified periods.

The company's leading brand names include Polo by Ralph Lauren, Ralph Lauren Purple Label, Ralph Lauren Women's Collection, Black Label, Blue Label, Lauren by Ralph Lauren, RRL, RLX, Rugby, Ralph Lauren Childrenswear, American Living, Chaps, and Club Monaco.

Our initial discussions of Ralph Lauren as a potential investment began in late 2006 at a strategic offsite meeting in Montana. At the time, our investment team had embarked on an exercise to create a list of top global brands.

Not surprisingly, Ralph Lauren was on the list. We all agreed that Ralph Lauren was a great franchise and a company that we would someday like to own. At the time, however, Ralph Lauren stock (Nasdaq: RL) was not an undiscovered phenomenon. It was surging toward $100 per share after bottoming in the mid-$40s earlier that year. We decided to put Ralph Lauren on our "wish list" of stocks, hoping that Mr. Market would offer us a better purchase opportunity in the future.

In early August of 2007, the company failed to meet its revenue guidance for the first time in 14 consecutive quarters, growing "only" 12.5 percent versus mid-teens guidance. The stock dropped more than 12 percent that day. Our interest was piqued, and over the next five months we began monitoring the company more closely and intensified our research efforts. Investor fear about a substantial decline in consumer spending was building, and the stock continued to drift lower.

In January 2008, we purchased our initial position in Ralph Lauren at an average cost of $56 (see Figure 7.7). The stock had fallen precipitously from its July 6, 2007, peak of $102, with investor fear focused on a potential decline in consumer spending. At the time, RL was generating revenues of $4.3 billion and boasted the best financial metrics in the industry, with mid–50s gross margins, 15 percent operating margins, and returns on invested capital (ROIC) in the mid-teens. In addition, the company was moving forward with its long-stated strategy for international growth, which included significant capital investment.

Choosing to invest for long-term growth and disregarding its impact on near-term earnings momentum is a decision that modern-day CEOs rarely make. The pressure to appease short-term-oriented shareholders in an effort to manage the stock price all too often proves to be too great. But Ralph Lauren appeared to be leading the company with strategic vision.

Our initial purchase of RL offered our clients an expected return of 15.6 percent per year over our seven-year forecast period, well in excess of our 12 percent hurdle rate. This was determined by utilizing our Graham valuation framework to establish estimates for both current and future intrinsic value.

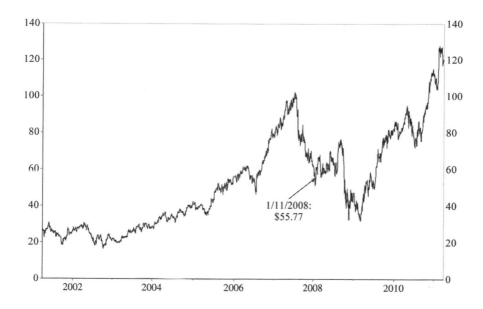

Figure 7.7 DGI Purchases: Ralph Lauren, January 11, 2008
Source: FactSet.

We incorporated the following assumptions into our model: 15 percent normalized operating margin, $3.66 in current normalized earnings per share, a 10 percent growth rate in earnings over our seven-year forecast period, and a terminal annual growth rate of 7 percent beyond Year 7. We arrived at a current intrinsic value of $104 by applying the Graham formula of 8.5 + 2G (G = 10%) to the normalized earnings per share of $3.66. The future intrinsic value of $160 was determined by applying the same formula to Year 7 earnings of $7.13, this time using the terminal growth rate of 7 percent.

Here's the valuation equation:

$$[8.5 + (2 \times 7\%)] \times \$7.13 = \$160.43 \text{ future intrinsic value}$$

Comparing the future intrinsic value of $160 to the stock price at the time of $58 yielded a 15.6 percent seven-year compound annual expected return.

During the course of 2008, the fears of diminished spending were realized as world economies entered a free fall. The financial crisis had taken its toll not only on Wall Street, but also on Main Street. By late 2008, the fear concerning the ability of consumers to make retail purchases was palpable. Wall Street had abandoned RL, and the naysayers were wondering, "Would Ralph Lauren ever sell another article of clothing?" The management team at RL didn't flinch and continued to execute against its stated long-term growth strategy.

We capitalized on the seemingly schizophrenic Mr. Market and added to our position at an average price of $48 at the end of October 2008 (see Figure 7.8). The expected return for RL had climbed to more than 20 percent using our original assumptions and updated financials. That, however, did not prevent the stock from falling more than 30 percent to its low of $32!

The ensuing recession caused a temporary decline in revenues and earnings at RL, but the company continued to invest heavily to build its presence outside of the U.S. market. These investments, along with the adherence to its

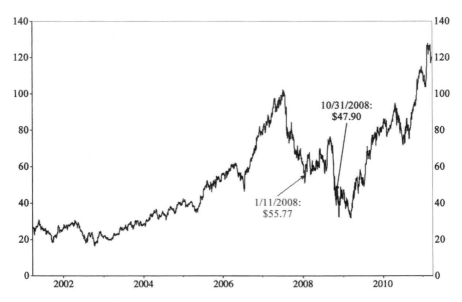

Figure 7.8 DGI Purchases: Ralph Lauren, October 31, 2008
Source: FactSet.

longer-term strategy, allowed Ralph Lauren to exit the recession in a much stronger competitive position relative to other branded apparel companies.

As Figure 7.8 illustrates, RL shares rebounded nicely in response to solid business execution and strong financial progress. The company has forged ahead with its international expansion plans in Europe and is now successfully replicating that strategy in Asia. In spite of this significant capital investment, the company has continued to register strong revenue and earnings growth accompanied by returns on invested capital approaching 30 percent.

As of this writing, shares of RL had reached $130 a share, which marked a 132 percent increase over our first purchase price and a 171 percent increase over our second purchase price. Yet, based on its current price and the Graham valuation formula, the stock continued to offer an annual expected return in excess of our 12 percent hurdle rate.

McLEODUSA

Founded in 1991, McLeodUSA began offering local and long-distance phone service in Iowa and Illinois in 1994. Within five years, the company had grown to become one of the largest regional phone companies in the country, with nearly 400,000 customers in 267 cities and towns.

By the time we purchased our first shares of McLeod in October 2000, it had become the nation's leading competitive local exchange carrier (CLEC), providing telephone and data services to small and medium-sized businesses. It had gained significant market share (more than 35 percent) in its core operating states and was the only CLEC that was generating positive operating cash flow. McLeod appeared to have ample funding to support its operations. Our internal assessment of the intrinsic value of the stock at the time was $25.

We utilized the Graham formula to determine the intrinsic value of McLeod. Although the company was generating positive operating cash flow at the time, it was not yet generating positive earnings per share because of heavy depreciation and amortization expense tied to its significant capital expenditures to build its nationwide network. We utilized a 20 percent normalized operating margin based on what we believed the company would achieve after its network build-out was completed and fully utilized. Applying the 20 percent operating margin to current normalized revenues of $1.4 billion resulted in normalized earnings per share of $0.57. We assumed that McLeod would grow normalized earnings by 18 percent. Applying these assumptions, the Graham formula looked like this:

[8.5 + (2 × 18%)] × $0.57 = $25.37 intrinsic value

Because of its strong position in the market, McLeod had gained the favor of Wall Street. The stock reached a high of $36 in March 2000—well above our assessment of its intrinsic value—but then dropped precipitously into the mid-teens over the following six months. We were able to buy the stock in October 2000 at an average price of $14.86. We added more shares to our position in November 2000 at a price of $12.96, which we believed to be about 50 percent of its intrinsic value. (See Figure 7.9.)

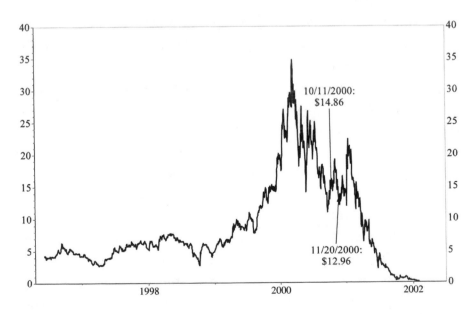

Figure 7.9 DGI Purchases: McLeodUSA, October 11 and November 20, 2000
Source: FactSet.

McLeod secured additional funding in January 2001, and the stock moved back up to $23 after our purchase. At about the same time, two competitors filed for bankruptcy, which bolstered our opinion that the industry was beginning to consolidate. Our investment in the company was looking very promising.

Beginning of the End

But in the spring of 2000, customer demand for telephone and data services from small and medium-sized businesses slowed sharply, and competition in the industry intensified. Our continual checks reaffirmed that McLeod was continuing to make fundamental progress, and the company reiterated its financial guidance on February 20, 2001.

The stock initially stabilized in the $13 to $15 level, then slid to $10 over the next two months. In May 2001, the company lowered its financial expectations, and the stock price dropped 40 percent to $6 in two trading days. At $6, McLeod represented a minor position in our portfolios, which left us with a tough decision: buy, sell, or hold. We chose not to sell the stock because we felt that the company could still turn things around, but we also chose not to buy more stock because of the company's elevated operational and financial risk profile.

Over the following four months, the stock gradually declined to less than $1 a share. We finally liquidated our entire position in the stock on October 11, 2001, at an average cost of about 50 cents. (See Figure 7.10.)

What Went Wrong?

To categorize the performance of McLeod as disappointing would be a gross understatement. Where did we go wrong? Our assessment of the risk characteristics of McLeod's operations was incorrect, and our financial forecasts for revenues, operating cash flow, and earnings turned out to be far more optimistic and variable than we thought. Our initial forecast for 2002 operating cash flow of $495 million proved to be 55 percent too high, as management ultimately guided it down to $225 million.

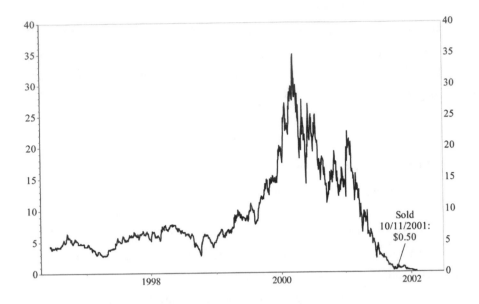

Figure 7.10 DGI Sale: McLeodUSA, October 11, 2001
Source: FactSet.

McLeod was in the seemingly stable telephone business, with very high market share in its core 25-state market. However, we underestimated the risk associated with rolling out a national data network. Prior to this rollout, McLeod had followed a prudent growth strategy of first acquiring customers and then adding the necessary infrastructure to support them. The acquisition of Splitrock in April 2000 allowed McLeod to complete its national data backbone, but it went against the company's tried-and-true strategy of measured, incremental growth. The company was now forced to get both existing and new customers to sign up for data services such as DSL in order to fill its state-of-the-art data network and cover its high fixed costs.

McLeod's small to medium-sized business customers were largely in rural areas and did not adopt data services as fast as McLeod had forecast. As a result, the data-related revenues that McLeod had hoped for did not materialize, and the company fell well short of our revenue and earnings forecasts. The high level of financial debt that the company carried on its balance sheet exacerbated the impact of this shortfall.

We are typically willing to take on higher levels of financial risk when they are accompanied by low levels of operational risk and vice versa. In the case of McLeod, because of our failure to accurately assess the operational risks the company faced, we ended up with high levels of both types of risk—financial and operational—and, as a result, suffered a painful loss.

PLEXUS CORP.

The contract manufacturing industry has undergone a dramatic transformation since Plexus Corp. entered the business in 1979. The Wisconsin-based operation has eschewed the traditional "screws and glue" approach to become what it terms a "product realization company." Plexus goes well beyond manufacturing, providing product development and design services, materials sourcing, procurement and supply chain management, prototyping and new product introduction, test equipment development, product configuration and logistics, and test and repair.

The company's unique approach to contract manufacturing has helped it earn profit margins two to three times the industry average. Its success is largely attributable to management and its quest for being the best at what the company does rather than the biggest. Dean Foate, the president and CEO, was schooled in engineering and engineering management and worked his way up the corporate ladder for 18 years prior to becoming CEO. His focus on competitive advantage for Plexus is anchored in building and maintaining a high-performance organization and culture. Like all members of the executive team and board of directors, Foate is required to own Plexus stock with a value equivalent to one year's base salary. This philosophy encourages a long-term approach to business decisions by the board and management of the company.

Historically, final assembly and shipment of products had been the job of the original manufacturer. Now, a contract manufacturer such as Plexus might be involved in nearly every phase of a new product, from design and engineering to final assembly and shipping. For instance, Plexus recently partnered with Coca-Cola to design, develop, and manufacture its game-changing Coca-Cola

Freestyle fountain dispenser, which is capable of dispensing up to 100 different brands of beverages.

One of the primary drawbacks of the contract manufacturing industry has been the high cost of maintaining a global network of expensive plants and equipment. Those costs tend to drive down margins and cut into the return on capital. The difficulty of executing this business model is evidenced in the industry's top four revenue generators, Sanmina-SCI, Celestica, Jabil Circuit, and Flextronics International, all of which typically report operating margins in the range of just 1 to 2.8 percent. But Plexus is a different story. Despite the challenges of the industry, Plexus has managed to maintain about a 5 percent operating margin, yielding a double-digit return on invested capital. This has been the direct result of two factors: (1) the company's deliberate focus on dominating the contract manufacturing industry's mid- to low-volume, higher-complexity product niche, which offers higher margin opportunities, and (2) the company's steadfast refusal to pursue revenue growth opportunities that are not accompanied by acceptable returns on invested capital. As a result, Plexus has successfully avoided the industrywide temptation of pursuing size at the expense of profitability.

Our first exposure to Plexus came at an investment conference in 1998. At the time, Plexus had sales of roughly $400 million and a market capitalization of under $300 million and was a potential candidate for our small-capitalization portfolios. The company was in the early stages of differentiating itself from an industry that had come to be known as a commodity-oriented, low-margin industry. Plexus was successfully pursuing its mid- to low-volume, high-complexity manufacturing strategy, but on a much smaller scale.

Buying Plexus

After completing our research and valuation work, we initiated a position in the stock at $9.50, which gave us a generous margin of safety. Two years later, that margin of safety quickly dissipated as the stock got swept up in the dot-com mania and traded into the $60s. We exited a significant portion of our position at that point, but planned to revisit the company again after the dust from the tech crash settled. The stock ultimately peaked at $80 in the fall of 2000 before cascading down with the rest of the tech market.

Plexus continued to forge ahead in the midst of the market turmoil and continued to grow both revenues and profits. As the stock sold off into the low $20s in mid-2002, we began to consider Plexus as a candidate for our mid-capitalization portfolios. Revenues were now approaching $1 billion, and the company was emerging as one of the stronger competitors in the industry. In June 2002, Dean Foate was promoted from COO to CEO of Plexus and began to articulate the strategy that would take Plexus from its current revenue base of $1 billion to $2 billion. The company would continue to focus on its core competency of designing and manufacturing higher-complexity, low-volume products for its customers while maintaining its industry-leading margins and returns on invested capital.

Mr. Market had again created an opportunity for the patient investor. We utilized the Graham valuation formula to determine an intrinsic value for Plexus. Because of the industry downturn, Plexus's profit margins and earnings were cyclically depressed. We used normalized revenues at the time of $920 million and normalized operating margins of 5 percent. This yielded normalized earnings per share for Plexus in June 2002 of $1.01. We arrived at a current intrinsic value of $39 by applying the Graham formula of 8.5 + 2G (G = 15%) to the normalized earnings per share of $1.01.

The future intrinsic value of $50 was determined by applying the same formula to Year 7 earnings of $2.68, this time using the terminal growth rate of 7 percent.

Here is the valuation equation:

[8.5 + (2 × 7%)] × $2.68 = $60.30 future intrinsic value

Comparing the future intrinsic value of $60 to the stock price at the time of $21 yielded a 16.2 percent seven-year compound annual projected return. The competitive advantages at Plexus along with an expected return well in excess of our 12 percent hurdle rate prompted us to purchase the stock on June 4, 2002 (see Figure 7.11).

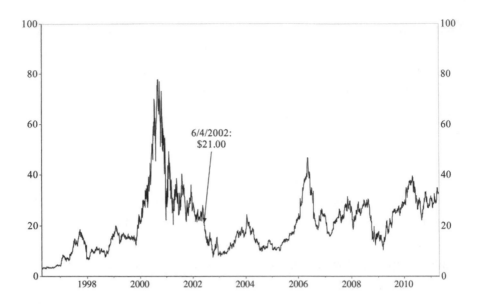

Figure 7.11 DGI Purchases: Plexus Corp., June 4, 2002
Source: FactSet.

In late July 2002, Plexus reported quarterly earnings that were in line with expectations, but lowered forward guidance because of continued weakness in the telecommunications and data networking industries, further fallout from the tech crash. The silver lining within the quarter was that the company generated $66 million in operating cash flow as a result of continued cost trimming by management. Dean Foate, the newly appointed CEO, was aggressively repositioning the company by cutting costs and reducing excess capacity in higher-cost regions. The end goal was to develop a more agile, flexible manufacturing model that would further strengthen the company's competitive advantage.

The price of Plexus stock, however, seemed to ignore these positive longer-term developments and instead dropped in response to the lowered guidance. We capitalized on this "time horizon arbitrage" opportunity that Mr. Market presented to us and added to our position in Plexus on August 9, 2002, at an average cost of $13.42, 36 percent *below* our previous purchase price (see Figure 7.12).

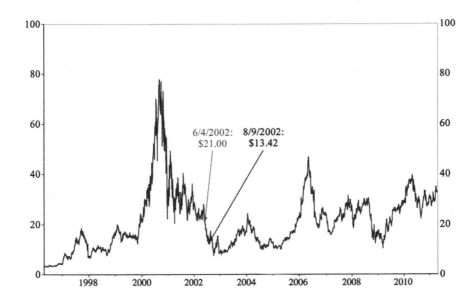

Figure 7.12 DGI Purchases: Plexus Corp., August 9, 2002
Source: FactSet.

Over the next five years, we had several opportunities to meet with management and tour the company's facilities to gain a better understanding of management's long-term operational and financial goals for Plexus. Over and over we heard a consistent message and strategy in the face of an industry that was undergoing significant turmoil. Plexus continued to execute against its plans and was quietly marching toward its goal of profitably growing revenues from $1 billion to $2 billion.

In mid-2007, the company eclipsed $1.5 billion in revenues by continuing to add significant new customers while retaining and growing existing customer relationships. The road to profitable growth, however, was not always smooth. Plexus had to endure the loss of a significant customer who defected to a "cheaper" competitor that Plexus was unwilling to match in price. A large, highly variable, and highly unpredictable manufacturing program for the Department of Defense added significantly to revenues, but also increased revenue variability and gave Wall Street near-term forecasting headaches. A marquee medical customer had to

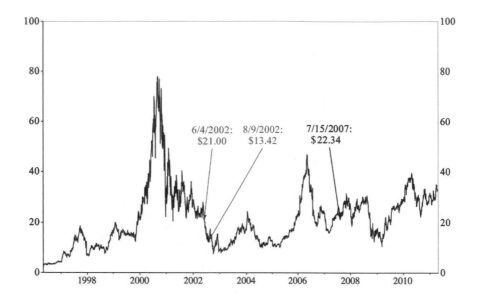

Figure 7.13 DGI Purchases: Plexus Corp., July 15, 2007
Source: FactSet.

halt production of a key product while dealing with an investigation by the FDA. And the company's expansion outside of the United States was not without its fits and starts. None of this, however, caused Plexus to take its eye off its goal of becoming the dominant global player in its chosen niche.

In the midst of all these crosscurrents and short-term uncertainty, we added to our position in Plexus on July 15, 2007, at an average cost of $22.34 (see Figure 7.13).

Over the next year and a half, the headlines began to be dominated by the ensuing financial crisis and economic downturn. In the fall of 2008, the financial crisis reached its nadir with the fall of Lehman Brothers and AIG and the near collapse of the commercial paper market. Wall Street analysts ran for the hills on Plexus, cutting their estimates and dropping their recommendations on the stock. The price of Plexus stock dropped nearly 40 percent in less than a month. We capitalized on the price weakness created by the fears surrounding the macroeconomic environment

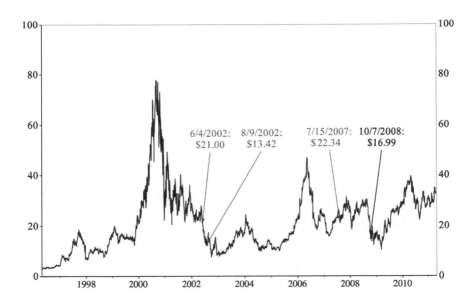

Figure 7.14 DGI Purchases: Plexus Corp., October 7, 2008
Source: FactSet.

and made our final purchase of Plexus shares on October 7, 2008, at an average cost of $16.99 (see Figure 7.14).

At the time, the company's normalized revenues had grown to roughly $1.9 billion and normalized earnings per share to $1.79. By applying the same Graham valuation model assumptions used previously for normalized operating margin (5 percent) and earnings per share growth (15 percent for the next seven years and 7 percent thereafter), the expected return offered by purchasing shares at these levels was a staggering 30.1 percent *per year* over the seven-year forecast period!

Here is the valuation equation:

$$[8.5 + (2 \times 7\%)] \times \$4.76 = \$107.10 \text{ future intrinsic value}$$

Comparing the future intrinsic value of $107 to the stock price at the time of $17 yielded a 30.1 percent seven-year compound annual expected return—2.5 times our hurdle rate of 12 percent!

This astounding projected return for Plexus, however, did not prevent the stock from falling to its eventual low of $11.44 on March 6, 2009, significantly below *all* of our average purchase prices over the previous more than six years!

As you can see in Figure 7.14, the price of Plexus stock rebounded nicely from its March 2009 lows and was trading in the low $30s by April 2011. Although the stock finally moved well above all of our purchase points, it continued to offer an expected annual return of 21.6 percent. The management team at Plexus continued to focus on maintaining and enhancing the company's competitive advantages while adhering to the strict financial disciplines that had generated industry-leading financial metrics, a formula that we feel bodes well for Plexus shareholders.

MIDDLEBY CORP.

Led by its charismatic CEO, Selim Bassoul, Middleby Corp. has grown quickly by taking a fresh approach to a mature industry. Founded in 1888, Middleby manufactures and distributes a broad line of cooking, warming, and preparation equipment for the commercial restaurant and food processing industries. The company came to prominence in the 1980s when it introduced an innovative new pizza conveyor oven that has become a favorite of large pizza companies like Domino's and Papa John's.

Shortly after he was named as COO in 1999, Bassoul implemented a radical corporate strategy that included shedding nearly half of the company's 10,000 products in order to focus on higher-margin, technology-driven products. He also engineered a successful acquisition program that helped position Middleby to become the worldwide industry leader and drove sales growth to nearly 20 percent per year.

But it wasn't just the acquisitions that created that growth. The company has also been aggressively churning out innovative new products that help customers produce higher-quality food faster and at a lower cost. The goal was to make existing products obsolete every three years. By utilizing disruptive technology to introduce revolutionary new products, Middleby was able to gain market share and improve profits.

The Elgin, Illinois, operation manufactures fryers, convection ovens, broilers, combi ovens, steam equipment, griddles, charbroilers, catering equipment, toasters, and coffee- and beverage-dispensing equipment. Among its leading brand names are Middleby Marshall, TurboChef, Southbend, Toastmaster, Carter-Hoffmann, and Blodgett. In addition to its North American sales, Middleby has distribution divisions throughout Europe, Asia, and the Middle East.

Our first exposure to Middleby came at an investment conference in February 2007. At the time, the company was successfully pursuing its strategy of transforming the commercial cooking industry, and it was standing room only at the company's presentation to investors. The company's stock had nearly doubled over the previous six months and was trading at an all time high. The company's CEO did a good job at the conference of articulating the competitive advantages of Middleby and why he believed they were sustainable.

A Company on the Move

We were attracted to the fact that most of Middleby's branded products were either number one or number two in market share in the end markets that the company served. It became apparent to us that the key competitive advantage that drove this market share leadership was the company's laser focus on introducing disruptive new products to the industry.

In the highly competitive restaurant industry, Middleby's customers—including both fast-food and full-service restaurants—are under increasing pressure to maintain or improve their profitability by reducing fixed or variable costs. Middleby helps its customers attain this goal by offering new products that are more energy-efficient, cook faster, and reduce labor costs through automation and self-cleaning. The required investment by Middleby's customers is typically less than 1 percent of their operating budget and offers a return on investment payback of less than two years.

A good example of this is the new Middleby Marshall WOW! oven. It is a pizza conveyor oven that fully cooks a handmade pizza in five minutes compared to the previous standard of nine minutes and uses 30 to 80 percent less energy than traditional pizza ovens.

We were also impressed with the company's global footprint for manufacturing and distribution to serve its marquee customer base. Several of its largest customers, such as McDonald's, KFC, Domino's, Papa John's, and Subway, are expanding globally, and Middleby's ability to offer sales, service, and manufacturing capabilities in the international market allows the company to grow alongside its customer base and potentially increase market share.

Not surprisingly, Middleby also boasted industry-leading financial metrics, with high-teens operating margins, 25 percent return on invested capital, and nearly $80 million in operating cash flow on $600 million in sales!

We left the conference with a strong desire to own shares of Middleby, but we chose to add it to our wish list given the recent surge in the stock price. We continued with our fundamental research in the hope that Mr. Market would grant us a better entry point in the future.

A Visit from Bassoul

On May 30, 2007, we had the opportunity to meet with the CEO, Mr. Bassoul, in our offices in Minneapolis. We came away impressed by his enthusiasm and passion for the business. We were not surprised to learn that he had recently been crowned "most effective CEO in Chicago" by the *Chicago Sun-Times* because of what writer Ted Pincus referred to as "positive fanaticism." He reiterated the company's strategy to gain further market share and continue profitable growth.

But a key insight we gained from the meeting came from Bassoul's comments on corporate governance. "When you are interviewing a CEO," he explained, "the most important question to ask is, 'Do you own more than 1 percent of the company?' If the answer is no, then don't invest in the company." At the time of our meeting, Bassoul personally owned 396,856 shares (actual shares, not options) of Middleby worth $24.6 million, roughly 2.3 percent of the entire company. This clearly demonstrated to us that his interests were well aligned with those of the shareholders. He also explained his philosophy on management and employee compensation: offer reasonable fixed salaries with significant variable bonus opportunities based on transparent, objective performance metrics. Music to our ears.

We were now convinced that Middleby was a company that we someday wanted to own. Over the following nine months, we continued to monitor the company's fundamental progress and waited patiently for Mr. Market to grant us an opportunity.

Waiting for Mr. Market

That opportunity began to develop in May 2008 after Middleby reported its first-quarter results. Both sales and earnings fell short of Street expectations, which the company attributed to weaker end-market demand caused by macroeconomic uncertainty. In August, the company bounced back, reporting record quarterly sales and earnings, but the bounce in its stock price was short-lived as further macroeconomic fears mounted.

We capitalized on this opportunity and purchased our initial position in Middleby on September 29, 2008, at an average cost of $52 per share (see Figure 7.15). The projected return at this purchase price offered our clients an annual expected return of 19.3 percent, substantially higher than our 12 percent hurdle rate.

We calculated this expected return by utilizing our Graham valuation framework to establish estimates for both current and future intrinsic value. We used normalized revenues at the time of $530 million and normalized operating margins of 20 percent. This yielded normalized earnings per share for Middleby of $3.67. We assumed that earnings would grow at 12 percent over the following seven years. We arrived at a current intrinsic value of $119 by applying the Graham formula of $8.5 + 2G$ ($G = 12\%$) to the normalized earnings per share of $3.67.

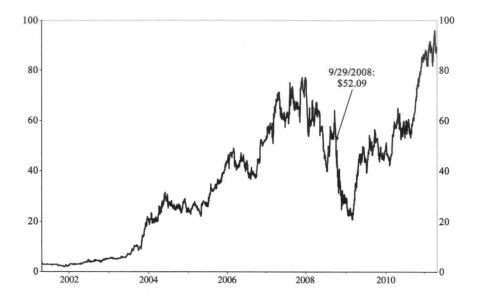

Figure 7.15 DGI Purchases: Middleby Corp., September 29, 2008
Source: FactSet.

Future intrinsic value of $182 was determined by applying the same formula to Year 7 earnings of $8.11, this time using the terminal growth rate of 7 percent.

Here is the valuation equation:

[8.5 + (2 × 7%)] × $8.11 = $182.48 future intrinsic value

Comparing the future intrinsic value of $182 to the stock price at the time of $52 yielded a 19.6 percent seven-year compound annual projected return.

Capitalizing on the Economic Downturn

Over the following three months, macroeconomic conditions continued to deteriorate, and access to credit for Middleby's customers came to a grinding halt. With end customers such as restaurants slowing their purchases of new cooking equipment, Middleby's sales and earnings continued to slow.

However, the company continued to invest heavily in research and development for its new product pipeline. Middleby also took advantage of the market weakness to acquire TurboChef, a leader in speed-cooking technology, one of the fastest-growing segments of the commercial food-service equipment market. On January 5, 2009, Middleby paid $5.10 per share for TurboChef, a 70 percent discount to where it had traded just one year earlier.

We were impressed by Middleby's strategic efforts to strengthen its competitive position in the midst of market turmoil. We added to our position at an average cost of $29 on January 7, 2009 (see Figure 7.16). The expected return for Middleby had now climbed to more than *30 percent* based on the same model assumptions we had utilized for our initial purchase.

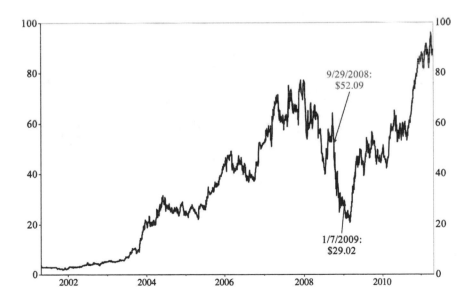

Figure 7.16 DGI Purchases: Middleby Corp., January 7, 2009

Source: FactSet.

As the credit markets began to thaw throughout 2009, Middleby's customer base slowly began to loosen its purse strings. For example, customers like Chipotle and Jason's Deli began growing their store base again, and large existing customers like Chili's looked to upgrade or replace aging equipment. Middleby's stock price rebounded sharply from its low of $21 back into the $50s.

In 2010, investments made by Middleby during the downturn to strengthen its presence outside of the United States began to pay off. Customers expanding aggressively in emerging markets contributed to international sales growth of 25 percent. With revenues approaching $700 million and earnings per share close to $4, Middleby had emerged from the downturn stronger than it had been when it entered.

Although the company was again firing on all cylinders, Middleby's stock price was still offering a handsome expected return of more than 20 percent based on our assessment of intrinsic value. We capitalized on that by making a final purchase of Middleby stock on August 9, 2010, at an average cost of $59 (see Figure 7.17).

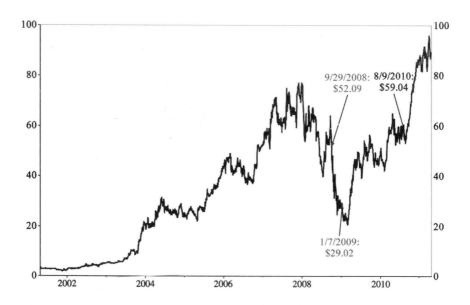

Figure 7.17 DGI Purchases: Middleby Corp., August 9, 2010

Source: FactSet.

As of April 2011, Middleby was trading at roughly $90 per share and continues to offer an expected return substantially above our 12 percent hurdle rate.

PERFECTION IS NOT AN OPTION

What lessons can you take from these stock-investing experiences? There are at least four important points to remember:

1. *Investing successfully takes time and patience.* As we demonstrated in the examples in this chapter, the process of researching a stock and building a position in that stock can take several years. And it may take several more years before those investments begin to pay off, as was the case with Apple. Investing successfully is not a quick process.

2. *There is no foolproof system for picking stocks.* Even the most experienced money managers on Wall Street and the most powerful computers equipped with the most sophisticated stock-trading programs still get it wrong from time to time. And so do we. And so will you. There are no exceptions.

3. *You don't have to get it right every time to achieve success in the market.* If you take the time and effort to ensure that there is an adequate margin of safety with every purchase of every stock that you make, you will enjoy success in the stock market over the long term.

4. *You'll give yourself higher odds of success if you follow the processes outlined in this book.* Although there are no perfect systems, you will give yourself a greater chance for success if you take the time to identify promising growth companies with a sustainable competitive advantage, use Graham's formula to value those stocks, and wait patiently for Mr. Market to bring you an opportunity to make your purchases. If you follow the principles discussed in this book, over time, you should be able to build a profitable portfolio of outstanding stocks. In the words of Vince Lombardi, "Perfection is not attainable. But if we chase perfection we can catch excellence."

8

▪ ▪ ▪

The Few, the Proud: Why So Few Investors Use Ben Graham's Principles and Methodology

The U.S. Marines pride themselves on being the toughest branch of the military. Often the first into battle, the Marines are a different breed of soldier. They enlist knowing that they will have to be tougher, train harder, and take more chances than any other branch of the military. But they're willing to put themselves through the rigors of the Marine Corps because they are driven to be the best.

That's why those who strive to be included among the best investors should use Graham's principles and methodology as the foundation of their investment strategy. Adhering to Graham's principles requires more work and more discipline than using other strategies. For money managers, utilizing Graham's methodology means that their results may be out of sync with the market, risking the occasional skepticism of their clients. This methodology gives all investors and their clients the best chance of success over the long term. And adherence to Graham's principles is especially important when investing in growth stocks.

We've spent the past seven chapters explaining in detail how to use Graham's formula to invest successfully, but one obvious question remains: if this methodology is so effective, why don't more investors use it?

Perhaps the most obvious reason is that very few investors are even aware of a key part of Graham's work: his valuation formula. Although it appeared in the 1962 edition of *Security Analysis* in a chapter entitled "Newer Methods for Valuing Growth Stocks," it was never published again. In subsequent editions of *Security Analysis* issued in 1988, 1996, and 2009, the chapter "Newer Methods for Valuing Growth Stocks" was omitted.

I was fortunate enough to come across the formula early in my career as an investment manager. Perhaps now that Graham's formula has been reintroduced to the investment public, its application will become more prevalent.

But regardless of how widely it's disseminated or how well it's accepted, many investment professionals will still choose to ignore not only Graham's formula, but also his pivotal insights on margin of safety for a variety of reasons. We'll explore the motivation behind those decisions in this chapter.

It's what you learn after you know it all that counts.
—JOHN WOODEN

Known as the "Wizard of Westwood," John Wooden was the most successful college basketball coach of all time, winning more national championships at UCLA than any other coach in history. Wooden learned the fundamentals of the game as a star in high school and college, then refined that knowledge as a high school coach in Ohio and Indiana. But even after moving on to UCLA, Wooden continued to add to his vast knowledge and understanding of the game, which had become increasingly complex since his playing days in the 1920s. Only by continuing to study the game throughout his life was Wooden able to convey the intricacies of basketball to his players in the simplest possible terms. "He broke basketball down to its basic elements," wrote Kareem Abdul-Jabbar in a *New York Times* article in 2000. Abdul-Jabbar, who led UCLA to three national championships under Wooden, added, "He always told us basketball was a simple game, but his ability to make the game simple was part of his genius."

To be at the top of any profession, you need to keep studying, keep learning, and keep trying new things. Complacency is not an option. As Coach Wooden once said, "Failure is not fatal, but failure to change might be."

Not everyone in the investment business approaches the profession with the level of commitment that Coach Wooden demanded. Once they reach a level of competence sufficient to allow them to operate adequately as investment professionals, they may not be interested in expanding their knowledge base or trying new methodologies. Shifts in strategy and new ideas do not always go over well with the clients, even if those strategies offer the promise of improved long-term returns.

Investment professionals should have an overriding allegiance to the profession and to their clients. If that allegiance becomes diluted by the purpose of making profits and perpetuating the enterprise, innovation could be stifled. When they cross that Rubicon, they are no longer serving the best interests of their clients.

A broker is someone who invests your money until it's gone.

—WOODY ALLEN

From our experience in the investment industry, we believe that financial institutions operate with three goals in mind:

1. To gather assets
2. To induce transactions
3. To improve the client's net worth

Unfortunately, the goal of improving the client's net worth is a distant third on this list and is subordinated to the first two goals. An individual who wants to develop and manage a successful investment program must recognize that financial institutions are not concerned about his situation. Brokers are in it for the transactions, and institutions (including mutual funds) are in it to gather as many assets and collect as many fees as possible from their clients. The best interest of their clients—including the implementation of any new strategy that could improve the long-term returns for those clients—often takes a backseat to their own priorities.

The idea that brokers, fund managers, and investment institutions are in business strictly to help their clients make money is a common misconception. Many people are attracted to the industry because of the high wages or hefty commissions it offers—the big payday. Although their intentions may be honorable, their clients' tepid results often reflect a more self-serving agenda.

You don't have to look far to find examples of investment institutions putting their own interests ahead of their clients'. In the days leading up to the global financial meltdown of 2008, there were reports that some Wall Street firms were instructing their brokers to ramp up the sale of mortgage-backed securities. But they weren't pushing the sale of those securities because they believed that this was in the best interest of their clients. They were pushing them because the mortgage market was on the verge of collapse and they had a vast inventory of highly leveraged mortgage-backed securities that they needed to unload. They were trying to minimize their losses and save their businesses by dumping those securities onto their unsuspecting clients before the bottom fell out of the market.

In 2000, with the stocks of high-tech companies near their all-time highs, Merrill Lynch was still publicly recommending the purchase of certain high-tech stocks that its technology analyst, Henry Blodget, was privately berating in his e-mails. The PBS Web site (http://www.pbs.org/now/politics/wallstreet.html) published some of the findings of the New York attorney general's investigation, including specific e-mails. For instance, on the same day the firm gave Excite@Home (ATHM) a positive rating of "buy" or "accumulate," Blodget sent a private e-mail that said, "ATHM is such a piece of crap!" The day after the firm gave Internet Capital Group a rating of "buy" or "accumulate," Blodget sent a private e-mail that said, "This has been a disaster. There really is no floor to the stock." Why was the firm publicly recommending stocks that Blodget privately disdained? Because those companies were investment banking clients that Merrill Lynch was reluctant to alienate. That breach of ethics cost Merrill Lynch $200 million in fines and other legal assessments, and it cost its clients untold millions in investment losses.

But Wall Street firms aren't the only ones known for putting their own interests ahead of their clients'. In the Midwest, Piper Jaffray established itself as one of the largest regionally based brokers in the United States during the 1980s and 1990s, specializing in stocks from the food, agricultural, and medical technology industries. In 1992, the Minneapolis-based firm ranked as the nation's fifth-largest securities underwriter.

The company also ran a bond trading operation that became one of the leading operations in the nation in the early 1990s. Worth Bruntjen, the manager of its successful Institutional Government Income Portfolio (a short-term bond mutual fund), was able to attract billions of dollars to the fund by enhancing its return through a complex trading strategy.

According to an account at www.fundinguniverse.com, Bruntjen "attempted to boost his funds' returns by using derivatives, a financial instrument in which the return is tied to—or 'derived from'—the performance of another instrument such as currencies, commodities, or bonds. Because the link between these interwoven instruments can be so substantial and so complex, the unexpected collapse of a derivative's underlying assets can quickly balloon into an enormous, snowballing loss. Bruntjen had invested as much as 90 percent of his funds' $3.5 billion assets into such derivatives (in his case, derivatives based on residential mortgages grouped together as securities) and exacerbated his risk by borrowing to fund his purchases."

Bruntjen had based his investment strategy on his expectation that interest rates would continue to decline, as they had in the previous two years.

But interest rates began to rise in 1994, giving the fund a $700 million paper loss.

What made the situation even worse for Piper Jaffray was that the firm had marketed the fund as a conservative strategy for risk-averse investors. The fallout from the debacle was devastating for Piper Jaffray, which ended up paying out more than $100 million in settlements to investors, as well as a fine of more than $1 million levied by the Securities and Exchange Commission. If Piper had relied instead on a conventional strategy for its bond fund, with a rate of return that was in line with the market averages, the firm would have avoided the firestorm that Bruntjen's funds ignited.

An examination of the practices of some of the leading mutual fund companies also illustrates all too clearly that the primary goal of these investment firms is to gather assets and generate fee income, while the needs of the customers come in a distant second.

Fidelity Investments is one of the leading names in the mutual fund business, with nearly 500 different mutual funds and about $1 trillion in investor assets. The fund that put Fidelity on the map was the Magellan Fund, managed by the legendary Peter Lynch. During his tenure, the fund grew from $18 million in 1977 to $14 billion in 1990 and achieved a 29.2 percent average annual return during that period—a phenomenal feat for any fund manager.

Lynch, who is also the author of the investment classic *One Up on Wall Street*, personalized the Magellan Fund in a unique way. His thinking and investment style was so straightforward that everyone could identify with his success. And, unlike many of his colleagues in the mutual fund business, he recognized the value of long-term investing. "Selling your winners and holding your losers," said Lynch, "is like cutting your flowers and watering your weeds."

By the time Lynch left the Magellan Fund, it had ballooned to more than $14 billion in assets with more than a thousand individual stock positions. It's little wonder that the performance of the fund has been pedestrian since Lynch's departure. According to Fidelity, the Magellan Fund earned an average annual return of 1.09 percent for the 10-year period ended February 28, 2011. The S&P 500 earned 2.62 percent per year during the same period. The expense ratio of the fund was 0.75 percent per year, which means that the investors in the fund received about 60 percent of the return from Magellan during that period, while the mutual fund company received nearly 40 percent. This does not seem like much of a deal to me.

In recent years, Fidelity has been touting the performance of its Contrafund. With a 10-year average annual return of 6.7 percent, the Contrafund has been performing far better than the Magellan Fund, but its expense ratio is also higher, at 0.92 percent. Higher fees might be justified until one considers that the Contrafund has more than $60 billion under management—more than three times the size of Magellan. Where are the economies of scale?

All investors—institutional and individual alike—must be careful not to get caught in the crossfire in the war between the mutual fund industry and the brokerage industry. Mutual funds want to gather assets; institutional brokers want transactions. Today we have the spectacle of the mutual funds using participants' fees to gather assets while their institutional brokers are pushing for more transactions. It appears that the brokers are winning the war—and, as usual, they're doing it at the expense of their customers. In addition to the customary fees that funds charge to cover transactions and to pay the salaries of the fund management team, many funds also tack on other fees that cut into the investors' total return. Many funds charge annual 12b–1 fees that can add 0.25 percent or more to the total cost of owning a fund. Those 12b–1 fees do nothing to contribute to the investors' performance, but are used, instead, strictly for the purpose of marketing the fund to other investors. Fund companies can use revenues generated by 12b–1 fees to place ads in newspapers and other publications, compensate sales professionals for providing services, cover the cost of printing prospectuses for prospective investors, and pay for other marketing initiatives aimed at attracting more investors to the fund.

In addition to the 12b–1 fees, fund companies may also charge investors another 0.4 percent of total assets each year to pay the cost of listing their funds on retail trading platforms, such as those of Charles Schwab or TD Ameritrade, in order to attract new investors.

Determining exactly how much you're paying in annual fees to your mutual fund company can be very difficult. Some of the most confusing language you will ever read can be found in the "expenses" section of a fund's prospectus. The confusing language makes it almost impossible to decipher exactly what you're going to be charged to own the fund. The important point to recognize is that financial services companies are not in business to make you wealthy. They are in business to make a profit—and that profit comes from fees paid by their customers. As an investor, it's important for you to identify the real costs of your broker-client relationship and to try to keep those costs to a minimum. After all, it's not what you make as an investor that matters—it's what you keep.

Don't just do something—stand there.

—CLINT EASTWOOD

Clint Eastwood is one of my favorite actors. Patient and deliberate, he takes his time assessing the situation and takes decisive action only when circumstances require it. If Mr. Eastwood is as patient and deliberate with his stock holdings as he is with his movie roles, I would bet he has built a successful portfolio.

Using Graham's strategy requires something that very few brokers and investment managers have been willing to try—long periods of inactivity. But as we've asserted throughout this book, a buy-and-hold strategy provides the greatest chance of superior long-term returns.

Patience, however, is not seen as a virtue in the transaction-driven investment profession. Taking a buy-and-hold approach and patiently waiting for the perfect time to invest in a stock contradicts the institutional imperative that inactivity is a bad thing. Your clients think you're not working for them if you're not making any trades. They want to know, "Why should I pay you for doing nothing?"

In fact, that call to action is music to the ears of the transaction-based brokers. They can't earn if they don't churn. Trades are the lifeblood of their business. They need to make transactions for their clients in order to make a living. The life of their firm also hinges on transactions. Without trades, those firms would be out of business. But what's good for your broker isn't necessarily what's best for you. As Ernest Hemingway once advised, "Never confuse motion for action." All of that activity in your brokerage account is probably not adding anything to your long-term performance. In fact, it is probably holding you back.

At our firm, we make our trades through institutional brokers. Those brokers tend to be very bright, very driven, and very persuasive. They are constantly pitching stock ideas to investment firms like ours, and offering very enticing incentives to the advisors who trade the most. There is no golf course you can't play, no ballgame or concert you can't attend, no trip you can't take if you're in the good graces of your institutional broker. And by all means, you mustn't let them meet your family. There are gifts for the kids, spas for the spouse, and family vacations to the most exotic spots on earth. When you understand the perks that come with an active trading strategy, it's easy to see why some investment managers would prefer an active trading strategy to a long-term buy-and-hold approach.

Ironically, even the transaction-based retail and institutional brokers could benefit from Graham's methodology. The formula could help them identify undervalued stocks that may be prime candidates for purchase and stocks within an investor's portfolio that might be priced well above their intrinsic values that the broker might justify selling. We strongly believe a buy-and-hold strategy with growth companies works best for the long term, but if you're intent on generating a high volume of transactions, you would be well served by using a valuation formula such as Graham's that puts the price of the stocks in the proper perspective.

Retail and institutional brokers who try to use Graham's methodology may find themselves in conflict with their own firm's recommended list of stocks.

Investors who want to use Graham's methodology can free themselves. They can choose to unbind themselves from their broker's advice.

[He] did nothing in particular and did it very well.
—W. S. GILBERT

To paraphrase Buffett, many, if not most, investors tend to be "more comfortable failing conventionally than succeeding unconventionally." Oddly enough, in their world, there's a good reason for that approach.

In Seth Klarman's book *Margin of Safety: Risk Averse Investing Strategies for the Thoughtful Investor*, he summarizes the issue very succinctly: "Individual and institutional investors alike frequently demonstrate an inability to make long-term investment decisions based on business fundamentals. There are a number of reasons for this. Among them are performance pressures, the compensation structure of Wall Street, the frenzied atmosphere of the financial markets. As a result, investors frequently become enmeshed in a short-term performance derby whereby temporary price fluctuations become the dominant focus."

Institutions often settle for mediocrity because that's what they think will help them retain clients. And client retention means fee income. And fee income means that the enterprise is successful. As long as the institution's investment performance is in line with the general market trends, it can justify its performance to its customers—whether their portfolios are moving up or moving down. If the stock market is down 20 percent and their portfolio is down 20 percent, the institutions can justify their own failings by pointing out that their performance is in line with the market average. But an investment manager who uses a consistent investment strategy will not always mirror the overall market averages. This manager will have a harder time justifying his strategy when his portfolio falls short of the market trends.

In this business, if you're going to split from the herd, you had better be right. If you're different and right, you're a hero. If you're different and wrong, you're a loser and a stiff. The challenge, of course, involves those times when the investor is right over the long term but wrong over the short term. Client scrutiny and skepticism increase when your performance is trailing the market. Clients will want to know what you're doing, why you're doing it, and why it's not working. That is a discussion that most of us would naturally prefer to avoid, which is why we are all tempted to use investment strategies that favor mediocrity over intelligent risk taking.

There is another, less flattering reason why institutional investment firms tend to favor mediocrity: their large base of institutional customers tends to favor that approach. The 401(k) market is a prime example. Most employers are content to offer a variety of mutual fund options to their employees, and the mutual fund companies have cleverly designed a variety of offerings designed to appeal to the whims of the 401(k) participants. The latest gimmick is "target-date funds." With these types of funds, investors are required only to pick a date on which they plan to retire, and, voilà, the fund automatically adjusts its asset mix as the investor's retirement age approaches. What could be simpler?

However, there are two critical missing pieces of data in this approach: what is the likely performance of the fund manager, and what are the fees? These are far more important considerations than the employee's retirement date.

By offering gimmick investments such as target-date funds, the fund managers are able to obscure their performance and their fees, which is not necessarily in the best interest of the clients. But that's the way the institutions have chosen to do it. Or as famed screenwriter Damon Runyon once put it, "The race is not always to the swift, nor the battle to the strong, but that's the way to bet."

At our firm, we rely on a disciplined buy-and-hold approach that doesn't always coincide with the movements of the market. When we're beating the averages, we rarely hear a word from our clients. They're quite content to beat the market. But there are times when our approach may trail the market averages for an uncomfortably long period.

During periods when our portfolio is trailing the market, we invariably get calls from some of our clients wondering whether we've lost our touch. We find ourselves explaining that we follow a strict discipline geared to the long term that may result in below-average returns during certain times in the market cycle. We must constantly reassure them that the short-term results are of little or no consequence, and that we expect our strategy to provide exceptional returns over the long term, as it has for the past three decades.

In the more than 30 years that we have been managing portfolios for clients, we have suffered only one short period in which our competence was questioned to the point that we lost clients. In late 1999 and most of 2000, our portfolios were not going up fast enough for some of our clients. But the clients who stayed with us helped build an even stronger long-term relationship. The strength of those relationships paid huge dividends after the market downturn in late 2008 and early 2009.

Dealing with clients and reassuring them during the down periods is part of the business. We are more than willing to continue to do that because we are confident in what we're doing and firm in our conviction that adhering to Graham's principles and methodology, including the margin of safety, is in the best interest of our clients over the long term.

Individual investors are subject to many of the same pressures as institutional money managers. Spouses can put the pressure on when your investments don't appear to be working out. What dutiful spouse wouldn't voice some concern when the family savings seemingly falls 25 percent? And relatives, who are often the source of bad marital advice, can be as bad or worse when it comes to investment advice. How many fathers have told their children that investing in stocks is gambling? Or that the stock market is rigged against the individual investor? How many parents have chided their children when their stocks declined along with the market? That's why it's important to have the courage of your convictions in order to stick with your strategy and Graham's principles when the market turns against you. As Rudyard Kipling wrote, "If you can keep your head when all about you are losing theirs . . . yours is the Earth and everything that's in it."

HUG YOUR MOTHER, NOT THE INDEX

This imperative in the institutional industry to "blend in" is sometimes referred to as "index hugging" or "benchmark hugging." It's a popular strategy with money managers because it's designed specifically to mirror the market averages. If they can sustain an average performance, that generally keeps their jobs secure. The index huggers present themselves as performance managers to justify their fees (true index funds command smaller annual fees than managed funds), but their strategy is very similar to that of the index funds. They build a portfolio with essentially the same sector allocation as the indexes so that their funds move in sync with the index funds. Whether the clients are making money or losing money is irrelevant.

Unfortunately, index hugging does little to reduce the clients' risk. If the market produces a nominal return over a 10-year period, clients of the index huggers will earn a nominal return (minus investment management fees). The manager faces a different type of risk from that faced by the clients. The risk to the clients is their money. The risk to the manager is her job. If she can cover her own risk by hugging the index, that takes precedence over her clients' risk of declining assets. Mirror the market, or hug the index, and the job is yours for as long as you wish.

BIFOCALS OR BINOCULARS?

Institutions grade their money managers on their performance every three months. It's a practice that's designed to enforce short-term compliance with a unified investment approach for their money managers, but it ultimately undermines the long-term returns for the client.

The quarterly review is a practice that contradicts the human ingredients of Graham's methodology—patience, courage, and a long-term perspective. There's no magic to three months, no special significance. Three months is meaningless in an investor's lifetime. It's just an arbitrary time frame that the institutions have adopted for their reviews that actually works against the best interests of the clients by stifling the use of intelligent, methodical strategies geared to the long term.

At our firm, we're also expected to issue quarterly reports for many of our clients, but we never base our investment decisions on quarterly performance.

If the last quarter was great, we are extremely careful about the next investment decision we make. If the last quarter was poor, we are extremely careful about the next investment decision we make.

Riding that train, high on cocaine

—GRATEFUL DEAD

Dopamine is a chemical that is naturally produced in the body and affects the function of the brain in a variety of ways. It is commonly associated with the pleasure system of the brain and is naturally released during pleasurable experiences such as eating and sex. It is also associated with the use of cocaine. Cocaine is considered a dopamine transporter blocker that actually creates an overabundance of dopamine in certain parts of the brain, leading to enhanced emotions.

Some experts have suggested that the movements of the stock market can have the same type of effect on the brain as cocaine, causing an increase in our emotional swings and a decrease in our ability to make rational decisions.

When the market is moving up and our stocks are increasing in price, the pleasure system of our brain is stimulated. We want more of this! During bull markets, investors tend to seek more pleasure by investing more money in stocks, even though those stocks are trading at higher prices.

Dopamine can also have the opposite effect during bear markets, when the account value is dropping on a daily or weekly basis. It triggers a fight-or-flight response in the brain that often compels us to sell our stocks as the market moves steadily lower.

Although those actions are a natural reaction of the brain, they have a counterproductive effect on our investment success. Instead of buying low and selling high, our natural reaction to the movements of the market is to buy high when the market is moving up and sell low as the market is tanking. The inability of investors to control their physiological makeup as the market is setting new highs or dipping to new lows can have a detrimental effect on their long-term performance.

These factors affect all investors—professionals and individual investors alike. If you can't maintain the proper discipline and keep your head during turbulent times, you'll have a difficult time making Graham's methodology work for you. We sympathize with anyone who seeks to become a professional in the investment management industry. Our lives vacillate between cocainelike highs and fight-or-flight fears. But we sympathize much less with those who call themselves professional investors but do not commit to using Graham's principles and methodologies to cope with the physiological demands of the stock market.

Individual investors need to deal with these challenges differently. On the one hand, they do not have the resources that are available to most professionals. They must manage their resources carefully. On the other hand, they do not have to worry about gathering assets or making trades. They can apply Graham's principles and methodologies free of the restraints and pressures of professional money managers.

The older I get the less time I have and the more patient I become.

—FRED MARTIN

When you commit to using Graham's formula as the centerpiece of your investment strategy, you're committing to a method that requires patience. The typical investor or investment professional may not want to put in the time and effort required to apply Graham's principles. More important, he may not have the temperament to pursue a strategy that requires him to stick with his plan through good times and bad.

One of the ironies of life is that young people have lots of time left in their lives but tend to be impatient. The pace and excitement of working on

Wall Street tends to reward impatience. The typical professional working on Wall Street tends to be fairly young and is able to become wealthy fairly quickly. These people get used to quick results and prefer a quick turnaround on their investments. They're not geared to the long term. They don't think in terms of years or decades or an entire lifetime, which is the focus of the long-term investor. They're geared to making something happen in a month or a week or even a day. The long term is a foreign concept.

The work required to apply Graham's methodology could be a deal killer for anyone who is not willing to be diligent in her investing practices. If she doesn't enjoy the painstaking effort of poring through 10-K reports, analyzing balance sheets and cash flow charts, and making careful projections, she may be unable to execute Graham's strategy effectively.

Many investors prefer "story stocks." Story stocks, as the name implies, are stocks that have a compelling story behind them that catches the fancy of the investing community. Maybe the company is developing the next great arthritis medication, or maybe it's developing the next great retail concept, or maybe it has a better way to browse the Web. What the stock is actually worth is irrelevant. If there's a good story behind it that finds its way to Wall Street, investors often plug the stock into their portfolios and see what happens.

Impatient investing is reflected in the portfolio turnover of many mutual funds, which often exceeds 100 percent per year. This is trading, not investing. If a portfolio manager turns his portfolio more than 100 percent per year, the average stock in the portfolio is held for one year or less. In fact, some mutual funds have a 200 percent turnover rate per year, leading to an average stock holding period of six months or less. If you are a mutual fund manager whose mutual fund owns 100 stocks and you turn your portfolio over 100 percent per year, you will own 100 new stocks every year. You will need to find a new stock every three working days.

Some mutual fund managers may respond to our analysis by saying that they "trade around positions." They claim to "take a little off the table" when a stock rises and add it back when the stock falls. So they really do not need

100 new ideas a year. Regardless, trading at such a high rate would be exhausting for the manager, the trading desk, and the support staff, and there is no evidence to suggest that such a trading strategy actually improves the performance of the fund. In fact, we believe it would be humanly impossible to maintain a 100 percent annual turnover rate and still have the time to calculate a reasonable margin of safety for every investment.

IF YOU WANT TO SHOOT AT A TARGET, GO TO A PRACTICE RANGE

Investment houses have another ploy that they like to use to convince clients to churn their accounts: target prices. When they issue a recommendation on a stock, they give a target price at which to buy the stock and a target price at which to sell it. Once the client owns the stock, the concept is that he should hold it until the stock reaches the target price, and then he should sell it. It's a practice that is prevalent across the industry. But what you may not understand about target prices is that neither the stock nor the stock price is the real target. The real target is the unwitting client, who is pressured to buy and sell these stocks based on this arbitrary target pricing system.

There is no magic to these target prices, and there is no real reason to sell a stock when it reaches a target price. There's no evidence to suggest that selling a stock at a "target price" and reinvesting in another stock is a good way to improve your returns. In fact, there is plenty of research that would suggest just the opposite, which is why we advocate a long-term buy-and-hold approach.

But analysts at the major investment houses are generally instructed to set a target sell price on every stock they recommend. It doesn't mean that the stock won't continue to go higher or that the company no longer belongs in your portfolio. It's simply an arbitrary price the analyst is required to set purely for the purpose of persuading the clients to sell their stocks.

What target prices really do is discourage investors from long holding periods. The investor is not engaged with the stock and is not looking at the value of the stock—she's just looking at the target price at which the broker tells her to sell. The target price process actually divorces the investor from the company underlying the stock. She's renting the stocks—not buying and not building a position in great companies that will pay off with big gains over the long term.

"There's only one thing I love more than money . . . OTHER PEOPLE'S MONEY."
—DANNY DeVITO, *OTHER PEOPLE'S MONEY*

The movie *Other People's Money* came out in 1991, when corporate board members lived in fear of corporate raiders like Carl Icahn, who was notorious for taking over companies, breaking them up, and selling them off in pieces. In the movie, Danny DeVito played "Larry the Liquidator," a small-time corporate raider who rationalized his practice of dismantling and decimating corporate targets by explaining, "It pleases me that I am called 'Larry the Liquidator.' You know why, fellow stockholders? Because at my funeral, you'll leave with a smile on your face and a few bucks in your pocket."

Investment institutions are in the business of using other people's money. They refer to it as "OPM," and they've elevated the practice to a fine art. OPM comes in many forms: fees, commissions, bond issues, public offerings, and venture capital, to name a few. In most cases, the investors are ignorant participants. They understand that the investment firm is using their money in exchange for a service or for access to an investment opportunity that could give them a fair return on their investment. But some investment houses have been known to cross the line and trade against their own clients to squeeze even more money from OPM.

The most common practice is known as "front running," the act of buying or selling a stock just before executing the same trade for the client. In other words, if a client puts in an order to buy a large block of a particular stock, the broker will place an order for the same stock just ahead of its client's order. Once the firm has made its purchase, it places its client's order at a slightly higher price, then immediately dumps its own shares to capture the profit. The very act of the broker dumping its shares typically drives the price of the stock down to its original price, giving its client an instant loss on the trade.

At our firm, we've seen this happen with our own orders many times. When we've placed an order to buy a large block of a certain stock, we've seen the price of that stock immediately go up by as much as a dollar per share because our broker was front running our trade. When we see a sudden spike like that in the shares we're buying, we typically pull the order, then watch as the price sinks back to its original level. We've learned that the best approach when acquiring a large block of a certain stock is to disguise our trades by buying in smaller lots spread out over time so that our orders don't trigger front running. Although the act of front running has been banned, we still hear reports of investment houses using creative ways to front-run their clients' trades. As Larry the Liquidator said, "You can change all the laws you want. You can't stop the game. I'll still be here. I adapt."

How could I have been so mistaken as to have trusted the experts?

—JOHN F. KENNEDY

In April 1961, just a few months into his presidency, John F. Kennedy ordered an invasion of Cuba that was intended to wrest control of the island nation from Fidel Castro. Known as the "Bay of Pigs," the invasion turned into a monumental disaster that led to dozens of deaths, the capture of more than a thousand prisoners by Cuban forces, and an embarrassing defeat for the United States.

Kennedy was mortified by the defeat, which has been widely regarded as the biggest blunder of his shortened tenure as president. His biggest mistake? He took the "experts" at their word, when, in fact, those experts were totally naïve in their expectations. They thought the invasion would be a cakewalk that would be met with little resistance. But, in fact, Cuban forces were well trained and well prepared to stamp out the invasion and defeat the invading forces.

Individual investors trust the experts every day when they put their money in the hands of brokers or professional money managers. Wall Street has proven repeatedly that it is not to be trusted. But if not Wall Street, whom should they trust? Most investors believe that they have nowhere else to turn.

All is not lost. The individual investor can arm himself by using the strategies described in this book and by reading *The Intelligent Investor* by Graham.

THE VALUE OF WASTED EFFORT

Applying Graham's principles and methodology requires a great deal of effort. We may spend weeks or months evaluating a stock, building a seven-year price projection, and tracking the stock before we ever make a decision on buying it. And the fact is, in many cases, we may end up deciding not to buy the stock. The price might rise before we're ready to buy, or we might see a red flag when we're evaluating the company that convinces us not to buy the stock.

If you're going to use Graham's formula to evaluate stocks, be prepared to see some of your work end in inaction. You're going to research a number of stocks that you are never going to buy. That's the value of wasted effort—not only to identify the stocks that you want to add to your portfolio at the price you want to pay, but also to identify stocks that you may never want in your portfolio.

To use Graham's formula successfully, you must be willing to put in a lot of time and effort on stocks that will never make it into your portfolio. But knowing what to buy and what not to buy is crucial to the long-term success of any investor.

We've used this book to explain the formula and explain how you can use it to build a successful portfolio, but not every investor will be willing to put in the time and effort to follow the strategy.

The secret of business is to know something no one else knows.

—ARISTOTLE ONASSIS

Aristotle Onassis was a prominent Greek shipping magnate and the founder of Olympic Airways. Through his astute business acumen in more than one industry, he became one of the richest men in the world prior to his death in 1975. Onassis was the source of many insightful quotes about business and success.

Although Onassis spoke several languages, we are going to assume that the quote given here was precisely stated, using the word *know* instead of the word *believe*. The Oxford American Dictionary defines *believe* as "to accept as true or as speaking or conveying truth." It defines *know* as "to have in one's mind or memory as a result of experience or learning or information."

Anyone who wants to achieve investment success must convert her beliefs into knowledge. If a belief leads to failure, it must be amended or discarded. It is only by repeated attempts to follow one's beliefs that enduring knowledge can be gained.

We believe most investors *believe* that long holding periods offer the best chance to earn average or superior returns from stocks. We suspect that most investors do not *know* how to hold stock positions for long periods of time. Here is a critical piece of knowledge that most investors lack: the most difficult time to own a stock is when the investor has a profit over his cost approaching 50 to 100 percent. The reason is that there is not a large enough cushion over his purchase price. He could easily lose his profits even in a normal market correction. If an investor buys a stock at $10 per share and the stock appreciates to $20 per share, the investor does not have much of a profit cushion if the stock should decline.

How do we know this? Our investment history with Dell Computer was an unfortunate, extremely expensive lesson for us. We owned the stock in the early and mid–1990s. I do not have all of the exact details of the transaction, but I can still remember the key decision moments as though they occurred yesterday. It was that painful and that educational.

In 1991, Michael Dell came through Minneapolis and talked to a bunch of investors. Mr. Dell was then at the ripe old age of 25 years old. He got up and explained Dell's direct selling model. It was a "lightbulb" moment for me. After the meeting, I went up to Mr. Dell. My question went something like this:" Mr. Dell, if your computer sells direct and Compaq sells through dealers, can you sell your product at about 25 percent cheaper than Compaq and still make good margins?" He said yes.

I went back to my office and reviewed the finances on Dell. The company had a decent balance sheet, and the stock was at about 10 times earnings. It was an easy decision to start a position in the stock.

About two years later, I sold the stock. I had a profit in the stock of about 200 percent, but the company was having quality problems and had had to withdraw a convertible debt offering. I thought perhaps its string of successes was coming to an end. I did not want to lose my profit in the stock.

The story gets worse. After I sold the stock, Compaq started making noise about changing its supplier relationship with Intel. Intel was the dominant supplier of microprocessors for personal computers. I thought Compaq's strategy was a long-term loser. Ironically, Dell's stock declined significantly after I sold it. I was feeling pretty good.

Even though Compaq was dominating the headlines and Wall Street was leaning toward Compaq instead of Dell, Dell's direct selling model remained a huge competitive edge for the company. The stock remained attractively valued. Yet I never bought the stock back.

How good was my decision making? I will let you decide. Until the end of 1994, Dell stock traded for less than 50 cents per share. In 1995, Dell stock began a climb that climaxed in 2000 at more than $50 per share, a gain of at least 100 times.

An expensive lesson, indeed.

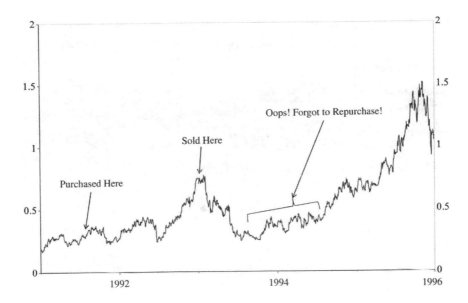

Figure 8.1 Dell Computer, 1991–1995

Source: FactSet.

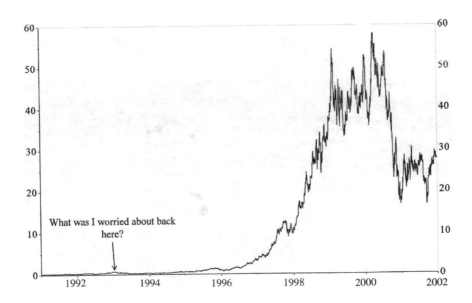

Figure 8.2 Dell Computer, 1991–2001

Source: FactSet.

When you consider our costly experience with Dell, perhaps you can understand that we know how difficult it can be to continue to hold a stock through a period of modest appreciation.

We continue to make mistakes; we hope those mistakes (and our successes) will help us to convert our beliefs into knowledge. We would prefer that they be a little less expensive than our Dell lesson.

9

...

Getting the Most from This Book

Knowing is not enough, we must apply. Willing is not enough, we must do.
—JOHANN VON GOETHE

This book lays out a thorough and meticulous strategy for investing successfully in growth stocks. You may not be able to apply every concept detailed in this book on every stock that you buy, but if, at the very least, you can incorporate the three most important concepts from this book into your own investment process, you will be well ahead of the vast majority of stock market investors. What are those three concepts?

1. *Margin of safety.* In a 1976 interview with the *Financial Analysts Journal*, Benjamin Graham was asked what he considered to be the most important rules of investing. The first rule he offered was to make sure that there is a margin of safety for every stock you buy. "He [the investor] should be able to justify every purchase he makes," said Graham, "and each price he pays by impersonal, objective reasoning that satisfies him that he is getting more than his money's worth for his purchase—in other words, *that he has a margin of safety*, in value terms, to protect his commitment."

2. *Mr. Market.* The incarnation of the entire universe of stock market investors, Mr. Market shows up every day willing to buy or sell any number of shares in any company. Sometimes the share prices are ridiculously high, and sometimes they are ridiculously low. It's the

fickle nature of Mr. Market that gives shrewd investors the occasional opportunity to buy stocks well below their intrinsic value. As Warren Buffett put it in a 1984 article in the *Columbia Business School Magazine*, "I'm convinced that there is much inefficiency in the market. When the price of a stock can be influenced by a 'herd' on Wall Street with prices set at the margin by the most emotional person, or the greediest person, or the most depressed person, it is hard to argue that the market always prices rationally. In fact, market prices are frequently nonsensical." For the alert investor, Mr. Market brings those nonsensical prices right to your door every business day.

3. *The power of compounding.* Albert Einstein and many, many others have marveled at the power of compound interest; it has been called "the most powerful force in the universe." Over a lifetime, a single percentage point can be worth millions of dollars through the power of compounding. That's why it's important to squeeze every possible percentage point out of every investment that you make.

This chapter is intended to suggest ways in which you might apply Graham's principles and the other investment concepts outlined in this book to your own investment process. Whether you're a student of investing, an individual investor, or a professional money manager, you can improve your personal investment success. If you want to learn more about Graham's investment strategies, we recommend that you also read his two classics, *The Intelligent Investor* and *Security Analysis*. We also recommend *The Selected Essays of Warren Buffett: Lessons for Corporate America*. If you are interested in pursuing growth stocks, we recommend our book and compound interest tables.

STUDENTS

Perhaps the most important lesson that students can take from this book is the power of investing in growth companies and the importance of patience in investing successfully over a lifetime. As you begin to invest and build your own portfolio, this book can serve as an important reference source to help you apply Graham's most important principles to investing in growth stocks.

INDIVIDUAL INVESTORS

First and foremost, this book is intended to help you invest successfully in an investment environment that often seems to be stacked against you by the financial services industry.

In fact, Graham believed that individuals actually have a greater chance for stock market success than the professionals. "The typical investor has a great advantage over the large institutions," explained Graham in the *Financial Analysts Journal* interview, "chiefly because these institutions have a relatively small field of common stocks to choose from—say 300 to 400 huge corporations and they are constrained more or less to concentrate their research and decisions on this much over-analyzed group. By contrast, most individuals can choose at any time among some 3000 issues listed in the Standard & Poor's Monthly Stock Guide. Following a wide variety of approaches and preferences, the individual investor should at all times be able to locate at least one percent of the total list—say, 30 issues or more—that offer attractive buying opportunities."

Not only is the selection process more favorable for individual investors, but the ability to hold stocks for long periods of time should also improve your long-term performance. Making the effort to establish and stick to your own hurdle rate will guide you in determining the proper price for every purchase. And conducting due diligence on every stock you analyze and insisting on an adequate margin of safety for every purchase you make will reduce the number of mistakes you make and set you apart from the pack.

This book should provide you with convincing evidence that growth companies offer the promise of superior long-term returns. For the individual investor, the after-tax effects of long-term holding periods can be significant. Many individual investors already own stocks through mutual funds. For those investors, we suggest that you convert your various funds into an

S&P 500 index fund with low management fees. As you uncover some great stock ideas, you can begin to move a larger portion of your investment assets from your mutual fund to individual stocks.

How many stocks should you own? You should own only the number of stocks for which you can calculate an adequate margin of safety. In many cases, that might be only four or five stocks. You might have 75 percent of your equity investments in an S&P 500 index fund and the remaining 25 percent invested in a handful of individual stocks. Over time, the more diligent investors may be able to increase the percentage of individual stocks in their portfolio as they uncover additional stocks that offer the potential for sustained growth and an acceptable margin of safety.

If you want to choose a stockbroker who can help you with the process, we suggest that you ask the following questions as part of the interview process:

1. How do you (the broker) calculate a margin of safety?
2. How do you view Mr. Market?
3. What is your investment time horizon?
4. What is your annual portfolio turnover ratio?

There is a range of acceptable answers to these questions. The worst answer would be, "Huh?" or "What are you talking about?"

Annual portfolio turnover is a key statistic. Annual portfolio turnover is the market value of your purchases and sales divided by 2 and then further divided by the market value of the portfolio. If a portfolio worth $100,000 had $100,000 in purchases and $100,000 in sales, then the portfolio turnover would be 100 percent.

Annual portfolio turnover can tell you the broker's actual investment time horizon. If his annual turnover is 100 percent, then his investment time horizon is one year. If his portfolio turnover is 50 percent, then his horizon is two years.

If you are looking for an investment manager who charges a fee based on a percentage of assets under management to manage your money (rather than

a commission-based broker), we would suggest adding two more questions to
your list:

1. What is your turnover of customers?
2. What is your turnover of employees?

Turnover of customers and employees tells a story similar to that told by
annual portfolio turnover. It is costly to lose clients and to have to bring on
new ones. The same is true of employees. These turnover statistics can tell
you a lot about how the manager treats his customers and his employees.

INVESTMENT PROFESSIONALS

What can institutional money managers, hedge fund managers, mutual fund
managers, and other professional investors take from this book?

We are going to split our suggestions into two groups. The first are things
that professional investors might prefer to use, but that are not critical. The
second group includes changes that all professional investors should take to
heart. Our industry has done a poor job of representing our clients. We have
to do better.

In this book, we have tried to explain the difference between growth
companies and stocks and value companies and stocks. We encourage professional investors to seek to clarify their own understanding of stocks.

We encourage professional investors to use our book to enhance their
proficiency when they are seeking to capitalize on the opportunities within
the growth company universe. We hope we have convinced you of the power
of combining Graham's principles and methodology with investing in
growth companies.

We encourage professional investors to use our book and Graham's model
to simplify their decision-making process. We sense that too many investment
managers have fallen prey to the notion that high mathematical proficiency is
better for investing. We would argue differently; we think that higher-level
math implies a level of precision that does not exist in the real world.

Along with a simplified process, we encourage professionals to set a fixed and public hurdle rate. Communicate this rate to your clients. Grade yourself on how well you perform relative to your hurdle rate.

There are many issues discussed in our book that we hope investment professionals will take to heart. Our industry's record of representing our clients has been generally poor. We are fiduciaries, and we should conduct our investment affairs accordingly.

We challenge investment professionals to lengthen their time horizon for owning stocks. Stocks are long-term investments. It is distressing to see mutual fund after mutual fund reporting annual portfolio turnover of 100 percent or higher. This is not investing! We challenge our peers to own stocks rather than rent them.

We challenge professional investors to put quarterly earnings reports in the proper perspective. They are just one data point. To own stocks rather than rent them, we challenge professional investors to develop their investment posture based on their best long-term thinking and stay with that posture even if the market temporarily disagrees with them. More often than not, if your investment posture is based on sound analysis, your clients will be rewarded over the long term.

We challenge investment professionals to own the same stocks in the same proportion as your clients. Eat your own cooking.

To own stocks rather than rent them.

Hug your mother, not the index.

We challenge investment professionals to avoid buying any stock unless they can calculate a satisfactory margin of safety on it.

Investment professionals must learn to handle the temptations of Wall Street brokers in a way that benefits their clients. Wall Street brokers perform a valuable service. They provide liquidity to the capital markets. They are aggressive, and they have many creative ideas. They will also ruin your clients' portfolios if you let them. Wall Street brokers have been this way ever since I entered the business in 1973; they will be this way long after I am gone. Deal with it.

We challenge investment professionals to examine our comments on the impact of fees on long-term compound returns. Our industry in general charges fees that are not supportable over the long run. Hedge fund fees are embarrassingly high. If you doubt this, look at the return over 50 years at 10 percent compounded. Then remove 2 percent annual fees and 20 percent of the remaining profits, the typical charge for a hedge fund. Only the rarest of hedge fund managers can justify such fees.

Fees for products delivered to the 401(k) market are too high, often 2 percent or higher per year. The participants are unlikely to achieve their long-term needs for retirement with such heavy fees.

CORPORATE EXECUTIVES

The lessons of this book, along with Graham's two classics and *The Selected Essays of Warren Buffett*, provide corporate executives with outstanding insights into what great investors expect from a corporate management team. You also might learn that even growth investors prize a high return on capital more than a high growth rate. And you might learn that any fool can grow a business; superior managers grow their businesses while maintaining an attractive return on invested capital.

You might also learn to focus more on building a sustainable competitive advantage instead of simply trying to beat the next quarter's earnings estimates.

Corporate executives might accept the idea that a fixed hurdle rate for internal investments and acquisitions is similar to a fixed hurdle rate for purchasing a stock. Executives should both preannounce their hurdle rate, especially for acquisitions, and report to their shareholders the performance of their acquisitions, adjusted by the size of the acquisition. Did the acquisitions in total achieve the company's preannounced hurdle rate? If not, why not?

We hope that corporate executives who read this book will renew their commitment to great corporate governance. Their actions, including a fair allocation of corporate cash flow to dividends, will attract long-term investors who seek to act as long-term partners with corporate managers. By examining Graham's methodology, corporate executives can learn to apply a more accurate hurdle rate to their potential acquisitions and understand the mentality of the long-term investor.

MARKET MAVENS

If you are a market maven, you're an individual investor who takes your investments very seriously and spends long hours each week assessing your portfolio and analyzing your next move.

If you fit that description, then this book is tailored to you. Before I entered the investment management business, I confess to having been a market maven, too. As a young investor nearly 50 years ago, I read every book on investing that I could find. I tried every technique. I remember using stop-loss orders in 1973. I was a naval officer back then. The Vietnam conflict had ended, and we stopped in Japan on our way back to Pearl Harbor. During the 10 days we were in transit from Japan to Pearl Harbor, Nixon devalued the dollar. The market sold off and then recovered. My stop-loss orders were activated. When I arrived back in port, my stocks had recovered their prices, but I had been sold out of all my positions! I have never used stop-loss orders since.

Ever so very slowly, I came to realize that the concept of investing was quite simple: Buy great companies when their stocks are priced at fair value or less. Then leave your holdings alone.

This book will give market mavens the tools they need to achieve investment success—and perhaps it will help make your learning process quicker than mine.

If you're a day trader and a key part of your strategy is to trade stocks rapidly, this book may be of limited value to you. Graham's growth stock principles are designed for use by long-term investors—not day traders. And the exhausting process necessary to find high-quality stocks and build a position in those stocks through Graham's methodology would probably take more time than you can devote. But Graham's formula could still serve as an important tool in valuing stocks and determining favorable points at which to buy and sell the stocks you're trading.

PUTTING THE PRINCIPLES INTO PRACTICE

This book can help you identify high-quality stocks and purchase them at advantageous prices. There are several steps to Graham's growth stock strategy that can help you achieve success. Following is a review of some of the most important elements of that strategy.

Step 1. Be Mindful of the Power of Compound Interest

Compound interest is a critically important principle of investing. In fact, we encourage every reader to keep compound interest tables handy when investing.

There is much to be learned from perusing these tables, including the fact that achieving a double-digit return over long periods of time makes one very rich. If you were to begin with $100,000 and compound it at 10 percent per year for 50 years, your investment would grow to $11,739,000. From this example, we can also deduce that very few people earn a return of 10 percent or greater because so few people get rich.

You can use the compound interest tables to establish a hurdle rate for yourself or to understand the devastation that can result from a 50 percent decline in value with no recovery. They help us recognize the importance of high compound returns when we have substantial amounts of assets under management.

Compound interest tables show the fallacy of using volatility as a measure of risk. Superior results produced by an additional 1 to 3 percent return per year over the market averages can be obscured by volatility over shorter time periods. If you look at your progress one year at a time, you may wonder why you are trying so hard to gain 1 to 3 percent. But viewed over long periods of time, superior incremental returns produce stunning differences in performance. If Investor A invests $100,000 and earns a compound return of 10 percent, at the end of 50 years, he will have $11,739,000. If Investor B earns 7 percent per year over the same time frame, his portfolio will be worth $2,945,670. Investor A's portfolio will be four times larger than Investor B's!

Compound interest tables can also illustrate the deadly effects of excessive investment fees and brokerage commissions. Investors A and B both earn a compound return of 10 percent on their portfolios over 50 years. Investor A pays no fees, while Investor B pays investment management and brokerage fees of 1.5 percent per year, reducing his net return to 8.5 percent per year. At the end of 50 years, Investor A's portfolio will be approximately double Investor B's portfolio. Investment management fees and brokerage costs are expensive!

Investors may also want to examine the effects of high turnover on portfolio returns. High turnover can generate short-term capital gains, which are taxed at higher rates than long-term capital gains. Higher tax payments can seriously diminish long-term performance. Consider the favorable impact on an investor who buys a stock and holds it for 50 years without paying capital gains taxes.

Step 2. Identify Companies with a Sustainable Competitive Advantage

The first step in selecting stocks for your portfolio is to identify companies that have a sustainable competitive advantage. Look for structural advantages, embedded in the underlying business model, that allow a company to stay ahead of the competition.

Don't confuse operational excellence with the durability of a sustainable competitive advantage. While operational excellence is essential in developing and enhancing a competitive advantage, in itself it is not enough to be considered a sustainable competitive advantage because the return differential will diminish as other companies close the execution gap.

Look for companies that not only have a structural competitive advantage, but have proven over time that they are willing to put in the effort required to maintain that advantage. The competitive advantage can be squandered over time by the management, which may make ill-advised decisions on the direction of the company or the reinvestment of corporate earnings. Once you've invested in a company, you need to continue to follow the progress of that company to make sure that it is maintaining a grip on its competitive advantage. If you notice a gradual degradation of that advantage, you should have ample opportunity to react before it completely vanishes. You also need to be vigilant for massive structural changes in the industry, changes in regulatory or political regimes, or disruptive technology, which can quickly undermine a company's competitive advantage.

Step 3. Use Graham's Formula to Set a Value for the Company

Once you've identified companies with a sustainable competitive advantage, the next step is to set a value for those companies so that you can determine an optimum price to pay those stocks.

Graham's formula is

[8.5 + (2 × growth)] × earnings per share = intrinsic stock value

---

The formula needs to be applied only once when valuing no-growth or slow-growth companies. Growth companies require the application of the formula twice—an estimate of today's intrinsic value and an estimate of a future intrinsic value. In our case, we forecast the intrinsic value of the company seven years out.

Determining today's intrinsic value gives you a current snapshot of the company; it shows you how the company operates, and it helps you determine the future value of the company. Calculating future intrinsic value gives you a key data point upon which to make a decision to buy, sell, or hold the stock.

You can estimate current earnings by analyzing the company's Securities and Exchange Commission (SEC) filings, such as the 10-K, 10-Q, and proxy reports. Once you've analyzed the company's financials and developed a thorough understanding of how the company operates, you can come up with a fair estimate of the company's normalized earnings per share and a viable growth rate for the ensuing years. We suggest that investors use the last trailing 12 months of earnings, adjusted for the current economic cycle.

By "normalizing" the current earnings, you can reduce the odds of buying a company at its cyclical peak in earnings or selling a company at its cyclical trough in earnings. It also helps you get a better focus on the company's true long-term growth rate, unaffected by current economic or industry conditions.

We suggest that you build a seven-year financial model for each company. When we analyze a company, we develop a forecast for the company by using the income statement, the cash flow statement, and the balance sheet. We assess the quality of corporate management; look at the size of the company, the size of the industry, and the potential for growth; and determine the potential profit margin. Only after we've examined the company's business model and financial returns can we make a reasonable projection of its future earnings seven years' hence. To account for declining growth rates, we have chosen to "freeze" the projected growth rate after seven years at 7 percent.

The intrinsic value of a company and its stock price rarely coincide, but as Graham put it, "In the short run the stock market is a voting machine; in the long run it is a weighing machine." Over time, the stock price should match up with the company's intrinsic value. As long as the underlying business performs at or near your expectations, investment success is simply a matter of patience. The intrinsic value of a growth company lies entirely in its future.

Step 4. Set a Hurdle Rate

In order to invest successfully, you need to decide what type of return you will need in order to meet your financial objectives. That's where your hurdle rate comes in. The "hurdle rate" is the average compounded annual return you hope to earn from each stock you buy. The hurdle rate is essential in helping you determine the price you need to pay for each stock you buy in order to reach your financial objectives.

The more ambitious your objectives, the higher your hurdle rate. The hurdle rate can vary significantly from one investor to another, depending on each investor's objectives. A conservative or short-term investor might be satisfied with a hurdle rate of 5 percent or less. More aggressive investors may have a hurdle rate of 8 or 10 percent. A select few investors with just the right temperament and investment savvy may shoot for a hurdle rate above 10 percent.

The two keys to setting a hurdle rate are your investment requirements and your ability to achieve those objectives. You should set a hurdle rate of about 2 percent above your long-term desired return in order to compensate for severe bear markets and/or extended periods of no return. Your hurdle rate will be important in every buying decision you make because it will determine the price you need to pay for a stock in order to achieve your desired return.

Step 5, Build In a Margin of Safety

When you make a decision to buy a stock, make sure you build in a margin of safety. The "margin of safety" is typically defined as the difference between the intrinsic value of a stock and its market price. In other words, a stock that is trading significantly below its intrinsic value has a wide margin of safety, while a stock that is trading at or above its intrinsic value has no margin of safety. The cheaper you can buy a stock relative to its intrinsic value, the bigger your margin of safety. Buying a stock with a margin of safety doesn't ensure that you will not have a loss on the stock—occasionally a company will fall out of favor for any of a variety of reasons and fall well below its previous trading level—but the margin of safety gives you a better chance of avoiding a loss on the stock.

For individual investors, a margin of safety is developed by strict adherence to quantitative analysis. You *must* play by the book. As you gain experience, qualitative factors can come into play. Before you purchase a stock, make sure you have a "warm and fuzzy feeling" in your gut.

Those who want to become great investors must understand that the next stock purchase should be regarded as a do-or-die effort. Just as in golf, the last shot you hit has little to do with your next shot. When you are investing, remember that a series of winning investments does not mean that the next one will work out, nor does a string of losers mean that the next one will be bad. Often the inverse is true, if you stick to the basics of Graham's methodology. Great investors insist on an adequate margin of safety for the next purchase, regardless of prior results.

Your ability to build an adequate margin of safety for each purchase determines how many stocks you should own.

Graham suggested that to determine an accurate margin of safety based on a true valuation of the company, an investor needs to evaluate the performance of the company over a period of several years—"including preferably a period of subnormal business."

We follow three key rules for setting a margin of safety for the growth companies we buy:

1. Know what you own.
2. Develop reasonable forecasts.
3. Set a reasonable hurdle rate.

For a value company, you can incorporate a margin of safety by buying the stock at a price below its intrinsic value. But with a growth company, investors need to take into account the future value of the company. The margin of safety shouldn't be predicated on the current intrinsic value of the stock, but rather on the future value. When we set a margin of safety for the stocks we buy, we base it on our projection of the company's intrinsic value seven years out.

At our firm, we have used a hurdle rate of 12 percent for years. If we miss our mark by a little bit and end up with a 10 percent rate of return, we are not happy, but we have still achieved a reasonable profit.

You may not always reach your targeted rate of return, but if you do a good job of building a seven-year financial model with a conservative projected intrinsic value, and if you build in a substantial margin of safety for every stock you buy, the odds of success will be in your favor.

Step 6. Take Advantage of Mr. Market

The behavioral characteristics of Mr. Market give the astute investor a continuing set of opportunities to purchase stocks at attractive prices. The ability to buy stocks at a moment's notice gives us the flexibility we need to take advantage of price declines and buy stocks at attractive prices.

Mr. Market's actions also tempt us to sell our positions needlessly. We can easily become distracted by the daily movements of the market. Astute investors need to become somewhat bipolar in their approach to the stock market. An investor should take advantage of the volatility in stock prices at the time of purchase. The rest of the time, however, the investor should ignore the market fluctuations and concentrate on the fundamental progress of the companies behind the stocks. The ability to do this requires discipline and preparation.

Only when the stock price rises so high as to threaten the margin of safety should an investor think about selling the stock.

Graham's insightful observation that a company's intrinsic value and its stock price can differ widely is critical to investment success—although it is often difficult to separate the two. This is especially critical when a stock is declining sharply on what is clearly bad news. In this situation, clear-headed thinking and defensible decisions can pay huge dividends.

If you want to succeed in the investment world, you must understand the difference between intrinsic value and stock prices. When stock prices fall, for whatever reason, we feel bad, but stocks are now cheaper. Our margin of safety is increasing. When stock prices rise, we feel better, but our margin of safety is decreasing.

We firmly believe that any investor who understands the difference between a stock price and the intrinsic value of the company behind the stock is on firmer ground than at least 75 percent of all investors. Learning to use Mr. Market to your advantage can help you buy great stocks at the best possible prices.

Step 7. Follow the Strategy to Build a Position in a Company over Time

You can rely on the volatility created by Wall Street to build your position in a stock over time. Once you've taken a position in a particular stock, you can look for opportune times when the stock drops in price to add to your position. Building a position over time also gives you a chance to evaluate the effectiveness of the management team. If management consistently meets its milestones, sticks to its business model, maintains its competitive advantage, and follows through on its business plan, you will have the confidence to add to your position in that company when the opportunities arise.

Long-term investors can use the market's volatility to build a position in a stock at favorable prices by holding when the stock price spikes and buying more when it drops.

As simple as this strategy appears, it requires great discipline. Using Graham's valuation formula and building a seven-year intrinsic value chart gives you the point of reference you need to keep your emotions in check and focus on the long term. You can take advantage of the short-term reactions of Mr. Market to build positions in great stocks at fair or less prices. During those rare instances where there is widespread and scary financial distress, you will have the opportunity to purchase great companies at truly bargain-basement prices. This is called "legalized grand theft."

Step 8. Invest for the Long Term

Stocks are traded daily, but they are long-term assets. Over the short term, stock market prices are random. Over the long term, they are ruthlessly efficient.

If you want to invest for the long term, you should never purchase a stock unless you intend to hold it forever.

Step 9. Overcome Outside Influences

Every investor, from the rank amateur to the seasoned pro, can expect to be buffeted by many outside influences over the course of her investing career.

Financial institutions will try to sell you expensive products that you do not need. Brokers will try to invest your money until it is gone. Your family will give you bad advice. The daily news headlines will tend to pull you in the wrong direction.

Every investor will suffer from both physiological and emotional factors while investing. That is part of the human condition.

The best investors have learned to focus on what is important and simply ignore the rest. Those who want to improve their investment effectiveness must learn this skill.

INVESTMENT SUCCESS IS AVAILABLE TO EVERYONE

One of the wonderful characteristics of public stock markets is that everyone can win. A rising tide lifts all boats. But investors who want to achieve investment success must develop a sound approach to investing. Understanding Mr. Market and the margin of safety gives investors a strong foundation for developing and implementing a successful investment process.

Perhaps the greatest benefit of using this methodology is that it simplifies the investment challenge. Once you determine the right price to pay for the stock you want, nothing else matters—not the market, not the economy, not the advice of your family or friends, not even your own emotions.

In his 1984 essay in the *Columbia Business School Magazine*, Buffett described the investment technique of his colleague, Walter Schloss, a fellow disciple of Graham's whom Buffett worked with at Graham-Newman Corp. in the 1950s: "He knows how to identify securities that sell at considerably less than their value to a private owner. *And that's all he does.* He doesn't worry about whether it's January, he doesn't worry about whether it's Monday, he doesn't worry about whether it's an election year. He simply says, if a business is worth a dollar and I can buy it for 40 cents, something good may happen to me. And he does it over and over and over again. He owns many more stocks than I do- -and is far less interested in the underlying nature of the business. I don't seem to have very much influence on Walter. That's one of his strengths: no one has much influence on him."

If you can implement the investment principles covered in this book through impartial analysis and cold calculation—while deflecting the many outside influences that tend to taint the stock selection process—you will enjoy a lifetime of success as a growth stock investor.

RENTING OUT YOUR MONEY

What is the real value of an investment? It's the *present value* of the *future cash flows* that the investment will yield you. A cash flow one year from now is worth less than cash in your pocket now, both because of the uncertainty of the value of that future cash flow and because of the "rent" that you demand to defer other uses of that cash for one year.

When we're determining the value of an investment, we use a 12 percent per year *hurdle rate*, or annual "rent," on our investment dollars to uniformly compensate us for both the risk of the investment and the deferral of the use of that investment. Using a 12 percent hurdle rate, $100 right now would have to grow to $112 by next year (the original $100 plus the $12 of rent) in order to justify an investment. Here is the equation:

Now	→	1 year from now
Present value: Present value × (hurdle rate + 1)		= future value
$100	$100 × (0.12 + 1)	= $112

You may also see the equation expressed in these ways:

$$PV(\$100) = FV_{1\ yr}(\$100 + \$12)$$
$$PV(\$100) = FV_{1\ yr}(\$100 \times 112\%)$$

All this means is that the value of $100 now is equal to the value of $112 one year from now.

To determine the future value out more than one year, you would simply repeat the above process. For example, if the hurdle rate, or rental rate, you would charge to use your money for one year is 12 percent, then you would demand at least $12 to rent out your $100 for the first year. In the third year, you would charge 12 percent of that $125.44, or $15.05. The equation would look like this:

Now	$\rightarrow$		3 years from now
Present value:	Present value +	=	Future value
	(three years of rent)		
$100	$100 × [(0.12 + 1) ×	=	$140.49
	(0.12 + 1) × (0.12 + 1)]		

You may also see the equation expressed in the following ways:

$$PV(\$100) = FV_{3\ yr}[\$100 + (\$12 + \$13.44 + \$15.05)]$$
$$PV(\$100) = FV_{3\ yr}[\$100 \times (112\% \times 112\% \times 112\%)]$$
$$PVy(\$100) = FV_{3\ yr}[\$100 \times (112\%^3)]$$

There are two things to note regarding these equations. First, the rent due increases every year because more money is "rented out" each year; this is the power of compounding. Second, in the last equation, notice that the 112 percent is raised to an exponent of 3. This is a shorthand manner of writing out all three years of rent; it simply means 112 percent × 112 percent × 112 percent, and it can also be used fractionally. For example, the future value of renting out

$100 for 2½ years at 12 percent could be written as $100 × 112 percent$^{2.5}$, or $132.75.

THE PRESENT VALUE OF A FUTURE CASH FLOW

The converse calculation discovers the worth of a future cash flow right now. Using the same 12 percent hurdle rate, how much would $100 one year from now be worth right now? Before, to calculate the value of $100 a year later, you multiplied $100 by 112 percent. To reverse this, you would divide $100 by 112 percent. The equation would look like this:

Now	←	1 year from now
Present value = future value ÷ (hurdle rate + 1)		Future value:
$89.29 – $100 ÷ (0.12 + 1)		$100

The equations can also be expressed as

$$FV_{1\,yr}(\$100) = PV(\$100 - \$10.71)$$
$$FV_{1\,yr}(\$100) = PV(\$100/112\%)$$

In this case, the $10.71 is 12 percent of $89.29; that is, it is the rent that would be charged to lend out that money for one year at a 12 percent rate. And, as with to the last set of equations, you can simply repeat the process to calculate the value of a cash flow several years from now:

Now	←	3 years from now
Present value =	future value ÷	Future value:
	(three years of rent)	
$71.18 =	$100 ÷ [(0.12 + 1)	$100
	× (0.12 + 1) × (0.12 + 1)]	

This can also be expressed as

$$FV_{3\ yr}(\$100) = PV[\$100 - (\$10.71 + \$9.57 + \$8.54)]$$
$$FV_{3\ yr}(\$100) = PV[\$100/(112\% \times 112\% \times 112\%)]$$
$$FV_{3\ yr}(\$100) = PV[\$100/(112\%^3)]$$

THE VALUE OF A SECURITY

Using these equations, if one can project the cash flows that a security will pay the holder in the future, then adding up the present value of all those future cash flows becomes a simple mathematical exercise. This summation of those cash flows is the value of the security. For example, if a bond were to pay you $10 per year for three years, and at the end of those three years, it also paid you the $100 in principal back, the value of that bond (using a 12 percent hurdle rate) would be

Present value of the payment in:					
Year 1		Year 2		Year 3	
($10/112%)	+	($10/112%²)	+	($110/112%³)	= ↓
$8.93	+	$7.97	+	$78.30	= $95.20

Valuing a stock requires two additional insights. First, the value of the future cash flows is uncertain, so they must be estimated (conservatively) before the value of the stock can be calculated. Second, in theory, the stock will produce cash flows into infinity, and so to avoid the work of calculating the present value of infinite future cash flows, a reduced equation to calculate the aggregate value of those infinite cash flows must be used.

As an example, imagine a stock that pays a dividend of $5. Imagine this dividend grows 5 percent every year—that is, it is $5 in the first year, $5.25 in the second year, and so on. The hurdle rate is still 12 percent. Without going through the derivation, the following equation can be used to calculate the total value of all the dividends of the stock:

Present value	=	Next year's dividend	÷	(hurdle rate	−	growth rate)
$75	=	$5.25	÷	(12%	−	5%)

Which can be generically expressed as

$$PV = [D_{0\,yr} \times (1 + g)]/(k - g)$$
$$PV = D_{1\,yr}/(k - g)$$

Where

   PV = present value

    D = dividends

    g = growth rate

    k = hurdle rate

This equation is called the Gordon growth model, and it is generally used to calculate what is called the *terminal value* of a stock. An example will make this easy to understand. Say an analyst has estimated the next three years of dividends for a stock at \$1.15, \$1.00, and \$1.25, and then assumes that those dividends will grow steadily at a 5 percent rate thereafter to infinity. The value of the stock can then be calculated to be

	Year 1		Year 2		Year 3		Years 4 to ∞		
Dividend	\$1.15	+	\$1.00	+	\$1.25	+	5% annual growth	=	↓
Present value	\$1.15/112%	+	\$1.00/112%²	+	\$1.25/112%³	+	[\$1.31/(12% − 5%)]/112%³	=	↓
Summation	\$1.03	+	\$0.80	+	\$0.89	+	\$13.32		= \$16.03

This concept is known as *discounting* cash flows in the future to value them today, and the body of equations used is known as the *discounted cash flow*, or DCF, model (see Chapter 3). It can be used to evaluate the worth of any investment, from stocks and bonds to internal projects within a company, and it is a staple of financial analysis.

Using this paradigm, one can then break down the value of a stock into its component time periods (for example, you could evaluate the worth of the first 10 years' cash flows against the worth of all the subsequent cash flows).

GROWTH VERSUS VALUE STOCKS

To demonstrate this, we'll compare two stocks. One is a growth stock, and one is a value stock. We'll call them G and V.

Assume that V pays a constant \$10 dividend every year, never growing. Assume that G pays a \$5 dividend, but grows that dividend by 4.75 percent per year. If the hurdle rate (or rental rate) is 10 percent per year, then the Gordon growth model introduced earlier will value both stocks at \$100 each:

V = (\$10 × 100%)/(10% − 0%) = \$100
G = (\$5 × 104.75%)/(10% − 4.75%) = \$100

Now, another way to look at it is to sum up the value of each dividend, year after year. For the value stock, this would look like

V = (\$10) + (\$10/110%^{1}) + (\$10/110%^{2}) + (\$10/110%^{3}) + . . .

while the growth stock would look like

G = (\$5) + (\$5.24/110%^{1}) + (\$5.49/110%^{2}) + (\$5.75/110%^{3}) + . . .

where the dividend keeps growing at 4.75 percent. An even easier way to show this is with charts. The future cash flows of V are displayed in Figure A.1.

Conversely, the future cash flows of G are shown in Figure A.2.

A value stock pays a higher dividend initially, but the identically valued growth stock pays a substantially higher dividend in future years. The reason they're identically valued is that a dividend sooner is *worth more* than a dividend later. If you look at the same charts as in Figures A.1 and A.2, but discount each dividend to its *present value* (as in the most recent set of equations given earlier), then V looks like Figure A.3, whereas the present values of G's dividends look like Figure A.4.

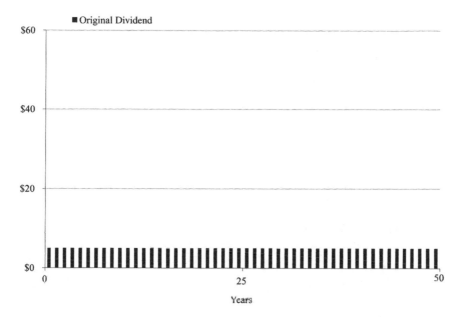

Figure A.1 The Future Value of the Cash Flows of a Value Company

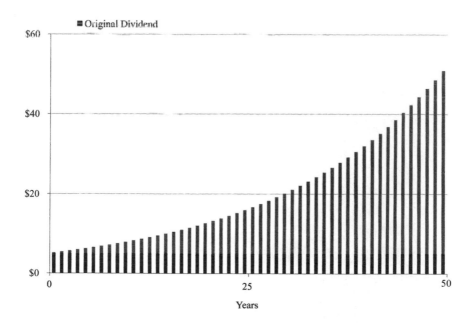

Figure A.2 The Future Value of the Cash Flows of a Growth Company

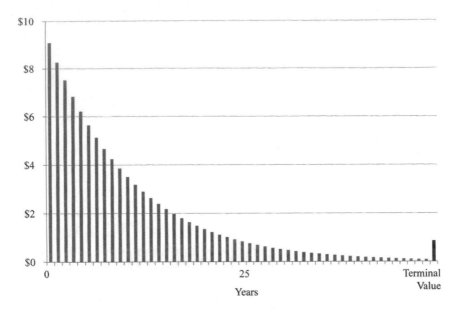

Figure A.3 Present Value of the Cash Flows of a Value Company

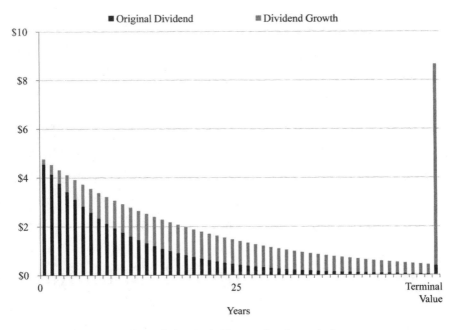

Figure A.4 Present Value of the Cash Flows of a Growth Company

The last column in both charts represents the *terminal value*, which is just the sum of the value of all dividends from year 51 to infinity {arrived at using the $PV = [D_{0\ yr} \times (1 + g)]/(k - g)$ equation}.

What these charts show is an important difference between G and V (our growth and value stocks).

While a growth stock pays you less money now, in the future it will both pay you more money and be worth more because of this higher payment. A value stock will simply pay you the same amount of money in perpetuity, and, assuming your hurdle rate never changes, it will always be worth the same amount of money. Therefore, a larger proportion of a value stock's worth is derived from the dividend it will pay over the next few years. Thus, to earn your hurdle rate consistently, you must reinvest these dividends in a similar opportunity that offers the same rate of return. The risk is that there won't be such opportunities perpetually available. This is called *reinvestment risk*, and our value stock has more of it than our growth stock.

So, while our growth stock has some reinvestment risk because it does pay a portion of its annual earnings out as a dividend, the reinvestment risk is not as great as that of a value stock. The rate of return of a growth stock will more be determined by the company's own *internal opportunities*, and less dependent on external reinvestment opportunities in the broader macroeconomic environment.

VALUING BONDS

To better illustrate this, let us use a simple annuity example. The value of an annuity depends on the existing interest rates. If the interest rate is 10 percent, then an annuity that pays $10 per year will be worth $100 (as $100 \times 10\% = $10). If interest rates drop to 5 percent, then the same annuity, which still pays $10 per year, will be worth $200 ($200 \times 5\% = $10).

Let's assume a couple of traditional structures for a 30-year bond. Our first bond, call it C, is a coupon bond, which pays a set interest payment for

30 years, and then, at the end of those 30 years, repays the principal amount in a lump sum. Our other bond, call it Z, is a zero coupon bond, which means that it does not make annual payments, but simply repays a fixed amount at the end of 30 years. The buyer of Z initially pays significantly less than the final payment and is compensated as her investment appreciates to that amount.

When evaluating the worth of bonds in the real world, one must consider not only the current interest rates, but also the rates that will exist when each coupon of the bond is received, as well as at the principal repayment at the end of the bond's life. If interest rates fluctuate up and down significantly during the life of bond C, then the rates at which the coupons can be reinvested will be subject to greater uncertainty, and the overall value of your initial investment 30 years from now is difficult to predict, since it will depend on all the reinvestments of interest you must make during that period. Bond Z is not vulnerable to this interim variation, so its value at the end of 30 years is far simpler to predict, but it still must be reinvested at the end of the period and so is dependent upon the existing interest rates.

There is a metric that is used to gauge a bond's exposure to this reinvestment risk, called *duration*. Duration measures the sensitivity of the price of a bond to changes in interest rates. Another interpretation of duration is to consider it to be simply the weighted-average maturity of the discounted cash flows you'll be paid if you purchase a bond, where *maturity* is the length of time until a given payment. So, bond Z has a duration of 30 years (one payment at year 30), while bond C might, depending on the coupon payments, principal payments, and prevailing interest rates, have a duration of around 15 years.

In essence, a shorter duration indicates that the eventual total value of an investment in a bond depends more heavily on near-term reinvestment opportunities within the prevailing macroeconomic environment. A longer duration signals that the eventual value of an investment in a bond will be more insulated from near-term fluctuations in reinvestment opportunities (although the price that could be achieved if that bond were liquidated instead of held may be *more* sensitive to near-term fluctuations in future expectations, since those near-term fluctuations are often perceived to have more significant long-term impacts).

THE ADVANTAGE OF GROWTH STOCKS

Returning to our stocks, G and V, it is evident that V (the value stock) has a shorter duration, and that the ultimate value of an investment in it is more dependent on the reinvestment opportunities, while G (the growth stock) has a longer duration and is more dependent on its own internal investment opportunities.

This is a very important distinction. If the price of V climbs and the economy as a whole offers less appealing investment opportunities, a long-term investor in V will be forced to evaluate either other stocks or other asset classes, such as cash, bonds, or even more exotic alternatives, or to reinvest in V at an inflated price and thus undermine the value of his entire investment. If there is significant uncertainty in the economy as a whole, across all asset classes, an investor in V may not have *any* attractive options for reinvestment, including, if inflation were a threat, in cash.

The long-term investor in G, while still somewhat vulnerable to reinvestment concerns, can rely more on the internal opportunities available to the company. G is master of its own destiny, while an investor in V is more dependent on the vagaries of the economy and market prices. If better market opportunities do occur, both value stock and growth stock investors might capitalize on them; if they do not, the growth stock investors are better protected by investments whose long-term value they understand.

This is one of the core arguments to be demonstrated throughout this book: diligent, savvy investors have a greater chance of successfully evaluating the long-term prospects of several high-quality, growing companies than of evaluating the immense complexity of the world's economy, and therefore they are better equipped to invest their time, effort, and money in these opportunities for the long run.

Index

About the Author

For nearly four decades, Fred Martin has relied on many of the investment principles of Benjamin Graham to earn a place among the best long-term-performing money managers in the United States. As the president and chief investment officer of Minneapolis-based Disciplined Growth Investors, Mr. Martin has compiled an outstanding record of double-digit average annual returns for his clients over the past 30-plus years. After graduating with a BA from Dartmouth College and an MBA from Amos Tuck School and serving four years in the U.S. Navy, Mr. Martin began his professional investment career in 1973 as an equity analyst for Northwestern National Bank in Minneapolis. In 1978 he moved to Chicago to join a branch of Mitchell Hutchins Asset Management, then a subsidiary of Paine Webber Inc. In 1984 Mr. Martin spearheaded the relocation of the Midwest office from Chicago to Minneapolis. By 1996 Mr. Martin led the Minneapolis office to assets under management of more than $2 billion. In 1997 Mr. Martin cofounded Disciplined Growth Investors (DGI). In 2001 Mr. Martin took over as majority owner of DGI and has served as president and CIO since then. DGI currently manages more than $2.5 billion of assets for institutions and individuals. Mr. Martin considers himself to be a pilot who honors the margin of safety. He is also an active financial supporter of those less fortunate than him.